Witch-Children

from Salem Witch-Hunts to Modern Courtrooms

HANS SEBALD, Ph.D.

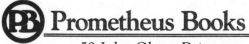 **Prometheus Books**

59 John Glenn Drive
Amherst, New York 14228-2197

Published 1995 by Prometheus Books

99 98 97 96 95   5 4 3 2 1

Library of Congress Cataloging-in-Publication Data

Sebald, Hans.
    Witch-children : from Salem witch-hunts to modern courtrooms / Hans Sebald.
        p.   cm.
    Includes bibliographical references and index.
    ISBN 0-87975-965-8
    1. Witchcraft—Massachusetts—Salem—History. 2. Trials (Witchcraft)—Massachusetts—Salem—History. 3. Witchcraft—Europe—History. 4. Trials (Witchcraft)—Europe—History. 5. Mythomania. 6. Abused children—Miscellanea. 7. Witches—Psychology. I. Title.
BF1576.S43   1995
133.4'3'083—dc20   94-44760
                                                                        CIP

Printed in the United States of America on acid-free paper.

The mold of the inquisitor

Whenever a man believes that he has the exact truth from God, there is in that man no spirit of compromise. He has not the modesty born of the imperfection of human nature: he has the arrogance of theological certainty and the tyranny born of ignorant assurance. Believing himself to be the slave of God, he imitates his master, and of all tyrants the worst is a slave in power.

—Robert Green Ingersoll

Contents

Introduction

This book is about a venomous chapter of Western civilization: the persecution of witches. The hunt extended over several centuries, from the Middle Ages into the early modern era. Although scholarly efforts have been made to understand this organized murder and a measure of valid insight into it has been gained, many aspects of the phenomenon remain mysterious.

This book hopes to shed light on some of the questions by: (1) exploring historical records that describe witch trials and the catalytic roles children played in a majority of them; (2) analyzing the heretofore unknown case of "Witchboy" to provide an intimate and detailed example of a child caught in the machinery of the inquisitorial witch-hunt; (3) showing children's behavior from the perspective of child psychology and in the light of modern research findings; and (4) comparing historical events to present-day issues, noting resemblances—"witch-hunt" here being used in its metaphorical sense, as applied to today's epidemic of accusations and denunciations by children claiming to have been molested or seduced, with or without the accessory of satanic cult practices. In short, this book presents history, case studies, and analysis.

The roles children played, either as the accused or as the accusers, were pivotal ones, linking the power of the inquisitor to the fates of a variety of people, many of whom became hapless victims to be devoured by a ravenous Inquisition. It is this nexus that serves as the focal point of this investigation; the way it worked is examined by looking at a number of historical witch trials, including those of colonial New England (Salem), England, Sweden, Austria, and especially of the German territories.

It is disquieting that the classical Salem syndrome is anything but past history; it is an ongoing potential and frequently reenacted in the modern courtroom as a time-honored tradition. We observe children as they play out (honestly or dishonestly, as the case may be) the nexus between prosecutor and defendant. Again, the child plays the powerful pivotal role. And a mythomaniacal child, not recognized as such by the authorities, is in a position to wreak havoc on the lives of innocent persons. It matters little whether the authorities are judges, juries, inquisitors, or the counselors and therapists of more recent vintage.[1] Part one of this book, "Little Actors and Actresses of Evil," will provide examples.

Literature has dwelled at length on the victimization of women during the witch-hunts and its underlying misogyny; inquiries into this problem have been more than justified. But few researchers have investigated the countless children who also have been involved in witch-hunts.[2] For example, one of the best-known works on the history of childhood in Europe, Philippe Ariès's *Centuries of Childhood* (1962), fails to touch on the vulnerability of children being drawn into the cauldrons of witch trials.

Children's vulnerability is of a peculiar sort and quite unlike that of women. In the persecution scenario children are more often victimizers than victims. A classic example is the case of "Witchboy," presented in the second part of this book.[3] The nine-year-old boy's "confession" abounds with a quality that is often special to children, namely, mythomania, or the obsessive telling of fantastic stories, especially when an audience expects exactly that type of exotic story and rewards its presentation. Witchboy's confession surpasses in phantasmagoria any of the many other confessions I have examined. Nonetheless, the inquisitors believed every word of it, including the boy's denunciations, with tragic consequences to totally innocent persons.

Witchboy also reveals vista after vista of life in early modern Europe, noting games and charades he and his peers played within the setting of seventeenth-century Franconia (a region of Germany), detailing his involvement in gang adventures that were mostly of unmitigated delinquent nature, and describing the way children lived during a disastrous period of European history—the Thirty Years'

War and the time of the Black Death—and the deteriorated socio-economic conditions that led to the formation of gangs of homeless children living in squalor and engaging in every conceivable crime. Further, we see how a child's thought and behavior mirror the metaphysical beliefs of the time, beliefs that today most of us would define as naive and superstitious. A significant part of these beliefs was the image of the witch and her nefarious deeds—notions of often lethal consequence. And, of course, there was the central figure of evil, the lord of the witches: the Devil. Witchboy's report gives a surprisingly comprehensive picture of the cosmology of his time, and his imaginative "confession" is an excellent medium through which to understand the seventeenth-century Christian worldview. By interweaving the ideas of witchcraft with his adventurous life as a street urchin, the boy conveys not merely information about his time, but inadvertently plunges the reader into an emotional experience as well.

Another phenomenon we cannot help noticing in the analysis is that power corrupts the human mind. Among the star players of the drama were the princes of the Roman Catholic church, a church professing love and forgiveness as foremost virtues. As we will see, the princes revelled in power and instead of love they bestowed death. With little hesitation they threw young children into dank dungeons or even had them executed, but most of all they used the children's mythomaniacal "confessions" as instruments to hunt down ever more victims and thus perpetuate the Inquisition.

There are further lessons to be learned from looking at the role of children within the framework of persecution. It seems that children's activities, especially in peer context, form a constant throughout history. Their playing, roaming, exploring, bravado pranks, and delinquent behavior have changed little over the ages. The major changes have been in the way people view and interpret the activities. During the totalitarian rule of the Inquisition, or of the Roman church in general, the meaning of a vast spectrum of youthful behavior was translated within a cosmology teeming with devils and demons. Today the scientifically minded would interpret the same behavior within a social-psychological framework. While the old interpretation demanded punishment, including the death penalty in its most horrific forms, the new view calls for therapy and rehabilitation.

This investigation does not mean to portray children as models of innocence or cast them into an idealistic frame, à la Rousseau, that assumes that they are endowed with an innate sense of fairness, honesty, and kindness. In fact, some characteristics of children can be of disastrous consequences to innocent persons. One such characteristic is children's unlimited talent for making up stories, especially in situations where they intuit what adults want to hear and what might net them approval or even laurels. During the time of the witch-hunt their confabulations tended to continue even when they knew that their stories endangered totally innocent persons and could get them burned at the stake. We will have opportunity to read children's lethal testimonies in various scenarios of the witch persecution. In part three, "Probing the Personae," issues of child psychology will be explored to help us understand the personality dynamics of children in extraordinary situations; the specific way mythomania works will receive thorough attention.

It is interesting that the present epidemic of children's mythomaniacal manifestations is not limited to the United States but appears to have spread and become a phenomenon of Western civilization. For example, new liberal laws in Germany allow, even encourage, children's testimonies in court. These testimonies have become crucial items in the context of divorce and custody battles. Children's fabrications of tendentious stories have become so widespread and have so seriously victimized many parents that the latter have found it advisable to rally in self-help organizations. It appears that the influence of lawyers and judges is responsible for enhancing the suggestibility of children to the degree of spreading confusion in the Teutonic court system.[4]

It is interesting that among the children accusing adults of magical or sexual perversion there is an overrepresentation of teenage girls. This was true of the witch persecutions of the sixteenth and seventeenth centuries and is true of today's wave of accusations of adult sexual abuse. Analysis of court records shows that older children are more prone to lying than younger children. "Nearly all false allegations had come from teenage girls" and had been directed against adults with whom they experienced strained relations, such as teachers, stepfathers, mothers' boyfriends,[5] and—as typically in the Salem episode—puritanical neighbors.

There is a striking parallel between the historical claim of "spiritual" abuse by witches and the new claim of sexual abuse by adults. Unlike many other crimes, child sexual abuse, like supernatural abuse ("bewitching" and the like), in most cases leaves no physical evidence and excludes other witnesses, thus pitting a child's word against that of the accused.

Finally, also on the political level, we see that the essence of the early modern witch-hunt is anything but antiquarian. Though the specific nomenclature has changed, new types of witch-hunts have filled the annals of the twentieth century with horrifying stories. Some of the mighty rulers, ephemeral as their reigns may be or may have been, have assigned the status of Satan's disciples to new groups of human beings—they were or still are the Jews; the Reds; the Kurds; the Croats; the Serbs; the Muslims; and, from the vista of fanatical Iranians, the Americans.[6]

The similarity between the new and the old witch-hunts becomes particularly evident when we look at a new genre of witch-hunting wherein the central figure of the old hunt has steadfastly—and in exactly the same theological framework—survived into our time: the Devil. According to true believers, the Devil is real and can have human conspirators—they call them satanists today, but they could just as well have continued calling them witches, because the two terms have the same meaning. Hence we can more correctly speak of a revival than a resemblance.

As we enter the twenty-first century, it appears that the social climate in the United States shows a strange persistence of the notion of a real Devil and his helpers. People who embrace the traditional dualistic theology of Christianity have little difficulty believing in the reality of the Devil. They find it logically acceptable that the Devil commands a host of demons, fallen angels, and evil spirits. For example, a 1993 Yankelovich survey found that about half of all adult Americans believe in the existence of fallen angels or devils.[7] Believers find it equally logical that these entities can recruit malicious helpers among human beings. It matters little what you call them. Witches or satanists will do. Hence those Christians who persist in believing in the existence of witches and their destructive works are anything but ridiculous—they practice a logical deduction from the core premises of their belief system.

It is therefore not surprising that the departments of public security of many communities have been offering lectures and seminars warning against what they perceive to be an epidemic conspiracy of satanic cults across the country.[8] For example, in Virginia alone, cult-crime officers gave at least fifty seminars in 1988.[9] I observed a lecture of this type in Mesa, Arizona, in which the lecturing police officer talked to an audience of worried parents about the "blood and urine" initiation rituals that presumably were going on in the community. Not one shred of factual data supporting the rituals' real occurrence could be provided, however. In 1991 a similar performance was given at the most prominent behavioral health institute of Arizona. A seminar on "Satanic Cults and Youth Subcultures" was fielded under the direction of a juvenile probation officer and a clinical psychotherapist. The same unsubstantiated claim of a widespread satanist conspiracy was presented, along with a packet describing satanic terminology, rituals, calendar, and crimes. The state's television media followed up on these suggestions and included warnings in their daily news programs of February 27 and 28, 1992, reporting that over fifteen satanic groups operated in the state. Anonymous and visually blocked-out "witnesses" asserted things like: "Children have to watch how their brothers and sisters are being tortured, raped, and killed." There were no identified witnesses and no documented evidence or official records of the missing or injured "brothers and sisters."

Seminars manifesting the belief in a new great conspiracy of satanists are held throughout the nation. Sociologist Jeffrey Victor describes a six-hour seminar sponsored by Harding Hospital in Worthington, Ohio, a suburb of Columbus. The seminar, "Culture, Cults and Psychotherapy: Exploring Satanic and Other Cult Behavior," was conducted by a social worker and a clinical psychologist, according to whom, "Organized satanic cults have existed as a secret 'countercultural religion' since ancient times."[10] They reported that teenage "dabblers" in black magic are recruited into witchcraft cults, which in turn grow "hard core" satanists, who specialize in such crimes as child pornography, "snuff porn," and the international drug trade. The ultimate goal of these secret satanists, according to the presenters, is "the infiltration on the highest levels of the power structure in all societies in order to undermine the moral order . . . [and] create international chaos in order to allow Satan to take over the world."[11] When it came to supporting these claims, highly questionable "circumstantial evidence" was introduced, mainly based on claims made by multiple personality disorder patients in the care of the clinical psychologist.

There have, of course, been a number of documented cases of satanic symbolism, many of them in the form of graffiti or in association with delinquent behavior. But the use of such symbols is no proof that an organized satanic conspiracy exists. Many of the symbols have achieved commercial merit—they are exploited by a wide range of commercial entertainment interests, from filmmakers to rock groups—and can easily be imitated by disturbed or maladjusted individuals without any cult affiliation.

The "exposing" of the Great Conspiracy has been conferred academic credibility by a professor writing a corroborating book. Carl Raschke, professor of religious studies at the University of Denver, wrote *Painted Black: From Drug Killings to Heavy Metal—The Alarming True Story of How Satanism Is Terrorizing Our Communities* (1990), in which he tries to persuade the reader that a grand conspiracy of Satanism is operating to destroy American society.

The mass media dwell on the subject with a vengeance, as exemplified by such television programs as NBC's Geraldo Rivera–hosted "Devil Worship: Exposing Satan's Underground," of November 1988. While the skeptical viewer recognizes the claims for the superficial sensationalisms they are, many viewers believe every word. That is not to say, however, that such cult groups won't subsequently develop and model themselves after the mass-media description. But that is a different story, and an ironic one at that.

The Satanism scare has assumed international dimensions. Sociologist James T. Richardson has found striking similarities among panics in England, New Zealand, and Australia. There is an interesting reason for the similarities: in all cases, the researcher detected an American-derived moral panic and found that prominent American "experts" on Satanism had been invited to these countries to enlighten social work professionals about the rising danger of Satanism. Regularly, "after such visits by American specialists, cases of ritual abuse were spotted by the newly trained social workers, who were looking for signs that ritual abuse was occurring on their home turf."[12]

It is not only the layperson or the social worker who often proves impressionable; it includes also law enforcement officers. For example,

Arizona law enforcement agencies have on several occasions called on me to help clear up events suspected as acts of witchcraft or crimes by satanic cults. In all cases, I had to disappoint credulous officers and report to them that my investigation had arrived at far less exotic and esoteric explanations—explanations that ordinarily should not require academic credentials to divine. One case dealt with what police officers initially described to me as "an altar in the desert near Phoenix, where the carcasses of a dozen or so stolen and slaughtered greyhounds were found, obviously sacrificed in some sort of satanic worship, and the place marked by occult signs carved into the desert floor." A closer look revealed a different story. First of all, there is no cult that would need more than one animal for ritualistic purposes. Second, the "altar" was nothing more than a simple platform of rocks on which the thieves had completed the tedious work of skinning the hounds. Third, the skinning of the large dogs had a very simple commercial purpose, namely, the selling of the hides south of the border for making leather goods ultimately sold back to unsuspecting American tourists delighted over bargain prices. Finally, the occult signs on the desert floor were nothing else than foot marks of working people.

The slightest suspicion that a certain behavior might be of cult origin seems to be sufficient reason for many people to jump to conclusions. The evidence is based on presumption and often on panic. The mass media have loosed barrages of reports on child molestations presumably committed by members of satanic cults, and prosecutors, let alone the public at large, have too often given unexamined credence to children's fanciful testimony.

As we turn into the third millennium, data from nationwide Gallup polls show that substantial percentages of Americans adhere to certain beliefs in supernatural phenomena: 55 percent firmly believe in the reality of the Devil, 8 percent aren't certain, and the remaining 37 percent disbelieve. In fact, 10 percent of adult Americans believe that they personally "were talking to or being talked to by the Devil." Forty-nine percent believe (and 22 percent are uncertain) that "people on this Earth are sometimes possessed by the Devil"; 29 percent believe (and 17% are uncertain) that "houses can be haunted"; 25 percent believe (and 19 percent are uncertain) that ghosts exist, and that spirits of dead people can come back in certain places and certain situations;

and 17 percent feel that they personally "have been in touch with someone who had died." Fourteen percent believe (and 8 percent are uncertain) that witches really exist; when teenagers aged sixteen to seventeen are singled out, the number of believers increases to 34 percent.[13]

There is no reason to expect a significant change of these statistics in the decades to come. Deeply ingrained religious beliefs, the heritage of hundreds if not thousands of years, claim a longevity unparalleled and almost unaffected by the changeability in the technological sector of the human venture.

This conjures up a déjà vu of high fidelity, merging the outlines of medieval and modern perceptions into perplexing oneness, and shows that an astounding percentage of modern people have retained the demonized cosmology of previous centuries. The previously mentioned Witchboy account has numerous modern counterparts. One of the most striking was the recent turmoil in the community of Olympia, Washington, where children's illusions of past events became "memories" of past events. Under pressure and repeated questioning, children "remembered" what persons of authority suggested they should remember. At the end, a devastating mixture of claims of incestuous and satanic-ritual abuse destroyed an entire family.[14] In another case, children's unproven allegations, again including claims of sexual and satanic-cult abuse, destroyed the California McMartin preschool. The denunciations resulted in personality assassination of teachers and manager, and netted the manager several years in prison *before* the trial was concluded. She was finally released because of lack of evidence. It turned out to have been the longest criminal trial ever in the United States.[15] It is noteworthy that among the "authorities" to which the children of the McMartin school had been exposed during the criminal investigation were counselors with a zest for suspecting satanic happenings.

This brings to mind an uncomfortable realization: The cessation of the witch-hunt was *not* accomplished by abandoning a psychotic thought structure or by humanitarian sentiments, but merely by separating the powers of the state from the powers of the church. Civil liberties, including the right to believe or disbelieve in religious credos, began to be safeguarded by secular law. It was this arrangement, and none other, that doused the flames of the witch persecution.

There was a further reason why the persecution came to an end: The machinery of the Inquisition got out of hand. By the end of the seventeenth century it became increasingly difficult to distinguish between true witches and merely defamed persons, innocent victims of denunciations often made under torture. After more and more tortured people pointed to the likes of priests, inquisitors, and even the bishops themselves, and asserted to have also seen them at the witches' sabbath, the cogs of the machinery got stuck. The industry of the witch-hunt threatened to devour itself.

Some of the challenges that this investigation arouses deal with elements endowed with such immense longevity and universality that they will continue to have compelling implications on modern life. These elements deserve more than academic attention. They demand public examination if we want to shed light on vital processes in our civilization and if we want to advance human dignity. Few of them, if any, are pleasant; but the obligation of the researcher of historical and sociological data is to report what in fact there is, not what we wish there would be.

This book will appeal particularly to readers refusing to acquiesce to the disclaimer that "those simply were the conditions of the day." Rather than facile escape into historical relativism, this book exercises a value approach in which respect and dignity for all human beings are the guiding principles.

Finally, it must be said that this book favors the dramaturgical metaphor since it facilitates clarity of description and perhaps even profundity of explanation. Shakespeare's adage, "All the world's a stage, and men and women merely players," is far more than a decorous phrase. It penetrates to the core of human personality and reminds us of the etymology of the word *persona*: a mask worn by players in antiquity. The human mind has always revealed itself in personae, manifesting the irrepressibly social nature of human beings. We can find comfort in the fact that we are persona-bound creatures, since this means that we are not destined to repeat past behavior, but can change our masks and select those that enact a nobler form of humanity. The language of the stage symbolizes the human ability to produce ever new personae with which to create fresh opportunity, initiate reform, and keep high the banner of hope. Cultural progress is nothing else than arranging new personae into a more creative play. And that may be the only vantage for returning from an excursion into a dismal era of history.

In sum, this book tries to present a holistic view of a dark side of humankind by examining: (1) *historical data* describing the witch-hunt in general and the role of children in particular; (2) the colorful *case study* of Witchboy; (3) *child-psychology research* explaining children as victims and victimizers; and (4) *implications on modern life* insofar as a revival of the witch-hunt is underway, with children again playing a prominent role.

Notes

1. Note the new dangers posed by new "authorities." Therapists and counselors have been found trying to help patients to "recall" past traumas but failing to realize that many of the details were illusions and fabrications brought on in part by the suggestive questioning of the therapist or counselor. See Martin Gardner, "The False Memory Syndrome," *Skeptical Inquirer* 17 (Summer 1993): 370–75.

2. Among the few are Hartwig Weber, *Kinderhexenprozesse* (Frankfurt, Insel, 1991); and Wolfgang Behringer, "Kinderhexenprozesse," *Zeitschrift für historische Forschung* 16 (1989): 31–47.

3. The selection of the Witchboy example was prompted not only by its revealing character but also because of a technical circumstance: its setting was Franconia and the language used by the court scribe in putting down the confession includes phrases in dialect intelligible to this author by merit of having grown up in the vicinity of the historical event. The archival material as such was discovered in the Department of Rare Books and Manuscripts at Cornell University.

4. "Schuldig auf Verdacht," *Der Spiegel* 47 (April 19, 1993): 111–21.

5. Cf. John Crewdson, *By Silence Betrayed: Sexual Abuse of Children in America* (Boston: Little, Brown, 1988), p. 170.

6. See generalized application of the witch-hunt concept in modern society, including the Red Scare, the McCarthy Era, the Great Purge, and the Holocaust in Jan Oplinger, *The Politics of Demonology* (London: Associated University Presses, 1990).

7. Nancy Gibbs, "Angels Among Us," *Time,* December 27, 1993, p. 61.

8. See research reports by James T. Richardson et al., eds., *The Satanism Scare* (Hawthorne, N.Y.: Aldine de Gruyter, 1991); Jeffrey S. Victor, "A Rumor-Panic About a Dangerous Satanic Cult in Western New York,"

New York Folklore 15 (1989): 23–49 and, "Satanic Cult Rumors as Contemporary Legend," *Western Folklore* 49 (January 1990): 51–81, and "The Spread of Satanic-Cult Rumors," *Skeptical Inquirer* 14 (Spring 1990): 287–91.

9. Robert D. Hicks, "Police Pursuit of Satanic Crimes," *Skeptical Inquirer* 14 (Spring 1990): 276, and *In Pursuit of Satan: The Police and the Occult* (Amherst, N.Y.: Prometheus Books, 1991).

10. Jeffrey S. Victor, "Satanic Cult 'Survivor' Stories," *Skeptical Inquirer* 15 (Spring 1991): 278, and *Satanic Panic: The Creation of a Contemporary Legend* (Peru, Ill.: Open Court, 1993).

11. Victor, "Satanic Cult 'Survivor' Stories," p. 279.

12. James T. Richardson, "Deconstructing the Satanism Scare: Understanding an International Social Problem," Research paper presented at the annual meeting of the Association for the Sociology of Religion, Los Angeles, California, 1994, p. 19.

13. George H. Gallup, Jr., and Frank Newport, "Belief in Paranormal Phenomena among Adult Americans," *Skeptical Inquirer* 15 (Winter 1991): 137–146; plus a figure from the Gallup Youth Survey, Princeton, N.J., 1988.

14. Lawrence Wright, "Remember Satan," *New Yorker,* part 1 (May 17, 1993): 60–81; part 2 (May 24, 1993): 54–76.

15. Paul Eberle and Shirley Eberle, *The Abuse of Innocence: The McMartin Preschool Trial* (Amherst, N.Y.: Prometheus Books, 1993).

Part 1

Little Actors and Actresses of Evil

1

The Making of a Drama

A Civilization Obsessed

The stage of this drama was a civilization haunted by the fear that the most evil forces in the universe were conspiring to destroy it. It rallied itself to fight back, and one of the greatest organized killings of Western civilization began to take its course: the witch persecutions. The fiercest of these "holy battles" was fought in Christian Europe, turning society into a seething cauldron of mass hysteria and, over a period of nearly three hundred years, destroying the lives of hundreds of thousands of innocent victims. It was a time when people vividly imagined abominable malice emanating from a conspiracy initiated by the Devil[1] and carried out by his demons and his human helpers, the foul witches. This belief came to be a major concern not only of the authorities, secular and ecclesiastical, but also of the common people.

Christian cosmology teems with spirits and apparitions; some good, some bad. Anxiety about an onslaught of bad spirits was reflected in the pronouncement by a Catholic exorcist in 1697: "The majority of all creatures are oppressed by the demons, and that out of ten thousand [creatures or humans] more than nine thousand are so afflicted."[2]

Besides the threat by legions of nefarious supernatural entities, there were specific contemporary social problems that played weighty roles in the creation of early-modern witch persecution. Alas, satisfactory discussion of the causal constellation would burst the frame

25

of this work. Suffice it to say at this point that the religious and political turmoil of post-Reformation Europe may to a large extent explain the preoccupation with evil forces. There was a projection of endangerment by rival religions unto the theological level, reinforcing the fear of the Devil and his demons. Related factors were religious wars, such as the Thirty Years' War (during which the Witch-boy episode, discussed later in the book, took place). Johann Looshorn, chronicling the history of the bishopric of Bamberg, Germany, points out that in some localities governments changed five times within fewer than four generations and with them the religious affiliation of the people because the principle of *cujus regio, ejus religio* (the ruler determines the religion of the ruled) obligated them to adopt the religion of the ruler.[3]

Not that the sequence of conversion and reconversion made much difference insofar as hunting witches was concerned. All Christian factions persecuted witches; it was a pan-Christian pursuit, including Protestant and Reformed churches.[4] For example, the ruler of Geneva and one of the founders of the Reformed church, John Calvin, was probably as fanatic a witch-hunter as any Catholic bishop.

However, there are reasons for concentrating on the Inquisition as the epitome of the witch-hunt: (1) The Roman Catholic church formed the largest and most unified organization to engage in the hunt, while the Protestant camp was much more diversified, if for no other reason than for the very Protestant notion that religious authority is to be found in our individual consciences rather than in a church hierarchy. (2) Catholics proceeded with unparalleled mercilessness and cruelty. Not one Catholic jurisdiction chose to forego torture, whereas, for example, the Anglican church, or English law in general, would not allow it. (3) Catholic authorities started the persecution long before the Protestant Reformation, although Catholic apologists would like to blame Luther and other reformers for "causing" the witch persecution by the disturbance they initiated in presumably undisturbed pre-Reformation time.[5] This defense is as cynical as it is ludicrous, since the Inquisition was racking and burning heretics and witches already before Luther's time. For example, after decades of witch panics and ecclesiastical debates on the issue, *Malleus Maleficarum* ("The Witches' Hammer"), serving as the manual to eliminate witches, was published in 1487,[6] four years before Martin

Luther was born. (4) Whatever theological assumptions upheld the persecution spirit and whatever methodology developed, Catholic authorities created the models for Protestant imitation. (5) The basic theological assumptions making belief in the existence of the satanic witch possible lay deeply embedded in Catholic dogma and tradition, savagely overriding any humane principles.

Some people might be inclined to exculpate the witch-hunters by saying that they were the victims of the *Zeitgeist,* the spirit of the epoch. But trying to shrug off the witch-hunt as simply having been an unfortunate element of the *Zeitgeist* is a cowardly escape into historical relativism that eschews individual as well as organizational responsibility. In fact, it avoids historical analysis altogether and leaves matters pretty much the way they were and are, ignoring, as philosopher Paul Kurtz has put it, that "there is also a body of tested prima facie ethical principles and rules that may be generalizable to all human communities."[7]

In any case, people lived in great fear of the witches, but soon in even greater fear of the authorities who might at any time arrest and accuse them of being one of the Devil's accomplices. Ultimately no one could feel entirely safe from being cast into the crucible of the witch frenzy. And as sad a commentary on the human situation as it may be, it was not humanitarian consideration or some progress of enlightenment that prompted the cessation of the witch persecutions, but rather the increasing difficulty of distinguishing between the guilty and the innocent and of controlling the persecution machinery.

In a few instances mass hysteria ignited such fiery persecution that it decimated entire communities. For example, the town of Zeil, a witch-hunting outpost of the prince-bishops of Bamberg, was so depleted after years of arrests and executions that in 1630 Commissioner Georg Einwag, doctor of law, petitioned the prince to release him from his post, for there wasn't much to do anymore, he "was greatly bored," and felt uncomfortable having to face "the eerie emptiness which yawned from so many houses."[8] Another example was the small town of Oppenau in western Germany. Between June 1631 and March 1632 a sequence of witch trials took place that claimed 50 victims executed in eight separate burnings. During the same time an additional 170 members of the community had been accused of witchery. "In a town of only 650 inhabitants one can easily imagine what suspicion on that scale would mean to social bonds of trust."[9] It must be noted, however, that these examples represent extreme conditions and should not be generalized to all jurisdictions where witch persecutions took place.

A special Catholic organization, the Inquisition, was created and charged with leading the fight against witches and other enemies of Christendom. Established through papal decree in 1232, the Inquisition initially was directed mainly against heretical movements that threatened to burgeon within the Holy Roman Empire (which included practically all of Europe at the time). In the fifteenth century the Inquisition created the image of the Great Deviance, presumably a heretical organization of witches. A landmark of the witch-hunters in their fight against the imagined conspiracy was their manual, the *Malleus Maleficarum*. The responsibility of carrying out the persecution was primarily, but not exclusively, charged to the Order of St. Dominic. However, the Inquisition had regionally independent headquarters, such as the Spanish Suprema and the many prince-bishoprics, which could employ other holy orders and additional methods to carry out the witch-hunts.

The organization soon developed into a veritable industry in which a network of functions and positions had to be carried out. Once a suspect fell into the machinery of the industry, there was no escape. The process would most likely lead to conviction, and that could end with the most hideous of deaths: being burned alive. After their arrest suspects were secured in prisons, most of them equipped with torture chambers, and in them confessions were almost invariably obtained.[10] The human neural system simply could not withstand the pain inflicted by the torturers, whose arsenal of torture instruments was as imaginative as it was barbarous, ranging from thumbscrews to scalding with lime to being torn on the rack. Though this generalization is pretty much correct, slight modification can be added, inasmuch as the Inquisition showed some regional differences. For example, John Tedeschi has pointed out that the Roman Inquisition (charged with taking care of inquisitorial matters in the area of Italy) proceeded with a bit more caution than in many other places. Care was taken to provide defense counsel, limit torture, and regulate confiscation of property. The Roman procedures, adding up to some sort of due process, were disregarded in many regions. Among the most blatant violators were the Franconian prince-bishoprics, among them Bamberg. It is the Bamberg jurisdiction that served as research basis for much of this book, and hence significantly influenced the tenor of the presentation.[11]

In any case, a significant part of the confession was the "denunciation." This meant denouncing others as participants in diabolic witchcraft. The witch mania included the image of the so-called witches' sabbath, a time and place of the witches' gathering to frolic, celebrate, and fornicate with the Devil.[12] Grotesque descriptions as to what allegedly went on at such meetings kept erudite minds busy writing books, telling stories, and preaching terrorizing sermons.[13] Bamberg's suffragan bishop Fridrich Förner thundered sermons against witches with such passion as to inspire his prince-bishop, Johann Georg II, nicknamed *Hexenbischof* (witches' bishop) on account of his witch-hunting fanaticism, to grant imprimatur to a collection for distribution throughout the realm.

It was the idea of the witches' sabbath that led to the questions: Who else was there? Whom did you recognize among the celebrants? Torture usually achieved the answers and dozens of innocent people were named. Records show that most of the tortured initially tried to protect the innocent and named those members of the community who had already died or had been executed as witches.[14] But the inquisitors quickly caught on to the protective maneuver, and so started reapplying torture in order to get fresh denunciations, usually successfully expanding the list of suspects. Then the process would repeat itself: the newly arrested were in turn tortured and forced to denounce. Thus the witch-hunters equipped themselves with a perpetual system that continued operating for several hundred years, roughly from the fifteenth to the eighteenth century. This was particularly true in German regions; and there again with the greatest of fanaticism in the province of Franconia, where the prince-bishops of Würzburg and of Bamberg raged with such fanaticism as to incur the admonition of the emperor, although he himself believed in the reality of witches and merely reminded church leaders to observe due process.[15]

The identity and character of the victims of the Inquisition are still a topic of research by historians, sociologists, and psychologists. We know, however, that no status or age category was immune from witch accusation; it made no difference whether the accused was a young child or a senile oldster, a man or a woman, rich or poor. Though it is true that we can hardly talk of a run-of-the-mill witch, certain categories of persons were more vulnerable to accusation. The most likely victims of course were women. The ratio throughout Europe seemed to have been eight out of ten. Regional fluctuations must be noted. The Bamberg ratio, for instance, seems to lie around seven out of ten, mostly due, it appears, to the bishop's acquisitive motive whereby more was to be had from propertied men than from usually property-deprived women. But Bamberg was also noted for burgher-clergy conflict; a larger than normal proportion of men among the accused and convicted may have been the result of political intrigue. Property and political rivalry as the motivations for prosecution often conveniently coalesced. Another weighty consideration was the reputation of a family and how quarrelsome it was.[16]

It was the liberality with which one could accuse and the fear of being accused that were primary reasons why the witch-hunts had to be abandoned. The officials began to realize that accusations could no longer be controlled and that it became increasingly difficult to separate the guilty from the innocent. After the prince-bishops witnessed members of their staff and even members of their own families being accused, their priests denounced, and judges suspected, it slowly dawned on them that the industry of the hunt was beginning to devour itself.[17]

Admittedly, throughout the years of the persecution there were voices pleading for humanity and rationality.[18] Among them was the physician Johann Weyer, who thought that most of the so-called witches were deluded women suffering from mental disturbances.[19] These voices failed in their effort to introduce alternative thinking about the witch phenomenon because they failed to remove from their argument a fateful Trojan horse, the ongoing belief in a personifiable Devil, who, according to Christian cosmology, was able to recruit humans for his evil work.

So much for a sketch of the larger stage on which the drama unfolded, a stage comprising the whole of Western civilization.[20] A more narrowly focused setting is outlined in chapter 6, "The Stage," in which Witchboy's environment, the Bamberg diocese, is described.

Children in a Dualistic Worldview

"The innocence of the little ones" is a phrase of dubious veracity since historical events suggest otherwise. Nowhere has this optimism stumbled over more obstinate obstacles than during the great witch-hunts of the sixteenth and seventeenth centuries. During those not-so-distant years vast numbers of children gave free rein to their imaginations. They played back the image of the witch, as it existed in the cosmology of their time, and substantially contributed to the witch-hunt. In harmony with supernatural assumptions of the Christian worldview, children denounced and brought to the stake uncounted thousands of innocent people, including neighbors, peers, and even members of their own families.

Questioning children's innocence is not popular. In a world that agonizes over perennial betrayal, cruelty, war, mass slaughter, and other failures of humanity, we passionately long for exemplars of unadulterated goodness. The child, like some sacred icon, has been traditionally placed upon an imaginary altar so that we might revere virtues lacking in ourselves. This is the benchmark of romanticism: to seek virtue and beauty in groups, places, and times that are remote and relatively unknown.

Ironically, if their behavior disappoints sacred expectations, revered categories of human beings can come to bear severe punishments at the hands of those romanticizing them. Much warranted commentary has been written about the victimization of women at the hands of male romanticists who quickly mutate into misogynists— a mutation that has energized many a witch-hunter.

Children have suffered a similar fate. When adults found them guilty of deviating from the romantic model, they were liable to suffer cruel punishment; after all, they defiled the altar upon which adults enshrined them to serve as symbols for the noble in the human race. It is to a large extent on the basis of the disappointment of romanticists that many children became vulnerable, were labeled as evil, and eventually were persecuted as witches. In most cases, their punishment was no less barbaric than the one meted out to adults.

Ambivalence about the nature of children resulted in vacillating reactions toward them. A child could be a pure, innocent soul or a corrupt collaborator of the Devil, and the problem that often arose was how to tell one from the other. It was the church with its claim of infallibility that came to the fore and insisted that it knew how to tell the difference. If need be, the truth could be extracted by means of torture.

Christian teaching bolstered this dualistic way of looking at children. Besides allowing for the category of the immaculate and innocent child, it also allowed demonological interpretation of a child's behavior. As a consequence, a child who today would be diagnosed as learning disabled or as delinquent was defined as evil, an accomplice in Satan's plan to wreak havoc in God's creation.

The dualism was carried to an extreme when its advocates allowed for the possibility that someone could be *born* a witch, the product of demonic intercourse. Another possible scenario was that immediately after birth, the Devil or an evil midwife substituted a demonic infant. "Learned doctors" of the church such as Thomas Aquinas and Jerome had worked out detailed ruminations on these possibilities. Among those most fervently believing them were the inquisitors, who presumed to know how to find out who was what.

As a consequence, troublesome children ran the risk of being considered devilish "changelings" (or *Wechselbälge,* as the German inquisitors called them). Conditions such as hydrocephaly,* for example, were often seen as signs that the child was a satanic creature and not really the one born to the parents. Rather, as such famous preachers as Geiler von Kaisersberg let it be known, at birth the Devil stole the real one and substituted the malformed.[21] The moral of the theory was that not every child could be trusted or taken at face value. Parents steeped in the dualistic cosmology had at times abandoned their "changeling" babies by turning them over to orphanages, leaving them at doorsteps, or, in extreme instances, practicing forms of infanticide not recognized as such.[22]

Sometimes parents recognized a child's deformity or disability as a sign of evil and thus mistreated the child or felt justified to abandon it. Generally the church did little to counteract such abuse. On the contrary, some historians feel that during the time of the witch persecutions great injustice was committed by the church against scores of handicapped or learning-disabled children, who were con-

---

*An enlarged head at birth as a result of water on the brain.

demned instead of helped. Uta Ranke-Heinemann, a historian of religion, says in her provocative book *Eunuchs for the Kingdom of Heaven*: "In the course of human history the handicapped could hardly have experienced more prejudice, or as much disdain, intolerance, and inhumanity as they did in the Christian world." She specifically refers to children born deaf and mute, who, according to Augustine, "can never receive faith, for faith comes from preaching, from what is heard."[23]

It would be misleading, however, to single out any specific group of children as being the exclusive target of inquisitorial suspicion. Quite the contrary is true: children of any appearance, gender, age, or social background could be drawn into the machinery of persecution. It was the child as child who usually drew the attention of the Inquisition. A child's behavior that we today would understand as reasonably normal was quite vulnerable to demonological interpretation. Such behavior might have included bragging about real or imaginary things and accomplishments, playing pranks, or belonging to a gang, but most significant, as we shall see, was children's flair for telling tall tales.

Before presenting historiographical material that describes the involvement of children in witch panics and trials, two contingencies must first be noted: the time dimension and regional differences.

Geography and Chronicity of Children's Trials

The severity and the duration of the witch-hunt differed in various territories. Southern European countries, including Spain and Italy, had severe, but short spells of persecution hysteria. Much has been written about the dread of the Spanish Inquisition, but it probably executed no more than one hundred witches, starting in 1498 and ending in 1611 when the Suprema, the sovereign Spanish branch of the Holy Inquisition, listened to the enlightened opinion of one of its prominent inquisitors, the Jesuit Alonso de Salazar y Frias, and put an end to the persecution, declaring witchcraft a mere illusion. (A distinction was made, however, between witches, on the one hand, and sorcerers and apostates, including Moriscos and Jews, on the other. Though actual witch-hunts were few in number, the

Inquisition continued a merciless persecution of the latter categories of people.)

The Spanish experience contrasts with that of the German territories, where the persecution started slowly, but lasted into the eighteenth century, reaching its climax during the first third of the seventeenth century. The Franconian prince-bishops of central Germany stand out as having stoked the fiercest and most enduring flames of the witch-hunts; for instance, the *Hexenbischof* burned approximately six hundred witches during his reign, which ran from 1623 to 1633.

The contagious witch panic even spread to the New World. North America was a late-comer to the family of witch-hunting countries, possibly because of the territory's preoccupation with other problems, its semi-isolation from the hot spots of European witch persecution, and the influence of the more moderate English witch persecutions.

On the European continent, persecution assumed devastating proportions. It is impossible to state exactly how many persons were executed as witches during the persecution, roughly beginning in the mid-1400s and ending in the mid-1700s. Many of the court documents have not survived, and of those that have, considerable numbers have not yet been evaluated. Furthermore, there are still archives closed to academic scholars, such as those in the possession of bishops, who, not surprisingly, have little interest in providing additional figures and information about the church's role in the persecution. A case in point is the archive belonging to the archdiocese of Bamberg, where access is barred not only to academics but even to priests, unless they receive the personal permission of the archbishop. Another example is mentioned by historian John Tedeschi, describing the difficulty he encountered when he tried to gain access to the archives of the Holy Office in Rome.[24]

Hence the estimates about how many witches have been executed are uncertain and vary wildly. Some put them into the millions; others reduce them to a few hundred thousand. Among the most conservative estimates, and therefore probably suggesting an absolute minimum, is the one by historian Brian P. Levack, who put the figure at under one hundred thousand.[25] We must, however, keep in mind that this estimate, derived from official records, refers to executions only, and excludes victims who died in prison or under torture or for whom there simply are no records.[26] Some experts, for example, the Catholic priest Hans Küng, therefore speak of nine million victims.[27] For this pronouncement and other "betrayals" of the church Küng was subsequently denied the privilege of teaching at Catholic schools. Readers interested in a scholarly assessment of the *total* number of victims (besides witches) of Christianity's persecutions and crusades, including Jews, heretics, Muslims, and other groups, should consult the bold work by Karlheinz Deschner, *Kriminalgeschichte des Christentums* (The Criminal History of Christendom), with sequential volumes in progress.[28]

The focus of the witch-hunts during their very early stages in the fourteenth and fifteenth centuries was less centered on individuals and more directed against heretical organizations, as, for example, the Knights Templars, who started out as a Catholic Order, but later were accused of heresy and systematically liquidated by the Inquisition during the 1330s. Over time, the fear of heretics spread into the private lives of the citizens, where it poisoned interpersonal relationships. Accusations evolved from the inevitable frictions innate in everyday interaction between family members, neighbors, and other people in the community. Common human conditions and emotions, such as ignorance, fear, greed, revenge, and often pure malice, became major catalysts for accusations. It was then that the witch image became a family and neighborhood phenomenon and that children began to assume an important role.

During the fifteenth and the early sixteenth centuries, as trials gradually increased, few trials featured children. The roles assigned to them were passive ones, usually casting children as innocent victims, being sacrificed by witches, slaughtered, and made into a black-magic broth. Such macabre lore was described or insinuated in the *Malleus Maleficarum.*

Nonetheless, *Malleus* did open the door to a more active role for children inasmuch as they could be introduced to the Devil and his demons by mothers or midwives who were witches. Indeed, witchcraft could infect an entire family. It was not until the late sixteenth century that a notable turning point was reached. Starting in the 1580s, the role of children turned active and assumed epidemic proportion. From that time until the mid-eighteenth century, the vast majority of the witch trials involved children, either as victims, victimizers, or both. A vast majority of these trials featured children implicating close relatives, especially mothers. At the center of some of the last trials resulting in execution were girls between the ages of nine and seventeen, who voluntarily reported that either they themselves or close family members had been practicing witchery.[29] For example, the last victim of the witch persecution in Bavaria was a fourteen-year-old orphan girl, an abused child who became a street urchin and insisted on having committed the most damnable sacrilegious crime the Catholic church could imagine: the desecration of the Holy Eucharist by defiling the transubstantiated wafer. She was burned at the stake in 1756 in the town of Landshut.

A New Status for Children

Historian Wolfgang Behringer selects as the turning point the trials in the German city of Trier (or Treves).[30] Traditionally children had been known there, as elsewhere, as victims used by witches, sometimes being possessed by demons, and hence qualifying as blameless candidates for exorcism. But in 1585, scores of children, apparently agitated and inspired by the public witch burnings, came forward confessing to be witches themselves or claiming to having participated at the diabolic witches' sabbath. An eight-year-old boy, for instance, described in great detail how he had played the drum at the witches' dance and had seen a number of neighbor women dancing and carousing with the Devil. His testimony was sufficient for the government to prosecute and extract (by means of torture) confessions that resulted in sentencing the women to be burned at the stake. Another boy, the fifteen-year-old scion of a noble family and a page at the court of the elector[31] of Trier, confessed to having bewitched his lord and sickened him. During the ensuing exorcism, performed by the very busy Trier Jesuits, the boy implicated Dietrich Flade, the judge presiding over the witch trials, and claimed to have seen him at the witches' sabbath. Right away a total of twenty-three condemned Trier witches parroted the denunciation. After five different torture sessions, the former judge confessed, whereupon mercy was shown and he was strangled before being burned, staging his execution as one of the many public execution spectacles in the ancient city.[32]

These descriptions and denunciations started a chain reaction, and within a few years scores of children stepped forward with accusations. In 1587, a sixteen-year-old boy reported that he had been seduced by witches and sorcerers and had served them as musician at their dances. Among the persons he defamed were prominent citizens who in quick order were arrested by the prince-bishop, thrown into prison and, after confession under torture, burned at the stake.

The witch panic spread from Trier like a devouring fire engulfing the entire area. By 1589, three hundred witches had been burned; in one village all older women but two were put to death.[33]

Over the remaining years of the witch persecutions, a hundred years or so, the cases in which children were star players multiplied. They starred most frequently during the fiercest wave of the German persecution, from approximately 1600 to 1633.

After the first third of the seventeenth century, a number of things changed. Accusations were handled with somewhat greater care, evidence (*indicia*) was weighed more carefully, older women gained a bit in protection, and the ratio between men and women hauled before the judges changed from about two men in ten to about three in ten. This was particularly true in the Franconian prince-bishoprics, where the rulers achieved greater monetary gains by convicting men instead of the usually propertyless women.[34]

What did *not* change was the involvement of children in witch panics and witch trials. While the number of witch trials generally decreased, the number of child-related trials remained relatively constant; hence their significance increased proportionately.[35]

This calls for an explanation. What were the circumstances at the close of the sixteenth century that turned children into active players and moved them to center stage in the witch drama? An important factor among the many pieces of the etiological constellation was the Protestant Reformation, with its religious turmoil and political strife permeating the entire century and causing demoralization in nearly all sectors of life: religious, social, and cultural. Several generations suffered moral decline and social disintegration. It took tenacious efforts on the part of the main churches to recoup standards of moral behavior. Lutheran and Calvinist leaders strained to develop internal and external controls necessary to preserve and enlarge their newly won religious identity. The Catholic hierarchy felt similar needs and the measures of the Counter-Reformation tried to save what could be saved by clarifying principles in theology, defining norms for ritual, and promoting standards of moral behavior.

A fitting sociological concept for these and similar dynamics is *boundary maintenance*.[36] The social disorganization of the time, with its economic disasters and psychological tensions, forced a redefinition of what was proper behavior, what was correct belief, and who was inside or outside the proper socio-religious boundaries. This was the intense quest tormenting the minds of post-Reformation civilization. In the words of Steven Ozment: "Preoccupation with morals and discipline was a pervasive feature of the sixteenth and seventeenth centuries; in the minds of most thoughtful people an ordered life was the only free and secure life, the consequences of anarchy always seemed more dreadful than those of tyranny."[37]

Social disorganization invariably results in a tendency toward establishing and maintaining boundaries. In this sense, historical conditions such as the turmoil and the uncertainty of the sixteenth century can be understood as the *independent variable*, and the behavior of the masses elicited by these conditions as the *dependent variable*. In this conception, the Reformation and the Counter-Reformation forged a new order, to which the people had to adapt. The adaptive behavior called for a heavy emphasis on discipline, a discipline most noticeable *between* the generations, meaning that children bore the brunt of the harsh treatment. This did not remain unchallenged; children were not necessarily passive and sometimes they reacted against the impositions. What we are dealing with is a generational conflict, and typical of such pervasive dynamics, confrontation proceeded on the unconscious level, its symptoms nowhere closely understood by any of the parties involved. Instead of understanding them, the parties to the discord merely reacted blindly to what they perceived as disagreeable behavior in others.

Before further proceeding with this interpretation, a logical question must be solved: Since the confrontational behavior extended over several generations, how did the rebellious youth of one generation become the disciplining adults of the next? Sociological role theory suggests an answer: Entrance into a new status, such as adulthood and especially parenthood, stimulates certain changes in attitude and creates a different outlook on life. This, incidentally, is a timeless social-psychological process, certainly not limited to the sixteenth century, and observable as far back as the time of Aristotle (who complained bitterly about the behavior of the younger generation). Certainly this tendency is prevalent in the twentieth century. The differences that evolve between the status of the child and that of the adult and parent include a new authority, material possessions, and a large range of responsibilities. The isomorphic merging of the sociocultural role, on the one hand, and personality pattern, on the other, explains why and how the delinquent youth of one generation could become the law-abiding and norm-enforcing adults in the next. A déjà vu in the twentieth century describes it this way: "Sooner or later, the vast majority of rebellious youth will be swallowed up by the social structure of society and find positions that will soothe the hurt of adolescence and make them miraculously forget all about it. In fact, soon after they anchor their personal identities in the adult social structure, *they* in turn will be the older generation against which the resentment of the younger generation (including their own off-spring) will be directed."[38] These dynamics add up to a reinforcing pendulum of mutual disaffection, meaning that authoritarian measures by adults evoke resentful behavior in the young, and as the former quality increases, so does the latter.

This sociological theory illuminates the sixteenth-century situation. While, interestingly, the authority of husbands over wives moderated, parental authority reached new heights. The neglect of generations had to be repaired, and the brunt of remoralizing was aimed at the young. Church leaders of all denominations led the battle against "sinful" children, illustrated by Rev. Andreas Althamer's 1527 Nürnberg sermon. He compared young children's "sinfulness" to the inborn instincts of animals: as a fox craves chickens or a cat mice, so human infants are inclined in their hearts to adultery, fornication, lewdness, idol worship, belief in magic, anger, hostility, dissension, hatred, murder, drunkenness, gluttony, and many more vices.[39]

While to most modern readers such an indictment of the nature of young children appears excessive, if not outrageous, we must not lose sight of the fact that Christian theology provides it with solid underpinning. Theologian Hartwig Weber, also searching for the reasons of children's involvement in witch trials, feels that Christian theodicy depicts God and patriarch in child-killing modes: God-Father sacrificed His own son, presumably for the good of evil humankind, and Abraham was well on the way of slaying his son, as advised by God (Genesis 22:2-10). These stories of sacrificing children may not have been without impact on the believers' thinking and feeling; after all, they come from the Scriptures. Weber thinks that this type of Bible-sanctioned theodicy influenced people of all social ranks during the era of the witch-hunts: children became sacrificial objects who needed to be purged of sinfulness ("original sin") through the ritual of baptism and later through churchly education. The idea of disciplining children was an intrinsic argument of the clergy. It was thought that only through baptism and religious discipline were the young able to obtain access to the community of the saved. Children could not possibly be treated firmly enough if found disobedient or incorrigible; they could even be killed.[40] No wonder "corporal punishment was a regular and encouraged part of discipline both at home and in school."[41]

An aspect of youthful delinquency particularly abhorrent to the clergy was infraction of sexual morality. With voyeuristic regularity, the first questions the inquisitors asked the accused—children as well as adults—usually pertained to their sex lives, specifically their sexual involvement with witches, warlocks, demons, or the Devil personally. In this context, the description of the witches' sabbath was of grave significance, since it was thought that the wildest sexual excesses and perversions took place on those occasions. Children would report details with mythomaniacal glee, and the inquisitors would believe every word. Sexual transgressions would be punished with sadistic determination, especially those involving sodomy or bestiality. Statutes decrying these abominations proliferated during post-Reformation and Counter-Reformation times. Youths not having been the aggressors or perpetrators in the crime but merely cooperating participants, that is, they "suffered" the crime, were publically whipped and forced to view the execution of their more aggressive peers. Research in Swiss archives revealed that around the turn of the sixteenth century scores of twelve- and eleven-year-old boys were executed for sexual crimes.[42] Hartwig Weber suggests a psychoanalytic interpretation of the church's heavy repression of sexuality of any form. He sees the celibate clergy engaged in a *reaction formation,* whereby they came to hate what they actually ardently wished to have but were prohibited from having.[43]

A simple psychological truism emerges: Brutal treatment elicits a like response. Children acquired a blatant disregard for the welfare of others, particularly for disciplining adults. Thus children evolved into both victims and victimizers. The traditional immunity against being considered agents of the Devil was rescinded in light of the new harsh style of child-rearing. Children's revenge manifested itself in unconscionable denunciations and accusations of witchcraft. It was no coincidence that the impeccable citizen, the staunch churchgoer, the pious spinster were targets of children's defamations. In Europe, especially England, targets frequently included parents, siblings, and other close relatives. The accusation of witchcraft was a convenient weapon with which to exact revenge because it required little, if any, empirical proof.

In sum, children's reactions, often expressed in insolence and hostility, provoked adults to counter with ever stricter methods of child-rearing and religious penance. In the course of such confrontation the children's customary immunity against being accused of witchcraft weakened and ultimately was abandoned entirely.

An exacerbating condition should be mentioned. The disturbances of the sixteenth and seventeenth centuries created hordes of homeless youth. They roamed the countryside engaging in just about any delinquency and crime perceivable, from murder, arson, and highway robbery to taking advantage of people's superstitions by faking magic and sorcery and, more seriously, denouncing adults as witches and sorcerers. The plague of beggars was mostly a plague of beggar children described as groups of youngsters disturbing the peace by disrupting public festivals and ceremonies. The 1588 agenda of the city council of Nürnberg was burdened with this issue because the citizenry complained about beggar children creating too much noise and insecurity in streets and alleys.[44]

The point is that youth *in general* fell into ill repute and became a marginal population that added to the panic and fear of the townspeople. Gradually a new stereotype of youth evolved, one that could easily be demonized: their behavior indicated they were in cahoots with evil spirits. Here was a merging, with fatal consequences, of theological ideas and social ills. The manifestations of homeless and rootless youth contributed significantly to the disintegration of the image of childlike innocence that adults of previous ages may have cherished.

The New Script

Having children suddenly ascend to active participation in witch trials was an unforeseen event with which the inquisitors needed to come to grips. Theoretical demonology had not prepared them for such a turn of events. The new culpability of children presented the authorities with a *terra incognita* that needed to be provided with road signs. It was left to the cerebrations of Bishop Peter Binsfeld, who had taken an active part in the Trier trials, to solve the judicial-theological impasse and erect the signs directing to legitimate prosecution of minors accused of witchcraft. He concluded that witch-children below the age of fourteen should be spared capital punishment and instead be flogged. He suggested imprisonment for those under the age of sixteen, and when those so imprisoned reached sixteen, they should be reexamined to determine whether they had repented and were willing to embark on a Christian way of life. Delinquents sixteen or older, the bishop felt, should be subject to adult standards.[45]

As it turned out, the different jurisdictions varied widely in actual practice and many of them, particularly prince-bishoprics, disregarded the lower age limit, which meant that children of any age became subject to torture and capital punishment.

The pivotal concept in Binsfeld's reasoning was that witchcraft was a *crimen exceptum,* that is, an exceptional crime warranting suspension of traditional norms of jurisprudence, and therefore could justifiably modify three significant traditional norms: (1) exemption of minors from torture; (2) exemption of minors from capital punishment; and (3) barring children's testimony against adults in capital crime cases. These safeguards were now dropped; henceforth minors were subject to torture and the death penalty and their testimony was acceptable as valid *indicia.*

The involvement of children in witch trials naturally also became the concern of secular jurists. A standard work, Zedler's *Universal-Lexikon,* suggested norms of jurisprudence and advocated as late as the mid-eighteenth century that children involved in sorcery and witchcraft were punishable:

> Whereas a child under the age of seven, having been found to
> be a witch or sorcerer, is not rightfully subject to be punished by

the court, but should be punished and chastised by the schoolmaster so that the child converts to better manners. . . . However, a fourteen-year-old person, or one who is near that age, is subject to the regular [adult] punishment, i.e., according to the *Constitutio Criminalis Carolina* [code of law of the Holy Roman Empire issued by emperor Charles V in 1532], Article 164, especially if the person is of mean character and has become guilty of abhorrent and dangerous behavior. This is particularly true in cases where there is little hope of rehabilitating the malefactor.[46]

Zedler's lexicon represented judicial attitude in Germany as it approached the middle of the eighteenth century; it stated, for instance, that execution of "witch-children" was only reasonable.

As much as the new status exposed children to draconian punishment, it also empowered them. They now possessed judicial credibility. Not only could they testify in ongoing trials, they could actually initiate them. The new status elevated them to powerful heights—from which, alas, they could tumble into the fires of the Inquisition at any time. In any case, Binsfeld's 1591 manifesto, *Tractat von Bekanntnus der Zauberer und Hexen* (Treatise about the Confessions of Sorcerers and Witches), confirmed the unconditional credibility of children's reports, confessions, and denunciations.

The treatise remained anything but a local theory of legitimizing the prosecution of minors in Trier; it became a new and well-known addendum to the manuals of the witch-hunters everywhere. Its popularity is indicated by an undelayed second edition, printed in Munich in 1692. From then on, children's involvement in witch trials blossomed. Even during the mid-eighteenth century Binsfeld's treatise was regarded as valid judicial theory, allowing children's testimony in cases of sorcery and witchcraft.[47] The courts began to emphasize that in cases of "exceptional crimes" parents were obligated to report their children; and, vice versa, children were obligated to report their parents. This system was in perfect harmony with the admonitions in the *Malleus,* wherein the reporting of exceptional crimes committed by members of one's own family was appraised to be most becoming to a Christian.

Clerical Zeal versus Secular Moderation

The testimony of children received far greater credence by the Inquisition, or the ecclesiastical courts in general, than by magistrates or other secular judges. For example, the outlying community of Bobingen, subject to the authority of the prince-bishop of Augsburg but locally administrated by a magistrate, experienced a disturbance in 1589, when a fourteen-year-old boy bragged that he had been attending the witches' sabbath and knew a number of other persons who had been attending also. He concentrated on a certain townswoman and would not let rest his accusation. Finally the magistrate felt obliged to send a report to the prince-bishop, adding, however, that the boy's story should not be believed, for he was known to have a mischievous disposition. The ecclesiastical court chose to disregard the advice, accepted the boy's allegations as evidence, and proceeded to arrest not only the one woman but as many as forty-five others. The episode ended with the burning of twenty-seven women as witches.[48]

To be fair, it must be said that the court did not exclusively rely on the boy's testimony, but thoroughly questioned the suspects themselves and only then formulated the convictions. In any case, Prince-Bishop Marquard von Berg (1575–91) took advantage of the boy's claims to justify the beginning of a systematic witch-hunt, primarily directed against persons in poor standing with the church, persons whom he otherwise could not have touched. In essence, the boy became the bishop's tool. The youngster's defamatory behavior suited political plans and the bishop and chancellor Dr. Thomas Seld embarked on a course that aimed to exterminate the human vermin called witches. The Augsburg diocese was one of the places where the pressure to persecute witches came from above, i.e., emanated from the church's eagerness. This fervor was typical of the Inquisition, or the ecclesiastical courts in general, as patently demonstrated in Bamberg and Würzburg. In contrast, worldly governments often tried their best to avoid prosecution and even took steps to suppress popular demands, as, for example, in the case of Hagenau (discussed in the next chapter).

The ecclesiarchs of the Augsburg diocese wasted no time in working out the infrastructure necessary for a systematic persecution.

This included the establishment of an inquisitorial court in the town of Schwabmünchen because, unlike Bobingen, it had a resident executioner; the assignment of clergy to minister to the accused and condemned; the design of a lengthy questionnaire; the readying of the prison; and the calling in of additional torturers and executioners.

The call resulted in a macabre assembly of professional henchmen, who, like vultures attracted to carrion, flocked to the place, often with their entire households, anticipating plenty of work and plenty of wages. According to Behringer, at least one dozen executioners well known for their skills came to settle in Schwabmünchen, including master executioner Hans von Biberbach, famous throughout the empire for his torture skills.[49]

By the end of 1589, the stage for the trials was set and ready for the drama to unfold. The local magistrates of Schwabmünchen, just like those of Bobingen, showed little interest in the trials. Not even waiting for the first execution to take place, the leading magistrate petitioned to be transferred. Similar lack of interest was expressed by the local judge who, as one of the duties of his office, had to spend hours on end in the jail and bitterly complained about the "stench of the dungeons." Nevertheless, the prince-bishop and his court were undeterred and keen to start prosecution. So were the executioners, who were paid according to standard tariffs, received free room and board, and after every execution were served elaborate henchman's meals; in one case, a party of seven executioners savored their meal with fifty-four liters of gratis wine.[50]

Notes

1. Readers wishing to explore the historical evolution of the concept of the Devil may find useful material in the works of Jeffrey B. Russell: *The Devil: Perceptions of Evil from Antiquity to Primitive Christianity*, 1977; *Satan: The Early Christian Tradition*, 1981; *Lucifer: The Devil in the Middle Ages*, 1984; and *Mephistopheles: The Devil in the Modern World*, 1986; all are Ithaca, N.Y.: Cornell University Press. Also Alfonso di Nola, *Il diavolo: Le forme, la storia, le vicende di Satan* (Rome: Newton Compton, 1987).

2. Giovanni Levi, *Inheriting Power: The Story of an Exorcist* (Chicago: Chicago University Press, 1988), p. 4.

3. Johann Looshorn, *Das Bisthum Bamberg von 1623–1729,* vol. 6 (Bamberg, Germany: Handels-Druckerei, 1906), p. 98.

4. The Orthodox church of eastern and southeastern Europe was an exception, being nearly free of the witch persecution. The reasons still puzzle many historians.

5. The standard history book used in German Catholic seminaries is Johannes Janssen and Ludwig Pastor, *Geschichte des deutschen Volkes,* 8 vols. (Freiburg, Germany: Herder, 1890s). By 1924 it had gone through fifteen unchanged editions. The authors shift blame for the excesses of the witch-hunt onto Luther and his disturbance of theological peace. See vol. 8, pp. 378ff.

6. This manual of the witch hunters was written by two German priests, Heinrich Kramer and Jakob Sprenger, and went through many editions, becoming the most popular and prestigious of the demonological works. It is replete with suspicion, if not hatred, of women and any form of sexuality. It even threatens persons not believing in the existence of the devilish witch conspiracy with being, ipso facto, guilty of heresy. Astoundingly, the church has never revoked the book, nor even criticized it. In fact, one of the book's recent republications, freshly translated from the original Latin and augmented with various literary references by Montague Summers, a Catholic priest, carries a foreword in which the priest assures the reader that it is one of the finest, most uplifting, and evocative books of Christendom and it would behoove any good Christian to practice reading in it daily. See Montague Summers, ed. and trans., *Malleus Maleficarum* (New York: Dover, 1971, foreword of 1946), pp. ix–x.

7. Paul Kurtz, "The New Skepticism," *Skeptical Inquirer* 18 (Winter 1994): 141.

8. Looshorn, *Das Bisthum Bamberg,* vol. 6, p. 72.

9. H. Erik Midelfort, *Witch Hunting in Southwestern Germany 1562–1684* (Stanford, Calif.: Stanford University Press, 1972), p. 137.

10. Examples of specialized prisons, complete with torture chambers, were built by Prince-Bishop Johann Georg II, reigning 1623–33. Most of the time they were filled to capacity and the over six hundred persons executed by the bishop spent sad sojourns in them.

11. John Tedeschi, "Preliminary Observations on Writing a History of the Roman Inquisition," in F. F. Church and T. George, eds., *Continuity and Discontinuity in Church History* (Leiden, the Netherlands: Brill, 1979), pp. 232–49.

12. The tradition of Franconian and general German witch imagery rarely spoke of the witches' *sabbath,* but usually of the witches' *dance,* thereby differing from the nomenclature of other regions, as, for example, Spain. I am using the expressions synonymously.

13. Probably the most phantasmagoric book ever written on the nature of the witches' sabbath was Henri Boguet's *Discours des Sorciers* (1602). The author was inquisitor of the Swiss-French Jura region and evaluated with the greatest of credulity the "confessions" of the accused and tortured, dwelling on pornographic aspects of the witches' festivities. Demonological works with similar details and similar credulity could be added to present a long list of treatises illustrating the vivid imagination of the inquisitors about what they thought witches were doing when they got together.

14. See examples based on documents from Bamberg archives: Hans Sebald, "Witches' Confessions: Stereotypical Structure and Local Color," *Southern Humanities Review* 24 (Fall 1990): 301–19.

15. Several such original letters from the 1620s and signed by Emperor Ferdinand personally are in the Rare Books Department of the Cornell University Library: *Witchcraft Documents from Bamberg*, Mss. Bd. Wft., BF H63++.

16. See example: Hans Sebald, *Witchcraft—The Heritage of a Heresy* (New York: Elsevier North Holland, 1978), passim; E. William Monter, *European Witchcraft* (New York: Wiley, 1969), and *Witchcraft in France and Switzerland: The Borderlands during the Reformation* (Ithaca, N.Y.: Cornell University Press, 1976), passim.

17. For example, in November 1628 prince-bishop Johann Georg II saw it necessary to write a letter to the emperor defending the innocence of the dean of the cathedral and of his suffragan bishop, both of whom had been denounced for witchcraft. See Looshorn, *Das Bisthum Bamberg*, vol. 6, p. 49. Also see the account concerning a relative of the prince-bishop of Würzburg plus the naming of the prince-bishop himself as members of the witches' conspiracy in W. G. Soldan and H. Heppe, *Geschichte der Hexenprozesse*, vol. 2 (1880, reprint; Kettwig, Germany: Magnus-Verlag, 1986), pp. 52–54. Note a somewhat different interpretation of the episode by Friedrich Merzbacher, *Die Hexenprozesse in Franken* (Munich, Germany: Beck, 1979), p. 46. See also Midelfort, *Witch Hunting in Southwestern Germany*, passim.

18. Among them was the Jesuit Friedrich von Spee, who had served as father confessor to numbers of condemned witches and found all of them innocent. He penned his observations clandestinely: *Cautio criminalis* (Frankfurt, Germany: 1632).

19. Johannes Weyer, *De praestigiis daemonum* (Basel, Switzerland: 1563). The question emerges why the medical establishment of early modern Europe failed to halt the witch persecution. It has been argued that, instead of opposing the persecution, the physicians supported it. See the argument advanced by Leland L. Estes, "The Medical Origin of the European Witch

Craze: A Hypothesis," *Journal of Social History* 17 (1983): 271–84. A broader treatment trying to explain medical science's inability to stop the persecution is by Hans Sebald, "Fire for the Female, Medicine for the Male: Medical Science and Demonology during the Era of the Witch Hunt," in Rudolf Käser and Vera Pohland, eds., *Disease and Medicine in Modern German Culture* (Ithaca, N.Y.: Cornell University Western Societies Program, 1990), pp. 13–35.

20. For an introduction to the history of the witch persecution and research into twentieth-century remnants of witch belief, expecially as applicable to the Franconian region, see Hans Sebald, *Witchcraft—The Heritage of a Heresy* and *Hexen damals—und heute?* (Frankfurt, Germany: Gondrom, 1993). For insightful research in different parts of Europe see E. William Monter, *Witchcraft in France and Switzerland: The Borderlands during the Reformation*; H. Erik Midelfort, *Witch Hunting in Southwestern Germany 1562-1684*; Alan J. D. Macfarlane, *Witchcraft in Tudor and Stuart England* (New York: Harper, 1970). In addition, there are pioneer classics by Joseph Hansen, *Quellen und Untersuchungen zur Geschichte des Hexenwahns* (Hildesheim, Germany: Olms, 1901); Henry C. Lea, *A History of the Inquisition of the Middle Ages* (London: 1988), and *Materials toward a History of Witchcraft* (New York: Yoseloff, 1957); and W. G. Soldan and H. Heppe, *Geschichte der Hexenprozesse*. The latter authors were early bushwhackers in the jungle of history of the witch persecution and have unabashedly shown indignation at the church's involvement. As a consequence, their passion sometimes has been criticized as lacking objectivity. (See, for example, John Tedeschi, "Preliminary Observations on Writing a History of the Roman Inquisition," in F. F. Church and T. George, eds., *Continuity and Discontinuity in Church History* [Leiden, the Netherlands: Brill, 1979], pp. 232–49).

21. Cf. Hartwig Weber, *Kinderhexenprozesse* (Frankfurt, Germany: Insel, 1991), pp. 123, 143–44. Jean Bodin, a renowned authority on international law during the sixteenth and seventeenth centuries, had a different interpretation concerning malformed infants: they were God's revenge against sinful parents. *De daemonomania* (Strasbourg, France: 1581), pp. 62, 64, 160.

22. John Boswell, *The Kindness of Strangers* (New York: Vintage Books, 1990), pp. 379–80.

23. Uta Ranke-Heinemann, *Eunuchs for the Kingdom of God: Women, Sexuality and the Catholic Church* (New York: Doubleday, 1990), p. 242. (The author was banned by the Vatican from Catholic schools because she raised questions not only about the humanity of the church, but also about the reality of Mary's virgin birth.

24. Tedeschi, "Preliminary Observations," p. 238.

25. Brian P. Levack, *The Witch-Hunt in Early Modern Europe* (New York: Longman, 1987), p. 21.

26. Examples where accused have been found dead in prison cells after torture sessions were reported by G. von Lamberg, *Criminal-Verfahren vorzüglich im ehemaligen Bisthum Bamberg während der Jahre 1624 bis 1630* (Nürnberg, Germany: Riegel & Wiessner, 1835, Beilage R.), p. 22; and Herbert Pohl, "Hexenglaube und Hexenverfolgung im Kurfürstentum Mainz," *Geschichtliche Landeskunde* 22 (Universität Mainz, 1988), pp. 69, 163.

27. Hans Küng, "Kardinal Ratzinger, Papst Wojtyla und die Angst vor der Freiheit," in Beate Kuckertz, ed., *Kreuz-Feuer: Die Kritik an der Kirche* (Munich, Germany: Wilhelm Heyne, 1991), p. 150.

28. First volumes have appeared by Reinbeck/Hamburg, Rowohlt, 1987.

29. Wolfgang Behringer, *Hexenverfolgung in Bayern* (Munich, Germany: Oldenbourg, 1987), pp. 359–63.

30. See, for example, the reasoning by Wolfgang Behringer, "Kinderhexenprozesse," *Zeitschrift für historische Forschung* 16 (1989): 31–47.

31. An elector was a prince-bishop or secular ruler holding office in the council of the Holy Roman Empire of German Nation empowered to elect the emperor of Germany.

32. Emil Zens, *Ein Opfer des Hexenwahns: Dr. Dietrich Flade* (Trier, Germany: Spee-Verlag, 1977).

33. From a Strasbourg document, quoted in Wolfgang Behringer, *Hexen und Hexenprozesse* (Munich, Germany: dtv, 1988), p. 204.

34. Sebald, *Witchcraft*, pp. 46–47.

35. Behringer, "Kinderhexenprozesse," p. 39.

36. See insightful discussions as to how the desire for "closure" or boundary maintenance expressed itself during the Reformation era: Dieter Harmening, *Zauberei im Abendland* (Würzburg, Germany: Königshausen & Neumann, 1991), p. 57–59; Hartwig Weber, *Kinderhexenprozesse* (Frankfurt, Germany: Insel, 1991), pp. 193ff.

37. Steven Ozment, *When Fathers Ruled—Family Life in Reformation Europe* (Cambridge, Mass.: Harvard University Press, 1983), p. 135.

38. Hans Sebald, *Adolescence—A Social-Psychological Analysis* (Englewood Cliffs, N.J.: Prentice-Hall, 1992), p. 329.

39. Ozment, *When Fathers Ruled*, p. 164.

40. Weber, *Kinderhexenprozesse*, pp. 193–94.

41. Ozment, *When Fathers Ruled*, p. 149.

42. Weber, *Kinderhexenprozesse*, pp. 233, 234n.

43. Ibid., p. 196.

44. Ibid., pp. 219ff.

45. See Sigmund von Riezler, *Geschichte der Hexenprozesse in Bayern* (1896; reprint, Aalen, Germany: Scientia Verlag, 1968), p. 271.

46. Translation of Zedler, *Grosses vollständiges Universal-Lexikon,* vol. 61 (Leipzig, Germany: 1732–54), p. 97, as cited by Behringer, "Kinderhexenprozesse," p. 135.

47. Zedler, vol. 61 (1749), p. 97.

48. Behringer, *Hexenverfolgung in Bayern,* pp. 175–79.

49. Ibid., pp. 44–45.

50. Ibid., p. 136.

2

Variations on a Basic Plot

Different Versions of Children's Trials

During the early-modern period (roughly from the sixteenth to eighteenth centuries) the European countries, especially the German lands (see map, pages 52–53), experienced a profusion of different jurisdictions. Diversity was reflected in inconsistent and confused reactions to the novel status of children. Some rulers felt encouraged to treat juvenile offenders more harshly, as, for example, the bishops of Würzburg and Bamberg; others adhered, at least initially, to older standards and granted children mitigation; and still others were undecided and sought advice from authorities pretending to know what to do.

An example of the latter category was the tiny jurisdiction of the Count-Palatine of Neuburg, which experienced a number of witch-children trials: a ten-year-old girl in 1629, a seven-year-old girl in 1699, and a thirteen-year-old boy in 1700.[1] At the time of the first trial, the Count-Palatine was confused about how to handle the situation of a ten-year-old imprisoned witch-girl whose mother, Ursula Zoller, had already been burned as a witch. The count's chancellor, Zeschlin, sought advice from the neighboring prince-bishops of Würzburg and Bamberg, both of whom were known to have had firsthand experiences with witch-children. Ironically, the Würzburg prelate, though having ordered dozens of executions of children himself, suggested that the girl be punished with a thorough spanking and then sent home. The Bamberg prelate, on the other hand, suggested that children, like this girl, should be thrown into prison, kept there until they reached adult status (twelve years of age), and then executed.[2] Fortunately, the count chose a different course of action and ordered that the girl receive a Christian education under tight clerical supervision.

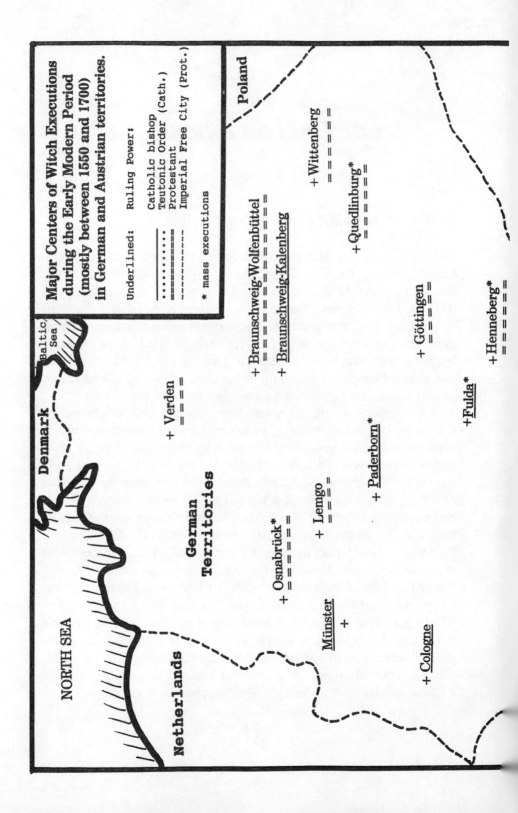

Major Centers of Witch Executions during the Early Modern Period (mostly between 1550 and 1700) in German and Austrian territories.

Underlined: Ruling Power:

    Catholic bishop
    Teutonic Order (Cath.)
    Protestant
    Imperial Free City (Prot.)

* mass executions

NORTH SEA

Baltic Sea

Denmark

Poland

Netherlands

German Territories

+ Osnabrück*

+ Lemgo

+ Münster

+ Paderborn*

+ Verden

+ Braunschweig-Wolfenbüttel

+ Braunschweig-Kalenberg

+ Wittenberg

+ Quedlinburg*

+ Göttingen

+ Fulda*

+ Henneberg*

+ Cologne

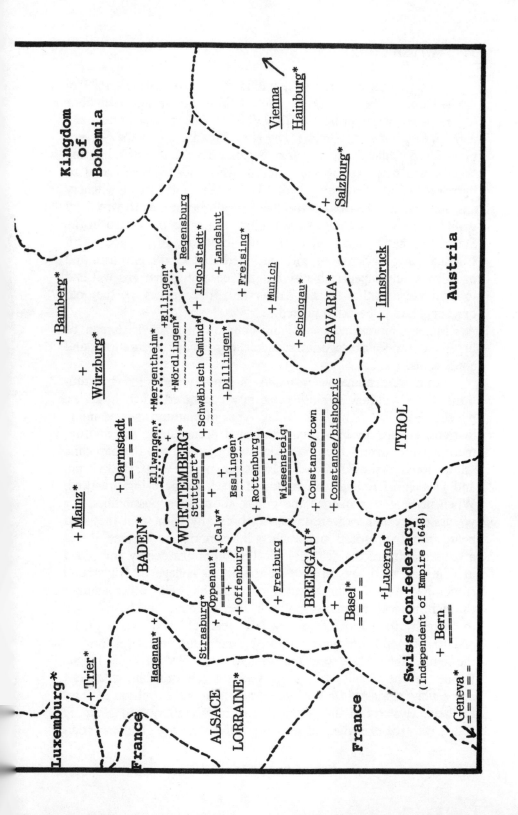

Concern was reflected in a public flyer distributed in 1629 in Aschaffenburg, the residence of the archbishop of Mainz, neighbor of the Würzburger bishopric. Its title was *Newer Tractat von der verführten Kinder Zaubergy* ("The New Treatise about the Sorcery of Seduced Children").[3] The text began with the author admitting that he was perplexed to see children, who outwardly appeared so harmless and innocent, being involved in so damnable a vice as witchery and sorcery. He then raised the theological question as to why God would allow such a thing, since nothing seems to be written in the Scriptures that would explain this phenomenon. In harmony with Christian theology, the author concluded that God's purposes and providence are impenetrable by human reasoning; that His will had to be done; and that the Devil's servants, the witches, be they old or young, had to be exterminated.

Major circumstances involving children in witch trials can be organized into four categories: scandals, possessions, accusations, and confessions.

There were numerous *scandals* in schools and similar institutions where children in close proximity concocted witch hysterias. Rivalry, jealousy, enmity, and other types of emotions stirred imaginations, created hysteria, and motivated accusations. An environment patently prone to eruptions of such hysteria was the parochial school. Records show Jesuit schools in Cologne, Eichstätt, Hildesheim, and Düsseldorf roiling with rumor of black magic being practiced. When investigators queried the pupils about such possibilities, the youngsters' responses were in perfect harmony with what they had heard from their priests and teachers in sermons and lectures. It was a confirmation of the demonological assumptions deeply embedded in Christian theology. In 1604 at the Jesuit college in Hildesheim rumor had it that pupils created mice, rabbits, and other animals through magical incantations, which, they claimed, had been taught to them by the Devil personally. The scandal prompted a gleeful reaction among Protestants, reinforcing their long-held suspicion that the Jesuits themselves were the ones who dabbled in black magic. Panics in the Jesuit college in Eichstätt resulted in witchcraft accusations against dozens of youngsters and the expulsion of forty of them. Hysteria in the Jesuit schools in Würzburg and Neuburg ended with the execution of several pupils.[4] And the children's trials at Trier, the turning point in defining children's status, was another example of this circumstance.

Under the thralls of *possession,* children could identify witches with impunity, and indeed could even benefit from the compassion of the inquisitor, who eagerly extended every form of exorcism to rid the young of demons. Possession offered psychological comfort to the participating persons. To the allegedly tormented child it gave license to accuse disliked persons, even close family members, and to do so without appearing cruel or ungrateful. To the exorcist it was a rewarding challenge to defeat the Devil and to purge the Christian community. The only recorded case of a witch execution in Vienna, for example, was the consequence of a sixteen-year-old possessed girl denouncing her grandmother as the agent of her affliction.[5]

Accusations of witchcraft commonly implicated members of the community against whom children held a grudge and against whom they could not apply other means of revenge and punishment. Sometimes accusations may have been forms of camouflaged rebellion or revenge against authority in general.

Numbers of children presented the courts with *confessions* that glittered with the vile ornaments of the contemporary image of witchcraft. Many of these children sparkled with a flair for mythomaniacal make-believe, the talent to fabricate convincingly and colorfully. Even though they probably realized initially that they were lying, they ended up believing what they claimed. A classic example is Witchboy, the case study to be described later in this book. Another example is young Catalina, who came to the Spanish inquisitor Alonso de Salazar y Frias and told him that she was a witch and had had sex with the Devil, during which she almost bled to death. Salazar, more circumspect than most of his colleagues, ordered matrons of the town to examine the girl. The women established that she was a virgin. This prompted the inquisitor to warn the girl against making up such stories, explaining the dire consequences that could have happened had another inquisitor heard them. Salazar then sent the girl home. Catalina was not the only one claiming such things; scores of other maidens pretended to identical debauchery.[6]

The scenarios show that children played diverse roles: they could be victims or victimizers, or, in many cases, a complex mixture of both. The following historical episodes illustrate the different versions.

One constant throughout all of them is the assumption that children can be guilty of plotting blasphemous and evil deeds with the Devil.

Playing the Double Role: The Hagenau Case

The town of Hagenau, about eighty miles southeast of Trier, in the province of Alsace, suffered a witch panic in 1627 that demonstrated the social-psychological dynamics whereby a victimized child turned into a victimizer. The violence of the Thirty Years' War had ravished the region and a bad harvest had caused starvation. Social order and cohesiveness were in ruins, and the confused and starving townspeople envisioned conspirators and malefactors lurking everywhere.

In their search for scapegoats they hit upon witches as the culprits of most of their troubles. Three women and a fourteen-year-old girl were implicated and, after a hurried trial, executed in July. Before the girl, Marie Niethin, was put to death, she denounced a score of townspeople, among them thirteen-year-old Peter Roller. In the hands of the Inquisition, the boy confessed and implicated additional townspeople, including just about everyone he knew. They all, he claimed, had attended the witches' sabbath and were active malefactors in the service of the Devil. The boy, with studied detail and rich imagery, persuasively established connections between community disasters and certain diabolic conspirators. The usual chain reaction took its course: When arrested and tortured, the accused admitted to all accusations and in turn named accomplice after accomplice. In the meantime the boy claimed to be bewitched and hence an innocent victim of the Devil's servants. He declared himself more than willing to be cured. Here was an exceptional youngster who knew what sort of role would help him to survive. Instead of going to the death cell, he went to the hospital. During the sixteenth and seventeenth centuries, most hospitals were run by religious orders, notably by the Order of St. John, dedicated to the care of the sick. As such they were subinstitutions of the church and cooperated with the Inquisition. Besides patients with medical problems and such non-patients as paupers, pilgrims, vagrants, and the resident monks or nuns, these hospitals also accommodated "patients" with spiritual problems.[7]

When Peter was reexamined nine months later, in March 1628, he reported that, in the name of Christ, he had just driven away the Devil who had tried to reenlist him. The inquisitors thought his resistance brave and a sign that he was on the way to rehabilitation. To complete the reinstitution into God's good graces, Peter was remanded to the care of two Capuchin monks. Two months later, Peter was considered purged of all demons and no longer a risk to the kingdom of heaven. He was freed and returned home. "This thirteen-year-old boy was responsible for twenty-four people being burned, three suicides in prison, and three being dismissed after torture—permanently crippled."[8]

High Drama at Würzburg

One of the most dangerous places for children to grow up during the time of the persecutions was in the prince-bishopric of Würzburg. Research by historian H. Erik Midelfort shows that more than a quarter of the 160 witches executed between 1627 and 1629 were children.[9] A roster listing the names of, or mostly nameless references to, over 200 persons executed during those few years includes such items as the following:[10]

a little girl twelve years of age from out of town;
a little girl of nine or ten years;
her younger sister;
a boy of twelve;
a boy of ten years;
a boy of eleven years;
a boy of ten years;
a pupil in the fifth grade, who knew several languages and was an accomplished musician in voice and instrument;
two boys, twelve years old, from the new monastery school;
a boy from out of town;
the two sons of the prince-bishop's cook, one fourteen and the other ten;
the bailiff from the Brennerbacher Hof and his apprentice;
two boys from the Spital school;
two boys from out of town;

a little blind girl; and
the twelve-year-old son of David Croten.

The witch persecution in Würzburg was so fierce that within an eight-year period (1623–31) of Prince-Bishop Philipp Adolf von Ehrenberg's reign nine hundred victims were executed. Many of them were burned at the stake or died under torture. Not even the bishop's blood relatives were spared accusation and prosecution. For example, Ernst von Ehrenberg, a young boy from the prelate's family, had to stand trial. Soon after the boy's execution, a number of persons included in their confessions the denunciation of the prince-bishop himself as well as his chancellor. The defamations claimed that these prominent persons had been seen dancing at the witches' sabbath. The unforeseen accusations jolted the prince-bishop into realizing the unreliability of the court procedures and prompted him to order moderation of the hunts.[11]

The unreliability of accusations became a pattern toward the end of the first third of the seventeenth century. Midelfort's studies of the witch panics in regions adjoining the Würzburg diocese found that the panics usually began with accusations against socially deviant and lower-class individuals, but then escalated rapidly and engulfed more and more prominent persons, even persons of high authority holding leading positions in the witch prosecutions.[12]

Although reaction to the von Ehrenberg case sedated the fever of the hunt and brought the largest wave of the persecutions to an end, it did not end the hunts completely. In Würzburg the succeeding princes of the church resumed the persecutions, executing a witch as late as 1749.

A Modern Exorcism

A notorious 1976 exorcism in Würzburg demonstrates the need to think in terms of historical continuity instead of discrete historical eras. It would be wrong to assume that possession and exorcism were phenomena restricted to past centuries. A striking example is the case of Anneliese Michel, a twenty-two-year-old student at the University of Würzburg, who symptomized what her family considered satanic possession. The woman's symptoms included spasms, writhing, speaking in devilish tongues, and other signs construed by the devout Catholic family as possession. The archbishop of Würzburg concurred with their diagnosis and entrusted two experienced priests with performing the Great Exorcism from the seventeenth-century *Rituale Romanum.* The Devil, as it turned out, personified himself as five different demons: Cain, Judas, Nero, Hitler, and Lucifer. A desperate fight, lasting several months, ensued between the exorcists and the presumed demons in the body of the young woman. In the end, the woman died. A medical doctor, called when it was too late, attributed her death to starvation. Michel, formerly strong and five feet, eight inches tall, weighed a mere seventy pounds at her death, for the exorcists had added the discipline of fasting to the other means employed to drive out the demons. (They may have relied on Matthew 4:1–2, where it is said that Jesus prepared himself to withstand the Devil's temptation by fasting.) At this juncture, the district attorney stepped in and ordered a thorough investigation, which resulted in the 1978 indictment of the priests and the woman's parents on charges of negligent manslaughter. The priests were convicted and sentenced to prison terms. This outcome shows that modern society, unlike society during previous eras, observes the separation of the powers of state from the powers of church.

A retrospective psychiatric assessment of the woman's symptoms diagnosed a pathology composed of epilepsy on the physiological level and high-fidelity role-playing on the social-psychological level. If we add a masked talent for spontaneously ventriloquizing voices as though they billowed from the belly, the woman's performance was persuasive and absolutely equal to that of Linda Blair in *The Exorcist,* which, incidentally, had been screened in the Würzburg region just prior to the onset of Michel's possession. (*The Exorcist,* by the way, is a bona fide depiction of symptoms the Catholic church still accepts as credible criteria of possession.)

Despite the tangible, natural explanation of the woman's affliction and the mass media's nationwide presentation of it, many believers have persisted in seeing the episode as a supernatural phenomenon. Noteworthy among them is Felicitas D. Goodman, an American anthropologist who claims that she can "prove" that this was a case of true possession and that new types of demons are presently active. When Goodman talks of demons, she doesn't mean it symbolically;

she depicts them as active "entities." Goodman was one of the first authors to publish an evaluation of the Michel case and made an impression on German readers by flaunting her academic credentials (including a doctorate from Ohio State University).[13] Goodman's writing contributed to the division and confusion of a German public that was not—and still is not—sure what to think of the event.

Panic in Mora

The witch panic in Mora, a town in northern Sweden, serves as a classic example of the double role of children.[14] During the 1660s and 1670s many northern Swedish communities experienced witch scare and more than two hundred persons were executed. Sermons by Protestant ministers thundered against the Devil and his human conspirators and brought public madness to a crescendo. It took little cerebral work to combine ancient Nordic mythology, according to which the witches congregated at a place called Blokulla, with contemporary Christian ideas and to inspire scores of children with vivid imaginations and dangerous mischief. They reported to the authorities that they had observed hordes of local townspeople at the diabolic witches' dance. Not to be outdone by the denunciations, many adults retaliated by claiming that the children themselves had participated. Finally, the cauldron fed by both parties produced a scenario in which adults had seduced the children to participate.

Rumors and scandals had grown by 1669 to such proportions that King Charles XI appointed a commission to redeem the errant citizens by prayer instead of by separating their souls from their bodies. However, despite royal concern and fervent prayer, fear and panic did anything but abate. The result was a sterner approach and the identification of seventy witches. Although a royal degree forbade torture, historians suspect that the commissioners nonetheless applied it. How else to explain that of the seventy accused persons, twenty-three confessed right away and were condemned and burned within a matter of weeks? The remainder were sent to prison in Falun, where they were later burned. On the basis of the adults' testimonies, fifteen children were burned; thirty-six others between the ages of nine and fifteen were sentenced to run the gauntlet (having to pass between rows of switch-wielding parishioners) in addition to being lashed with the rod across their hands once a week for an entire year; twenty others were spared the gauntlet because they were under nine years of age, but were caned at the church door every Sunday for a number of weeks. Levels of punishment were determined according to severity of denunciations brought against them.

When, on August 25, 1669, the Falun condemned were carted to the place of execution and, as procedure demanded, asked to publicly confess their crimes before being put to death, almost all confirmed the details of the accusations. Yet previously, when they had been asked individually, they consistently denied them. It appears that the unanimity demonstrates the power of collectivity and the contagious element of confessing en masse. In any case, regardless of their last-minute confession, they were put to death.

The details of the accusations and the confessions illustrate how mythomaniacal talent intertwined with traditional image. According to the children, the witches carried them, dressed in red or blue, on goats, sticks, or sleeping men to the nocturnal celebrations. The witches had no problem in exiting or entering the children's homes through windows because the Devil had previously removed the glass for unimpaired passage. Later, as they began to renounce the conspiracy, repent their participation, and reveal the names of witches, the children claimed to have been flogged at the witches' gatherings. Yet, as much as the commissioners examined the children's bodies, they could not find a trace or mark of the lashes. This was quickly explained as a sign of the witches' shrewdness: they caused the marks to disappear magically in order to abolish the evidence.

Blokulla seemed to consist of a vast meadow with a house in the middle. Part of the meadow was fenced and served as corral and pasture for the beasts that had carried them there. The diabolic rites that supposedly took place there included eight acts: denial of God by writing one's name with one's blood in the Devil's book; being baptized by the Devil; swearing an oath of allegiance to the Devil; sitting down to a lavish banquet; music and dancing; fornication with one another; building a stone house to shelter the witches on the Day of Judgment (the walls were perpetually falling down); and promising the Devil to do evil deeds in the community.

Testimony was given to the reality of the last item by the minister of Elfdale, who attributed his chronic headache to the malice of witches. Hardly had he pronounced this diagnosis when one of the accused witches admitted that the Devil had sent her to torment the minister: one night she had stolen into his bed chamber and tried to hammer a nail into his skull—hence the headache.

The lord's commissioners tried to investigate thoroughly and took great pains to persuade the witches to show them some of their tricks, but to no avail, for the accused witches declared unanimously that their magical powers had vanished at the moment of confession.

The panic did not end with the conclusion of the trials, but spread over the next six years to the Swedish-speaking provinces of Finland and to Stockholm. In the Swedish capital it was stopped in its earliest stage by the remonstrations of an enlightened medical doctor, Urban Häjrne, who succeeded in demonstrating that the hysteria was fueled by morbid imagination, confused thoughts, pure malice, and the desire to get attention. Nonetheless, there was a flare-up of the witch scare about sixty years later, during the 1720s, when a thirteen-year-old Norwegian girl, Siri Jorgensdatter, tried to duplicate the Mora details about which she had heard or read, and started to accuse several old women of witchcraft.

An Upper-Class Trial

A scenario quite different from that of the Mora case stars a young nobleman in training to become a knight. This time it is not a community affair, but a very private family tragedy. It is the case of Ernst von Ehrenberg, a member of the family of the Würzburg prince-bishop. The case shows that accusations thrived in educational institutions, that a minor could become a victim without turning into victimizer, that no socioeconomic class was exempt, and that trial and execution could be a hushed-up affair.

The case is described unctuously and in great detail by the Jesuit charged with the physical as well as spiritual care of the young knight-to-be. Little did the Jesuit know that this responsibility would turn him into the youth's executioner.[15] The style of the narration must thus be understood as written from the point of view of the youth's priestly tutor. Whereas today we would diagnose the boy's trouble as adolescent confusion and rebelliousness, his contemporaries, clergy as well as lay people, saw his behavior as inspired by the Devil, warranting the conviction of witchcraft.

The Jesuit begins his story with the assurance that young Ernst used to be a diligent and pious boy, until the time he entered into an intimate affair with an older cousin. She evidently seduced him, and from then on he neglected his studies, failed to attend worship services, and became more interested in girls than in scholarly or religious pursuits. Würzburg judges, busy with some unrelated witch trials, happened to hear explanations for the impious behavior: several of Ernst's peers confessed (under torture) that, through the evil wiles of the cousin, Ernst had committed himself to the Devil, put spells on his enemies, and seduced his friends. Upon hearing this, the prince-bishop turned Ernst over to the learned Jesuits, ordering them to rehabilitate the young renegade. It was made clear to the boy that the *indicia* were sufficient to burn him at the stake, but that the prelate's mercy would give him a chance for remorse and penance. In order to save his life, however, he must first confess. The unexpected confrontation came as a shock to the boy; he was thoroughly frightened, confessed readily, and promised to return to Christian ways. He was taken to the house of the Jesuits, where he was closely supervised and provided with all the sacraments of the church, including such liturgical weapons as blessed amulets, relics of saints, and holy water. At the beginning, Ernst cooperated willingly, almost eagerly, but his hasty zest for salvation and monastic lifestyle soon dwindled and he began to regress to his negligent ways. The Jesuits suspected that during the night Ernst would put aside all the sacred paraphernalia, let the Devil come into his cell, and depart with him for the witches' dance. Nothing was more difficult, his tutors now realized, than to fight the evils of witchcraft.

Again the boy was confronted. Sobbing, he confessed that he was still experiencing miraculous things, but readily renewed the promise to mend his ways. The promise was of short duration, and soon he was found to have again departed from Christian ways. Now the Jesuits started to develop self-doubts concerning their pedagogic capabilities and decided to turn the troubled adolescent over to the Franciscans, hoping they could do a better job.

Unfortunately Ernst proved as intractable for them as he had been for the Jesuits. At this stage, a report was submitted to the prince-bishop declaring the young nobleman beyond hope and betterment. In response, the prelate had a judge sentence the boy to die. The Jesuits were ordered to arrange the execution. A delegation of Jesuits, among them the narrator, went to the boy's cell and spoke in rather ambiguous terms, alluding to a better life that was awaiting him. They asked him to come along to the castle, and, failing to recognize the real meaning behind the obtuseness of pious parlance, Ernst accompanied them, sharing some cheerful recollections of his childhood while walking through the castle's familiar corridors. (At this passage the narrator seemed to show sentiments of being moved.) Finally Ernst's ineffectual teachers ushered him into a hall with walls curtained in black and a scaffold in the center. All at once the boy understood the situation and, as the executioner was about to lay hands on him, he began to wail, sob, and beg for mercy with such sincerity that everyone present felt sorry for him. They decided to stop the proceedings and to petition the prince-bishop for mercy and another chance at redemption.

The Würzburg ecclesiarch agreed to a reprieve and sent a personal delegate to his young cousin to convey his willingness to forgive him on the condition that he make a holy promise to revert to a Christian life. It is not certain what exactly transpired in the boy's cell and how the interview proceeded; but in any case the report of the delegate was totally negative: Ernst had refused to promise anything and had the effrontery to declare his desire to stay the way he was, claiming that if he weren't already that way, he would certainly want to become so. In short, the delegate reported, the Devil had hardened Ernst's heart beyond reach.

This was the end of the Würzburg hierarch's patience. Angrily he reordered the execution and insisted that justice take its course without delay. They dragged the adolescent boy into the black hall; two Jesuits flanked him and implored him to repent, but Ernst rejected their exhortations, replying that he was in no need of repentance. Again he cried to have his life spared and sobbed and begged, all the while trying to fight off the executioner attempting to get a hold of him. The undignified melee finally ended when the executioner, taking advantage of the boy's exhaustion, swiftly swung his sword, severing the youth's head.

The Jesuit narrator concluded by noting that the boy fell without an utterance of repentance and that he hoped the errant knight-to-be would be spared eternal hellfire.

Notes

1. Sigmund von Riezler, *Geschichte der Hexenprozesse in Bayern* (Aalen, Germany: Scientia, 1968), pp. 228–29.

2. Wolfgang Behringer, "Kinderhexenprozesse," *Zeitschrift für historische Forschung* 16 (1989): 38.

3. (Anonymous), *Newer Tractat von der verführten Kinder Zaubery* (Aschaffenburg, Germany: Quirin Botzer, 1629).

4. Hartwig Weber, *Kinderhexenprozesse* (Frankfurt, Germany: Insel, 1991), p. 244n.

5. Heide Dienst, "Hexenverfolgung," in *Hexen und Zauberer,* ed. H. Valentinitsch (Graz, Austria: Akademische Druck-M. Verlagsanstalt, 1987), pp. 268–71.

6. Julio C. Baroja, *The World of Witches* (Chicago: University of Chicago Press, 1965), p. 186.

7. Cf. Adalbert Mischlewski, "Alltag im Spital zu Beginn des 16. Jahrhunderts," in *Alltag im 16. Jahrhundert,* eds. A. Kohler and H. Lutz (Vienna, Austria: Verlag für Geschichte unde Politik, 1987), pp. 152–73; and Hartwig Weber, *Kinderhexenprozesse* (Frankfurt, Germany: Insel, 1991), pp. 265, 270, 272.

8. Rossell H. Robbins, *The Encyclopedia of Witchcraft and Demonology* (New York: Crown, 1959), p. 94.

9. H. Erik Midelfort, "Witch-Hunting and the Domino Theory," in *Religion and the People, 800 to 1700,* ed. James Oberkevich (Chapel Hill: University of North Carolina Press, 1979), p. 283.

10. W. G. Soldan and H. Heppe, *Geschichte der Hexenprozesse* (Kettwig, Germany: Magnus-Verlag, 1986 [a revised edition of the 1880 Cotta publication]), pp. 45–51.

11. Ibid., p. 54.

12. H. Erik Midelfort, *The Witch Hunt in Southwestern Germany 1562–1684* (Stanford, Calif.: Stanford University Press, 1972).

13. Felicitas D. Goodman, *Anneliese Michel und ihre Dämonen. Der Fall Klingenberg in wissenschaftlicher Sicht* (Stein a. Rhein, Switzerland: Christiana-Verlag, 1980). An English version by the same author appeared a year later: *The Exorcism of Anneliese Michel* (Garden City, N.Y.: Double-

day, 1980). Supporting Goodman's "true possession" theory is Georg Siegmund, ed., *Von Wemding nach Klingenberg* (Stein a. Rhein, Switzerland: Christiana-Verlag, 1985). The latter publication is remarkable for choosing as foreword a statement by Joseph Cardinal Ratzinger, a pontiff second only in authority to the pope and heading the Congregation of the Faith, the erstwhile office of the Holy Inquisition. In this foreword (p. 6) we have it on highest authority that "the Devil is an enigmatic but real and personifiable being and *not* merely a symbolic figure" (emphasis added).

14. I am basing the Mora description on Robbins, *The Encyclopedia of Witchcraft and Demonology,* pp. 348–50, and Brian P. Levack, *The Witch-Hunt in Early Modern Europe* (New York: Longman, 1987), pp. 191–92.

15. I am relying on the German rendition, a translation from Latin, by W. G. Soldan and H. Heppe, *Geschichte der Hexenprozesse,* pp. 52–54.

3

America: The Devil in Salem

The Setting

The witch trials best known to American readers are of course the Salem trials of 1692, in which children were victimizers under the guise of being possessed. Since this discussion focuses rather narrowly on the role of the children, the many and complex ramifications of the Salem episode cannot be done justice here. A few brief comments must suffice to sketch the larger setting.

It seems that the Puritans of New England were more Devil-fearing than God-fearing. They had undergone extraordinary hardship and danger in the New World and hence had become hypersensitive to fears and superstitious beliefs. It must be emphasized, however, that the decisive factors powering the witch panic existed as inherent parts of the culture the Puritans had brought with them from the Old World, specifically from England, which, at the time, was replete with the typical stories, written and oral, about the evils of witchcraft. Almost all the supernatural symbolism observable in Salem was of English background,[1] notwithstanding the fact that the last English witch had been executed in 1684.[2]

The Salem episode is characterized by a number of features uncommon to European persecution: (1) The persecution came on fast, like a tornado, tore through the community, and was gone within about a year's time. Its ephemeral nature is remarkable when compared with Europe's witch-hunts, which literally stretched over several centuries. (2) In their wake the Salem witch-hunts left a noteworthy sociological phenomenon: the institutions of church and court completed the break between religion and magic; henceforth, witchcraft was no longer considered a civil deviance, a punishable crime. (3) After sanity returned to the community, restitution and official declarations of regret were made to the victims or to the victims' families. This was unique in the annals of the witch persecution in Western civilization. One regret was noticeably late, exactly three hundred years late. It was not until September 1992 that members of the First Church of Salem voted to readmit Rebecca Nurse and Giles Cory, excommunicated in 1692 during the witchcraft hysteria. The vote by the Unitarian parish was part of the three hundredth anniversary of the trials. Nurse was hung, while Cory was killed by stones being piled on him.[3] (4) The accused were not characterized by deviant reputation or lower-class standing, as in most parts of Europe (excepting certain regions of Germany). On the contrary, they tended to be models of Christian lifestyle and respected members of the village. (5) The persons standing trial appear to have been highly individualistic personalities, not merely because of careful court records, but mainly because they were expressive and assertive persons to begin with, quite unlike most of the muted personalities of their European counterparts. (6) The episode undoubtedly became the most thoroughly analyzed and publicized account of any witch trial, whereas, in comparison, the trials in European regions have received far less intense attention.[4] The Salem saga has become an item of American national identity to a much greater extent than its equivalents in other nations ever have.[5]

Some features definitely were *not* exceptional: (1) the children's hysteria and accusations; (2) the unquestioned credibility granted to children's testimonies; (3) the dealing out of death sentences on short order (though the number of victims—fourteen men and five women hanged, four others died in jail) is minuscule compared with European statistics; (4) the role of neighbors' quarrels and denunciations.

Children as Classic Victimizers

The witch panic started with the reaction of suggestible young girls to certain stories told by the slave Tituba in the house of the Rev.

Samuel Parris. His daughter Elisabeth (Betty), aged nine, and her cousin Abigail Williams, aged eleven, became regular and avid listeners and responded to the lore with extraordinary emotionality. They soon developed the symptoms of suffering under spells, having become thoroughly acquainted with the symptoms through the stories they had been hearing or reading.

Among the stories was one that evidently affected them most profoundly. It described what happened four years earlier to the Goodwin children in Boston. In the family of the God- and Devil-fearing mason John Goodwin, four young children had developed agonized fits, crazed behavior, and blasphemous outbursts so outrageously and publicly as to cause a general scare in Boston's North End quarters, which, at the time, was under the spiritual care of the Rev. Cotton Mather. Without much delay, the affliction was blamed on an evil spell cast by an Irish washerwoman known as the Witch Glover. Since the concerted prayers of four ministers failed to lift the suffering of the children, a more radical action was taken— the Witch Glover was tried and hanged. Predictably, the details of the episode spread across the land and became well known in Salem Village. In fact, Rev. Mather had published his observations on diabolism under the title of *Memorable Providences Relating to Witchcraft and Possession*. The book had achieved a wide circulation and left a deep impression in the colonies. A copy of the book was in the Parris home. Indeed, it is quite possible that the entire Parris family had been firsthand witnesses of the case, for they lived in Boston at the time. They might have seen the actual hanging, taking along, as tradition allowed, little Betty.[6]

To the credit of the clergyman it must be said that he initially hesitated to accept a supernatural explanation and refused to equate the meaning of the girls' expressions with that of the Goodwin children's; instead he took the afflicted to a medical doctor. Dr. Griggs tried his best to diagnose the strange malady within the limited frame of medical science available at the time.[7] After he had ruled out epilepsy and observed the ineffectuality of his medicines, he concluded that the Devil had something to do with it and suspected witchcraft. The news of the suspicion traveled like wildfire throughout the village, and the girls became the center of attention. Soon thereafter the strange affliction spread, like a contagious disease, to other young people in the community, enveloping with particular ferocity eight supposed ringleaders ranging in age from twelve to twenty: Ann Putnam, Elisabeth Hubbard, Mary Walcott, Mary Warren, Elisabeth Proctor, Mercy Lewis, Susan Sheldon, and Elisabeth Booth.

Because they were judged to be possessed—which included the understanding that they suffered innocently and against their will—the girls' behavior remained unpunished and even escalated into ever greater hysteria, as they took advantage of the opportunity to rebel against the restrictions imposed by tradition and adult society. Only the villagers' unshakable belief in the reality and the power of the Devil can explain why they felt pity and compassion for the "poor, suffering children," instead of punishing them for offensive behavior. In fact, the hysterical youths achieved the status of celebrities.

The Dimensions of Possession

The "state of possession" flung open the doors of an armory filled with weapons and strategies designed to accuse people with impunity and submit the most exotic "evidence" with credibility.

The Display of Diabolic Torment

First, the children displayed intense pain and discomfort for which no one knew a natural cause, and so everyone assumed a supernatural origin: spells by witches. The girls wept, uttered short choking sounds, jerked all over as if they were being pinched or pricked by needles, got down on all fours and ran under the furniture, barking and braying, convulsing, writhing, and screeching. The prayers of the frightened audiences seemed to be ineffectual; indeed, they seemed to make matters worse, as Betty, who had been known as the gentlest of little girls, would shriek wildly at the mere sound of "Our Father in Heaven. . . ." And Abigail would cover her ears, stamp her feet and scream at the top of her voice in order to drown out the sound of pious words. On one occasion, Betty even hurled a Bible across the room. The rage would increase or decrease, depending on who was present.

Targeting Accusations

It is interesting that the victims of the children's denunciations were persons in good standing in the community, persons with impeccable reputations and substantial properties. Quite clearly, the only way to tarnish their status was through accusing them of indefensible crimes of supernatural nature, such as witchcraft. For example, eighteen-year-old Elisabeth Booth testified in a sworn deposition before the court that the "appearance" (spirit) of her neighbor, Goodman John Proctor, had tormented her grievously. Not only had she been tormented, the girl continued to assert, but also her friends, Mary, Mercy, and Ann; she had seen Proctor's "appearance" inflicting such torments as pinching, twisting, and almost choking them to death.[8] Sixteen-year-old Mary Walcott accused Goodwife Abigail Faulkner of the same misdeeds, swearing before the court that, "I saw Abigail Faulkner, or her appearance, most grievously afflict and torment Sarah Phelps and Ann Putnam. And I verily believe in my heart that [she] is a witch, and that she has often afflicted me . . . by acts of witchcraft."[9] Both the denounced were condemned and sentenced to die. Proctor was hanged. Faulkner pleaded pregnancy and thus was spared. The depositions of all the young women were so similar that the only differences were the names of the accused—the form of torment and "evidence" established remained nearly identical.

Drawing an Audience

The girls' affliction was not only public knowledge, but also public spectacle. Their seizures were not limited to the family setting, but could be seen and heard at court hearings, where they regularly attracted a large audience—an audience, it must be emphasized, mostly sympathetic to the girls, considering them innocent martyrs of wicked spells. And here we have arrived at the key concept: the audience. It was and is the sine qua non of the enactment of possession. There is no possession on record that took place in private, with an audience absent. An audience would provide the girls with the right cues to start acting. If no audience was present, or if the audience failed to give the right cues, such as failing to show signs of credulity, the girls' acts either shriveled pitifully or didn't materialize at all. An example was the girls' encounter with citizens of Ipswich, a community that didn't want to have anything to do with the hysterical youths. As the girls almost automatically fell into their fits in front of them, the people literally turned their backs on the youthful actresses, depriving them of familiar cues and aborting their performance. As Marion Starkey poignantly put it: "Being ignored was a therapy that had rarely been tried upon these girls."[10] Audiences at other places, however, continued to reinforce the girls' behavior and supported their denunciations.

"Spectral Evidence"

A possessed person was believed to be clairvoyant and prescient, sometimes referred to as "having the second sight." This, in essence, meant that the girls could see spirits and gain vision of the usually invisible world of witches. There was a lethal twist to this notion: the Devil cannot assume the "shape" or "appearance" (spirit form) of an *innocent* person. Hence the persons visible to the girls' "second sight" were by definition devils or witches. Thanks to the people's belief in this phenomenon, the girls' testimonies and accusations were taken at face value, instead of as hoaxes or hallucinations. The court accepted the girls' stories as proof, and many villagers realized that against this sort of proof there was no defense, and no alibi. The power of the belief in spectral evidence was such that, when the panic spread to the neighbor community of Andover and the local justice of the peace refused to sign any more warrants for arrest, he, too, was denounced by the girls. They claimed spectral evidence that he and his wife had committed nine murders. Rather than fighting the people's tenacious belief in the phenomenon and risking their lives, the justice and his family, as well as other denounced individuals, decided to pack up and leave the community.[11]

Identifying Witches by Touch

As is typical of all communities that suspect witches in their midst, Salem and the neighbor community of Andover became obsessed with the goal of identifying them. The girls' gift of spectral evidence was not the only means to accomplish that task; an additional technique was identification by touch, whereby persons to be tested for witch-craft had to join hands with the girls, who, by then, had established themselves as infallible mediums. Community meetings were arranged, where scores of villagers were ordered to stand in virtual police lineups to be tested. Then the girls were brought into the hall in the throes of full possession and the ritualistic contact of hands was made, with the audience giving all the rewarding cues. Surprising things happened. Not all of the persons in the lineup had been suspected, but had been included in the interest of impartiality. Yet the girls' reactions indiscriminately identified suspects and nonsuspects. When, at the touching of the hands, a girl would draw a sobbing breath and relax her seizure, the entire assembly perceived the act as evidence that a witch had drawn the demon from the afflicted.[12] This sort of testing was repeated again and again. No one had expected that more than a few witches would be discovered in Andover; yet within a short time forty warrants were issued. On one occasion, one of the young girls gave an unearthly shriek of agony and fell to the floor in convulsions as she approached an accused matron. The fits would not cease until two officers of the court picked her up and carried her to the accused. "Then one officer would twist the prisoner's head so that she could not 'overlook' her victim and the other would guide her hand to the afflicted girl's, so that her touch might draw her devil back to her. That done, the afflicted one was pronounced officially out of danger."[13] Later the touch technique was used to (temporarily) restore the health of several of the girls.

Salem's method of taking children on a virtual circuit of the community to identify witches had a 1527 precedent in Spain. The judges of Pamplona were confronted by two girls, one nine, the other twelve, who asserted that they could recognize a witch by look-ing into her left eye. Finding the opportunity irresistible, the judges scanned the entire countryside with the children determining in each community which of the suspects truly were witches. In no time, 150 witches and warlocks were arrested. And in equally short time the Inquisition extracted confessions, according to which they all were members of covens dedicated to Satan and celebrating orgiastic sabbaths.[14]

The Power of Concurrence

It probably was by tacit and spontaneous agreement, rather than by prepared conspiracy, that at testing sessions and at hearings the girls would agree with one another about who was and who was not a witch. They were talented actresses, perfectly able to improvise on a theme and carry it to a victorious crescendo. Such behavior in concert is best described as the result of mutual reinforcement, seeing the identical action in others and deriving from it a feeling of power that at times can reach heights of ecstasy.

The Salem trials were not unique in conjuring up manifestations of the power of collective reinforcement. Hartwig Weber reports a 1666 episode of hysterical behavior among the adolescents in the orphanage of the community of Horn in the Netherlands. Off and on, the entire group would erupt into an insane choreography of writhing, flailing limbs, and rolling on the ground, accompanied by bellowing and gnashing teeth. Whenever one youngster started the action, the others followed suit. Their contortions were carried out with such force that it took several adults to hold down just one adolescent. All efforts at remedy failed. Least effectual proved to be religious measures, such as prayer services, which worsened the condition, as the intonation of prayers and litanies seemed to inspire the congregated youths to turn immediately into a writhing mob. In desperation, the authorities finally removed the youngsters from the orphanage and placed each one individually into foster homes throughout the town. With one stroke the entire spook vanished: not one of the children continued to display any sign of the previous affliction.[15]

A typical Salem example comes from a hearing at which the matron Martha Cory was to be questioned. As she tried to defend her innocence and assured the magistrates that she certainly was a faithful "gospel woman," one of the girls screamed: "Gospel witch!" Immediately all the girls took up the cry. "Gospel witch! Gospel witch!" An earsplitting pandemonium broke out. After order was restored, Martha Cory continued the attempt to defend herself. All at once, the girls commenced to imitate every movement and action of the accused, and a classic example of echomania ensued: "What Martha did now they all did. If she shifted her feet they did so, too, and fell to stamping with such force as to rock the meeting-house. If she bit her lips, they yelled that she had bitten theirs, and came running up to the magistrates to show how they bled."[16] When Martha persisted in her innocence and called on the magistrates not to believe the "distracted children," one of the magistrates turned on her angrily and pointed out that the girls' present torment was nothing less than further proof that even while she defended herself, her devils were continuing to torment the girls. There simply was no defense against the accusations of the girls, who had become confirmed mediums. Such demonstrations of accusations in concert tended to intimidate witnesses, even officials, who might have been inclined to hold different definitions of the situation. For example, a number of people (thirty-one friends in Ipswich and twenty-one neighbors in Salem Village) were afraid of risking the revenge of the determined girls after they had signed their names to a petition, letting the court know of their faith in John Proctor's good conduct. Their testimony was manifestly disregarded. Not even the status of clergy was sufficient protection against the concerted onslaught of the girls. When Rev. George Burroughs stood trial for witchcraft, his courageous defense was not merely a personal one but turned against the total idea of the reality of witchcraft. In an oral as well as written statement he addressed the jury and tried to persuade them to see the situation as it really was: a delusion. He declared, in essence, that there were not nor had there ever been witches who made pacts with the Devil and tormented human beings. The response of the girls was swift and merciless. They appeared before the court, claiming that Rev. Burroughs had sent his "shape" on the very eve of the trial to torment and bite them severely. They all had teeth marks on their arms to show the judges, who delayed taking their words for it until Rev. Burroughs's teeth had been examined and compared to the sets of marks. Not only did they compare his teeth but also the teeth of others present in the courtroom with the evident marks. "It was thereby established beyond doubt that Rev. Burroughs and Rev. Burroughs alone had bitten the girls."[17] Burroughs was hanged.

Contagious Hysteria

Personality dynamics similar to those that energize concerted action also cause imitation. Persons who up to that time had neither belonged to the conspirators' circle nor even shown any of their symptoms started to imitate the girls upon experiencing direct contact with them. On several occasions the girls were led from house to house to focus their tranced glare on the sickbed in order to identify the nature of the malady. In most cases they claimed repeatedly to have had the same vision: seeing a witch standing at the patient's head, another at the patient's feet. As they modeled their gifted "second sight" with the usual embellishment of fits and seizures, young people in the house often joined them in their demeanor, breaking into howls and barking, suffering instant convulsions, and claiming that their eyes suddenly also had acquired "second vision." Contagious emotionality has been aptly described and explained by such pioneers of social psychology as Gustave LeBon and Charles Mackay, with the latter employing the analytic framework to understand actual cases of English witch hysteria.[18]

So much for the deadly role of the children in the Salem episode. After agonizing months of hunting witches under the guidance of accomplished young actresses, the death of almost two dozen people, and the imprisonment of over 150 witches awaiting trial, the hysteria, like a vile fever, had run its course and sanity slowly returned to the community. The curtain came down on a drama in which the stars had played their roles with lethal skill and so convinced the audience that it confused stage with reality. As the play ended, the audience realized their confusion and dispersed, embarrassed, contrite, and with a parting feeble attempt at restitution.

Notes

1. See descriptions of English witchcraft trials in Alan Macfarlane, *Witchcraft in Tudor and Stuart England* (London: Routledge & Kegan Paul, 1970).

2. There is a question as to the exact year. Christina Hole refers to 1684 (*Witchcraft in England* [Totowa, N.J.: Rowman, 1977], p. 18), Rossell H. Robbins to 1685 (*The Encyclopedia of Witchcraft and Demonology* [New York: Crown, 1959], p. 429), and Charles Mackay to 1716 (*Extraordinary Popular Delusions and the Madness of Crowds* [1841, reprint, New York: Noonday Press, 1974], p. 521).

3. *USA Today,* September 21, 1992, p. 3A.

4. The neverending interest in Salem has produced volume after volume of research work, beginning in the nineteenth century and continuing to the present. To mention just a few: Charles W. Upshaw, *Salem Witchcraft* (Boston: Wiggins & Lunt, 1867), 2 vols. (an esteemed pioneer work); Marion L. Starkey, *The Devil in Massachusetts* (New York: Time Inc., 1949 and 1963); P. Boyer and S. Nissenbaum, *Salem Possessed: The Social Origins of Witchcraft* (Cambridge, Mass.: Harvard University Press, 1974); John Putnam Demos, *Entertaining Satan: Witchcraft and the Culture of Early New England* (New York: Oxford University Press, 1982), though this is a treatment of the larger setting of New England.

5. No other country that experienced witch persecution is celebrating the anniversary of trials; no other country has an organization like the Daughters of Early American Witches, an organization that, among other things, rallied to festivities and orations at the occasion of the three-hundredth anniversary of the Salem witch trials. *Miami Herald,* March 15, 1992.

6. Starkey, *The Devil in Massachusetts,* p. 22.

7. Some researchers have since suspected ergotism (poisoning through a hallucinogenic fungus) as the cause of the girls' bizarre behavior. Few historians think this notion merits attention. But even hallucinating minds are limited to roam within the cultural parameters with which they are familiar, in this case the witch images as they were generally perceived by the people at the time. Hence the possibility of ergotism does little to change the overall meaning of what was going on in Salem. See proponents of the ergotism theory: Linnda R. Caporael, "Ergotism: The Devil Loosed in Salem," *Science* 191 (April 2, 1976): 21–26, and Mary K. Matossian, "Ergot and the Salem Witchcraft Affair," *American Scientist* 70 (July/August 1982): 355–57.

8. Robbins, *The Encyclopedia of Witchcraft and Demonology,* p. 433.

9. Ibid.

10. Starkey, *The Devil in Massachusetts,* p. 237.

11. Ibid., p. 194.

12. Ibid., p. 190.

13. Ibid., p. 139.

14. Hartwig Weber, *Kinderhexenprozesse* (Frankfurt, Germany: Insel, 1991), pp. 200–201.

15. Ibid., pp. 202–203.

16. Starkey, *The Devil in Massachusetts,* p. 60.

17. Ibid., p. 203.

18. Gustave LeBon, *Psychologie des Foules* (Paris: Olean, 1895); Mackay, *Extraordinary Popular Delusions and the Madness of Crowds.*

4

The English Witches

The Bewitched Children of Warboys

The trials that significantly prefigured Salem, and may indeed have served as models for the Salem girls' behavior, dealt with the witches of Warboys. As was typical for English trials, disturbed children played the decisive, accusatory role. The Warboys trouble started in 1589 in the well-to-do Throckmorton family of Warboys in Huntingdon-shire. There were five daughters. Jane, the oldest and at that time about ten, began to suffer strange convulsions and contortions, which, in retrospect, appear to have been epileptic in nature. However, when a well-known Cambridge physician, Dr. Barrow, was called in to examine and treat the girl, he was unable to come up with a natural explanation and finally diagnosed witchcraft as the cause of her ills.[1]

This was a turning point in the meaning ascribed to the symptoms. Henceforth Jane herself, her four sisters, and gradually also her parents saw the affliction in a supernatural light. Soon the symptoms spread like an infectious disease. The four younger children developed identical fits; so did several of the servants, and finally an aunt of the girls in the nearby village of Ellington.

Almost at the same time the responsibility for the trouble was laid upon an elderly village woman, called Mother Samuel, who fit the image of the storybook witch: old, poor, and quite homely. Since there was no other reason, let alone evidence, to target her, it probably was her appearance that stimulated the accusations, which sprang forth with amazing unanimity from many sources. All the afflicted pointed the finger at the matron. Jane claimed that the first time she experienced the piercing pains was when she passed Mother Samuel's cottage and the old woman, sitting in front of the door knitting, looked up from her work and stared at her. Jane then knew right away that her pain derived from an evil spell. From that day on she told everyone who cared to listen that Mother Samuel had bewitched her. That made a deep impression on her younger sisters, who forthrightly exhibited the same odd fits as their older sister. The fits assumed particular savageness whenever they caught sight of the "witch." This continued for an incredible three and a half years, during which time the parents showed exemplary patience in a household that must have been hellish to live in. An unusual aspect of the case is that during these years the parents not only refrained from taking action against the old woman, but treated her in a friendly way and merely entreated her to confess her sorcery and remove the spell. This lenience may have been in part a consequence of their merely half-hearted belief in the accusations, although the sufferers incessantly repeated them.

Then something happened that escalated the affair. One day, Mrs. Cromwell, the rich landlady of both the Samuels and the Throckmortons, paid a visit to the latter. On that occasion she learned firsthand about the children's plight and decided to do something about it. Impulsively she sent for Mother Samuel and ordered her to appear immediately before her and, in front of the entire Throckmorton family, with the children shifting their fits into higher gear, roundly accused the woman of being an evil witch. Without giving her a chance to defend herself or to get away from her, Cromwell tore off the matron's cap and snipped off a strand of her hair. This she gave to Mrs. Throckmorton, telling her to burn it. The high-handed action understandably upset Mother Samuel, who responded by shouting: "Madam, why do you use me thus? I never did you any harm as yet."[2] The last two little words were to assume a fateful meaning at a later date, incriminating the speaker of evil intention. That night Cromwell experienced a nightmare featuring Mother Samuel and her cat, an understandable psychological reaction to an upsetting day. Cromwell's daughter-in-law, who was sleeping with her, later testified that she was awakened by the woman's cries and restlessness and saw her move frantically as if to fight off an attacker.

After that, Cromwell's health steadily deteriorated, and no one will ever know whether it was a consequence of the continued bad dreams or due to other causes. In any case, Cromwell died fifteen months later, in July 1592. Right away, the disturbed children spread the rumor that the death was caused by Mother Samuel's revenge curse.

Around the same time, Mother Samuel confessed to the Throckmortons that indeed she had been bewitching the children. At the time, the matron hadn't been feeling well, was exhausted, and apparently gave in to the entreaties to confess. Now she promised to make amends and appeared so repentant that the worn-out parents thought their troubles were over for good. Even the children were pleased and stopped their fits. But after getting a good night's sleep, Mother Samuel felt stronger and retracted her statement, saying that she had nothing to confess. This immediately prompted the children to explode into new fits of agony.

It was at this juncture that a new self-view began to take shape in Mother Samuel. Three different factors had slowly undermined her self-confidence and wrought a deviant self-concept. First, there was the ongoing barrage of exhortations by the Throckmortons to confess. Second was the children's persistent enactment of being bewitched and holding her responsible for it. And third was the death of Cromwell. In other words, the question took on substance in Mother Samuel herself: was she indeed a witch?

What followed must be seen in the light of this self-doubt. By now the parents of the raging girls had run out of patience and decided to complain to the bishop of Lincoln. Bishop William Wickham summoned Mother Samuel and subjected her to intense questioning. The frightened and confused woman again confessed, wildly expanding on her first statement by, for example, giving the names of her familiars, three dun chickens, Pluck, Catch, and White. Escorted by the constables back to Huntingdon, she was jailed along with her husband and daughter, Agnes. The latter two had by now also been denounced by the girls as conspirators in the murder of Cromwell and in various and sundry other malefactions.

The children had been busy in the meantime expanding the details of their accusations. They had invented a whole host of evil spirits, knew their names, and claimed they were sent by Mother Samuel to torment them continuously. She had raised from hell seven particularly vicious demons: "First Smack," "Second Smack," "Third Smack," "Blue," "Catch," "Hardname," and "Pluck."[3] The children had been chiefly responsible for making the connection between the witch, her husband and daughter, and Cromwell's death. In harmony with the children's testimony, the court condemned all three and they were hanged.

The community was satisfied that justice had been done because they saw the proof in the fact that, thereafter, the girls stayed free of spell-caused fits and agonies.

The Warboys Girls as Role Models

The Warboys girls were perfect role models for the Salem girls. That the latter had knowledge of the episode is most likely, since the Warboys trials were some of the best known in England. Rossell H. Robbins considers them "the most widely discussed trials for witchcraft in England before 1600."[4] Even if the Salem actresses had no specific knowledge of this episode, there were plenty of others with almost identical features following the Warboys drama, and a general idea of plot, scripts, and acting must certainly have reached the English settlers in the New World. There are a number of noteworthy parallels: Daughters of well-to-do, or at least respected, families set the community on fire with accusations. The state of possession was played with the same persuasive skill, and in neither place was there any let-up in pursuing the script until the victims were destroyed.

The Essex Witches

Additional examples that prefigured the Salem style include those that were part of the series of trials taking place in Chelmsford, Essex. The Essex witches started to disturb the community in the 1560s and the disturbances did not subside until the 1640s. Ominously for the future history of witchcraft trials in England *and* New England, a number of characteristics crystallized around the trials: unquestioned acceptance of wildly imaginative stories by children under the age of fourteen, admission of spectral evidence (accepting claims of apparition as evidence), the witches' mark (consisting of any of a variety of skin blemishes, such as scars or moles), acceptance of un-verified confessions as facts, and the targeting of primarily older and poorer women of the community.

The concept of "spectral evidence" had an interesting twist to it. Spectral experiences were rarely claimed by adults, but seemed to have been the specialty of children in England and New England, evidently due to a communication link. (The concept was next to nonexistent on the European continent.) Claims of spectral experiences turned out to be lethal weapons in the hands of children because witch-hunters, who accepted their claims as being based on facts, believed that the Devil can assume the appearance of a given person only if that person is allied with him, meaning that he or she is a witch. Due to this belief, children's dreams, hallucinations, flights of fancy, or plain malice resulted in court as proof not of the state of mind of the accuser but of the behavior of the accused. Obviously this was the type of "proof" for which there was no disproof. No alibi could stand up against the belief that the Devil can make house calls in your "shape" while you were sleeping in your bed.

The beginning of the first set of the Essex trials featured Agnes Brown, twelve, who produced spectral evidence and accused the sixty-three-year-old widow Agnes Waterhouse of various misdeeds. Heavily featured in the case was the role of the Waterhouse cat, Sathan, that again and again appeared in the spectral visions of the Brown girl and represented the familiar of the witch. The girl's visions plus allegations by other parties resulted in Mother Waterhouse being hanged. Now Agnes Brown targeted the daughter of the executed widow, the eighteen-year-old Joan Waterhouse, who was accused of having afflicted her with a "decrepit right leg and right arm."[5] Again the cat Sathan played the instrumental role. Agnes claimed that, in the disguise of a black dog, the cat kept haunting her. The ending of the affair was exceptional: Joan threw herself on the mercy of the court, which, in an atypical ruling, left her unpunished.

The second major Chelmsford panic came in 1579. By then the community had grown so hypersensitive to the threat of witches that the mere cry of a dying four-year-old child "Away with the witch!" was sufficient to prosecute and execute a woman. At the moment of the child's death, the mother, Goodwife Webbe, perceived a thing like a black dog disappear through the door. Immediately she knew what it was—the death-bringing familiar of the murderous witch. Prosecution followed. The accused was Ellen Smith, whose mother had been executed as a witch five years previous, and the accusation was murder by witchcraft. She was convicted and executed like her mother.

The third wave of trials hit the community in 1589. Again children gave much of the "evidence," and out of one man and nine women accused, four were convicted and hanged. The children's spectral evidence was populated by scores of imps and familiars carrying out evil deeds. Two boys were praised by the judges for bringing to justice their unwed mother, Alice Cary, and their grandmother, Joan Prentice. Both women were executed within two hours of being sentenced.

The tradition of hunting witches in Chelmsford came to a climax during the fourth wave of trials, in the 1640s, when "Witch-Finder General" Matthew Hopkins made the discovery of witches his career. And this career, fanatically pursued, was well paid. Mostly through Hopkins's zeal thirty-two women were indicted and sixteen hanged in Chelmsford. His methods of identifying witches included finding and pricking the Devil's mark, floating the trussed-up suspect on her back to see whether she would sink, or depriving her of food and sleep for days and nights on end until she agreed to "confess." Hopkins prowled widely and stalked his prey in many other counties besides Essex; indeed, Chelmsford was not even the community with the greatest numbers executed during Hopkins's "finding" spree. Because Hopkins applied such finely tuned "discovery" methods, the need for outside denunciations, including those by children, became secondary, at least as long as his pursuits prevailed, which was roughly to the end of the 1640s.

Imitation via the Printed Word

About four years after the conclusion of the Warboys trial, a Leicester boy, William Somers, accused thirteen women of bewitching him. Fortunately, just before the young boy's testimony turned lethal, the judges found out that Somers had carefully studied a pamphlet describing the details of the Warboys trial for the purpose of learning to imitate the appropriate symptoms. The boy admitted that much, and the women were saved at the last moment.

A case of possession shook the community of North Moreton in Berkshire when, in 1604, fourteen-year-old Ann Gunter displayed hysterical fits and epileptic-like seizures and accused several women of having bewitched her. The diagnoses of several medical doctors fell short of natural explanations; they declared the condition a supernatural disorder. As in the Warboys situation (and later in Salem), Gunter's testimony rested on spectral evidence, in which she had visions of the witches' spirits and of their familiars. Gunter added new items to the array of mischief committed by witches: she voided and vomited pins, sometimes sneezed them, and (reputedly) refused food for ten to twelve days. Gunter's fits regularly grew worse when visitors came to view her and express commiseration. A temporary remedy was found when thatch from the roof of the suspect was snatched and brought to Ann's house, where it was ritually burned (symbolically in lieu of the witch). King James I heard of the case and took a personal interest in it. Hearings were initiated and the trials were in their beginning stages when the magistrates discovered that Gunter had studiously absorbed the description of the Warboys girls' symptoms from a pamphlet. The same chapbook that had so affected young Somers also played an inspirational role for Gunter, who tried to teach herself the way a bewitched child should act. Apparently this discovery changed the judges' minds and no decrees are known from the case. In the final analysis, nothing more seemed to have happened, except that both Gunter and three of the accused women were suspected of witchcraft or at least of the simulation of being bewitched.[6]

King James I and the Young Impostor

Another example features a Leicestershire boy, John Smith, scion of Sir Roger Smith, an ancestor of the earl of Derby. The boy, starting at the young age of five, regularly accused a number of women of bewitching him. As Smith's affliction continued—apparently a form of epilepsy that resembled the symptoms displayed by the Warboys girls—the authorities began to take the son of so prominent a family seriously and commenced to prosecute the accused. In 1614, when he was thirteen, the credulity of the judges brought nine persons to the gallows, and the trials weren't even finished yet. Either the prominence of the family involved or the persistence of the accusations drew the attention of King James I. After he had interviewed the boy and investigated the circumstances, the king arrived at the conclusion that the youngster was an impostor and his accusations a sham. Ironically, James I, author of *Demonology* (Edinburgh, 1597) and himself a notorious witch-hunter, dismissed the cases of nine surviving prisoners, thus preventing further mistrials, at least in that locality. The judges were royally rebuked and warned against lending credence to such lethal pranksters.

We can only guess what motivated the boy's denunciations. In his case it may well have been an innocuous attempt to explain the epileptic seizures by black magic curses. He might also have been seeking aggrandizement and enjoyment of the feeling of power through fabricating stories for which he obtained exceptional attention. And, of course, it could have been a complex mixture of these factors.

The Feuding Witches of Lancashire

The Lancashire trials came in waves, the first in 1612 and the second in 1634. The first is probably the most challenging witch episode for the researcher to understand fully. This is so because the accused may indeed have been consciously and intentionally practicing black magic, believing in their trade, and being consulted by people far and wide for assistance in witchcraft practices. At least this much can be deduced from the earliest description of the case, a relatively objective write-up by the court clerk, Thomas Potts, in a lengthy (188 pages) chapbook, *The Wonderful Discovery of Witches in the County of Lancaster* (London, 1613). Some of the suspects' activities may have stimulated occult interpretation. The location of the suspects' domicile alone, in forest seclusion, provided an aura of mystery and secretiveness; and their private gatherings for planning concerted actions, sharing meals, and celebrating family affairs were ascribed ritualistic character. These goings-on were interpreted as celebrations of the witches' sabbath and gave rise to persistent rumors in the region.

It was this sort of interpretation that prompted such modern writers as anthropologist Margaret Murray to jump to questionable generalizations. She used credulous observations to develop a theory assuming the existence of a continuous and ongoing community of witches in England, a community rooted in ancient, pre-Christian Celtic religion.[7]

But the so-called sabbath may have been nothing more than ordinary activities, such as would normally take place among friendly families. Historian Christina Hole, an expert on English witchcraft, preferred to leave the question open. The following sketch is based on her description of the episode.[8]

The people who ultimately became known as the Lancashire witches had originally been two friendly families in the secluded Pendle Forest area, plus a number of their friends and neighbors. About 1601, the matriarchs of the families, the Old Demdike and the Old Chattox, as their nicknames were, quarreled, and, never reconciling, split the "company of witches" into two feuding factions. Henceforth they did their best to cause harm to each other. As the knowledge of the various misdeeds spread and began to upset the community, the authorities stepped in and arrested Old Demdike.

She confessed to having made a pact with the Devil as far back as the 1590s. Her first encounter with him was in a stone quarry in the forest, where he stepped up to her disguised as a boy. Since then he had visited her frequently, always in disguise as a man, a brown dog, or a black cat. Thus having become a witch, she proceeded to seduce into witchcraft her family, including her son, daughter, two grandchildren, as well as the Old Chattox.

These allegations spelled trouble for Old Chattox and her family, many of whom now became implicated as well. In the subsequent hearings, the rivals spit venomous accusations at each other. The amazing thing was that neither side bothered to deny them. As a result, four persons from the two families ended up being imprisoned in Lancaster Castle to await trial.

This brought about an emergency meeting of the witches. They met at Malkin Tower, the homestead of Old Demdike, and, as they later readily admitted, tried to work out a strategy to free the imprisoned accomplices by killing the guards and blowing up the castle. Since the meeting started with a banquet of (stolen) mutton, some writers have referred to it as an example of the witches' sabbath. (There is, however, no evidence that magical rituals were performed. As mentioned above, the occasion may have been no more than a simple meal shared among conspirators.)

Soon additional members of the rival groups were arrested, until there were about twenty in custody awaiting trial. Some others fled; Old Demdike died in prison. The five major figures in the ensuing trial included Elisabeth Device (Old Demdike's daughter); her two daughters, nine-year-old Jennet and eleven-year-old Alison; her twenty-year-old son James; and Old Chattox. At the hearings, these persons accused each other prolifically, citing such magical murders as Alison's use of her familiar (in the shape of a black dog) to lame the peddler John Law, who had refused to let her have some pins. Alison freely admitted to the crime. In turn, she accused her grandmother of having bewitched the Baldwin baby so that it died, and of having destroyed by witchcraft the Nutters' ailing cow when she was called in to cure the animal.

All these prisoners testified freely against each other, in addition to admitting to all the allegations. But the star at the trial was Elisabeth Device's youngest child, Jennet, considered by the court too young to be a witch herself. She brought mountains of detailed allegations against her mother, brother, and sister, plus several other individuals who had been at the Malik Tower gathering. Despite the questionable legality of introducing testimony from a child under the age of fourteen, the court honored every word she spoke. In order that she could be clearly seen and heard by everyone present, little Jennet was placed on a table in the middle of the court room. There she stood and with amazing calmness swore away the lives of her closest relatives. The court found her to have been a "very observant child, blessed with a good memory, and totally devoid of any family loyalty."[9]

Finally, the judges found ten of the accused guilty of murder or of having committed grievous bodily harm, as, for example, Alison's laming of John Law. In all, some sixteen deaths in the neighborhood were attributed to their conjurations, as well as damage done to livestock and other property. Again, it is astounding that most of the accused freely admitted to all the charges. For example, James Device told the court that he had a familiar, a black dog by the name of Dandy, with whose help he killed Mistress Towneley. Not limiting heedlessness against himself, Device also reported that his grandmother tried to put him up to committing blasphemous acts. Allegedly, Old Demdike had asked him to go to church and receive communion, but not to eat the blessed bread, rather to save it and give it to a spirit who would wait for him on his way home. In spite of these instructions, James swallowed the bread. As he walked back from church he encountered a hare who demanded the bread from him. When James admitted that he had disobeyed his grandmother's order, the demon-hare exploded with rage and threatened to tear him asunder. Thereupon the boy quickly made the sign of the cross, and the demon vanished at once.

The ten convicted witches, including Jennet's mother, brother, and sister, received the death penalty. If Grandmother Demdike hadn't already died in her prison cell, she would have been hanged along with the others.

There are a number of noteworthy features in this episode. (1) We see again that, initially, old women were the more vulnerable persons to be accused of witchcraft. (2) The testimony of a young child, even underage according to English law, was granted credence. (3) If we can believe the allegations that the families had made witchcraft a way of life, then the accusing child, Jennet, in a sense was an insider. Yet, this circumstance did not seem to make any difference to her, and she proceeded with the typical behavior of children victimizing the powerless. Whether her allegations reflected the truth or were mere inventions is uncertain, perhaps unimportant. What is important is that the child voluntarily proceeded to victimize her entire family. (4) It is possible that the witches believed in their magical powers and saw them confirmed in certain events that reinforced their black-magic rituals. It is possible that such unrelated factors as putting a curse on an enemy and the coincidental misfortune of the enemy confirmed for them a cause-and-effect relationship. For example, Alison's anger at the peddler for not giving her some of his wares may have consciously (even ritualistically) or unconsciously triggered the wish to hurt him. Later, when the peddler fell ill (in retrospect it appeared that he had suffered a stroke) Alison saw in it confirmation of the curse and evidence of her magical powers.[10]

The Lancashire Trials of 1634

The second wave of witch panic in Lancashire had little to do with the previous one, except perhaps that the now-thirty-one-year-old Jennet Device was one of the accused. But in general it is an independent affair and is added here because it was one of those rare instances where the accuser was proven fraudulent and the suspects set free.

Edmund Robinson, a ten-year-old boy, got the accusations rolling. What is so interesting about the case is the authorities' use of the child as an esteemed medium, not unlike the situation enacted a few generations later in Salem, where several girls were accorded the same respectful role. As Rossell H. Robbins put it: "England was especially afflicted with such little monsters, and American children copied their antics."[11]

Little Robinson started his accusations by pointing the finger at Mother Dickinson, asserting that he knew her as a witch. His story is imaginative and colorful, a mythomaniacal masterpiece of which only a sketch can be given here. The boy told the magistrates that one day, as he roamed the glades and woods, he encountered two greyhounds who wouldn't respond to him in the manner of hunting dogs; rather they would, as he grew impatient with them and wanted to strike them with a switch, transform themselves into a woman and a little boy. He at once recognized in the woman the witch Mother Dickinson. First she offered him money to sell his soul to the Devil; but he refused. Then she drew a bridle from her pocket and waved it in a odd way over the head of the little boy who was accompanying her. Instantaneously, the child was changed into a horse. She swung Robinson up onto the horse, holding him in front of her, and off they flew swiftly like the wind over forests, moors, fields, and rivers. Finally they landed at a large barn. The witch took Robinson's hand and led him into the building where he beheld seven old women milking seven halters that hung from the rafters. As they stroked the halters, chunks of bacon, balls of butter, loaves of bread, bowls of milk, hot puddings, and other delicious food would drop to the floor. After so magically procuring the food, the witches engaged in a sumptuous feast, which was joined by additional witches, who appeared as soon as dinner was ready. Many of them Robinson knew and he provided the magistrates with their names.

Fantastic as the story is, the authorities at the time believed it. After all, Robinson had sworn to the truth of his story. Two magistrates, Richard Shuttleworth and John Starkie, both of whom remembered the trials of 1612, issued arrest warrants for a score of the denounced feasters. In order to identify the witches, Robinson was led from church to church so that he might point out the crones he had seen at the witches' feast. Relying on his word, the escorting constables hauled scores of women away to jail. About twenty were thrown into prison; they were heard before the Lenten Assizes in Lancaster, and seventeen were convicted.

Only one of the convicted women confessed to anything. All the others steadfastly denied having had anything to do with witch-craft. This is in conspicuous contrast to the confessions offered at the first Lancashire trial, where almost all those accused confessed willingly. The contrast supports the claims, as they had been made at that time by both the prosecuting authorities and the accused themselves, that the persons of the first episode had in fact been immersed in a lifestyle of witchcraft, and that when they confessed to it they spoke the truth.

The steadfastness of denial by the accused at the second trial caused the magistrates to have second thoughts about the nature of the affair, and they referred the case to the king in council. The bishop of Chester was asked to examine the prisoners. After he had reexamined four of them, including Mother Dickinson, he concluded that the charges were mainly based on malice and ignorance. None-theless, he sent them on to London, where they once more were examined by Dr. Harvey, the king's physician, who finally cleared them of the accusation of having the Devil's mark on their bodies. King Charles, like his father James I, took an interest in such matters and desired to look into the Lancaster affair personally. He interviewed the four prisoners and also their accuser, the boy Robinson. At that occasion, the boy broke down and admitted that he had made up the entire story. Spinning such a yarn out of local lore was of course easy, since the region was pregnant with ideas about witches, and the memory of the 1612 trials was still very much alive.

A villainous aspect to top off the account involved the boy's father. There is reason to believe that the senior Robinson directed the boy's accusations, or at least some of them. For example, it was hardly likely to be simple coincidence that the first person to be accused by Edmund was Mother Dickinson, with whose husband the elder Robinson had recently quarrelled. The father also tried to lend credibility to the son's story of having been taken to the witches' place by claiming that the boy had stormed home crying, mightily upset by the experience. There were also rumors that the elder Robinson "gained considerable sums by threatening persons who were rich enough to buy off exposure."[12]

Characteristics of English Trials

A long list of additional examples could be added, but they all have essentially the same ingredients and would hardly add further insight into the role children played. The role, as far as England was concerned, usually shows children as victimizers, taking advantage of people's belief in the reality of the Devil, his demons, human accomplices, and their own state of possession. The children played their roles superbly, knowing exactly how and when to enact the expected symptoms.

In sum, English trials can be noted for a number of interesting characteristics.

1. Children tended to display violent fits at the sight of presumed witches.

2. There usually was a search and almost always the discovery of the Devil's mark.

3. Children recovered remarkably quickly from their affliction as soon as witches confessed or were executed.

4. Torture was rarely applied, at least not lawfully so. (Scotland differed in this; when the authorities suspected witchcraft, they applied torture nearly routinely.)

5. English authorities relied on children's testimony to such an extent that it was unnecessary to apply torture to obtain a confession. Hence the testimony of a child was as deadly as torture in other countries.

6. A surprisingly large proportion of children playing the role of the possessed came from prominent, or at least well-to-do, families, whereas just the opposite was true on the Continent, where most of the possessed children came from the lower classes.

7. There was a prominent role of animals as demonic familiars, especially in the shape of cats, dogs, and hares. One author considers this an amusing commentary on the affectionate role pets have always played in English families.[13]

8. The most common targets of children's accusations were older and poorer women of the community.

9. Finally a general point. English witch trials, or, for that matter, English witch persecution in general, were not initiated or conducted by the Holy Inquisition. The prosecutions of witches was the responsibility of secular courts, with emphasis on presumed harm committed (*maleficia*) rather than on heresy or other purely religious offenses. In most of the rest of Europe it was the Inquisition that led the persecution and initiated trials, based on heresy as much as *maleficia*.

Notes

1. For discussions on the feeble role medical science had played in halting the witch persecution and on medical doctors' inability to diagnose "possession" as mental or physical illness during the early modern period see: Oskar Diethelm, "The Medical Teaching of Demonology in the Seventeenth and Eighteenth Centuries," *Journal of the History of the Behavioral Sciences* 6 (January 1970): 3–15, and Garfield Tourney, "The Physician and Witchcraft in Restoration England," *Medical History* 16 (April 1972): 143–55. One author goes as far as blaming the witch persecution on cooperating physicians: Leland L. Estes, "The Medical Origins of the European Witch Craze: A Hypothesis," *Journal of Social History* 17 (Winter 1983): 271–84. Another discussion focuses on the misogynous biases of both medical science and Christian theology: Hans Sebald, "Fire for the Female, Medicine for the Male: Medical Science and Demonology during the Witch Persecution," in *Modern German Culture,* eds. Rudolf Käser and Vera Pohland (Ithaca, N.Y.: Cornell University Western Societies Program, 1990), pp. 13–15.

2. Quoted after Christina Hole, *Witchcraft in England* (Totowa, N.J.: Rowman, 1977), p. 61.

3. Charles Mackay, *Extraordinary Popular Delusions and the Madness of Crowds* (New York: Noonday Press, 1974), p. 490.

4. Rossell H. Robbins, *The Encyclopedia of Witchcraft and Demonology* (New York: Crown, 1959), p. 527.

5. Ibid., p. 92.

6. Cecil H. Ewen, "A Noted Case of Witchcraft at North Moreton, Berks, in the Early Seventeenth Century," *Berkshire Archaeological Journal* 40 (1936).

7. Margaret Murray, *The Witch Cult in Western Europe* (Oxford, England: Oxford University Press, 1921).

8. Hole, *Witchcraft in England,* pp. 85–87, 100–106.

9. Ibid., p. 104.

10. Incidents where belief in and practice of black magic are prominent parts of family life are not limited to previous centuries and relegated to historical annals. Research has shown that still during the mid-twentieth century such situations have flourished in Western civilization. For example, the peasant culture of the Franconian Jura in central Germany was found not only to believe in the reality of witchcraft and to distinguish between white witches (healers) and black witches but also to adhere to a tradition whereby certain families were known to pass on black magic from generation to generation. During previous centuries, this sort of family would have been vulnerable to prosecution. See research data in Hans Sebald, *Witchcraft—The Heritage of a Heresy* (New York: Elsevier, 1978), or Hans Sebald, *Hexen damalss—und heute?* (Frankfurt, Germany: Gondrom, 1993).

11. Robbins, *The Encyclopedia of Witchcraft and Demonology,* p. 94.

12. Mackay, *Extraordinary Popular Delusions and the Madness of Crowds,* p. 510.

13. See a description of Sathan the cat, as it figured in the Essex witch trial, by Hole, *Witchcraft in England,* pp. 40ff.

5

As the Curtain Falls

Witch-Families

As the total number of witch trials gradually decreased toward the end of the age of the witch-hunts, the proportion of trials implicating entire families increased markedly. It was in such family-devouring trials that the role of children took on a deadly edge against parents and siblings. The type of callousness shown by Jennet toward her family in the first Lancaster trial was not unique; episodes with similar outcomes spread in England as well as on the continent during the last decades of the seventeenth and the first decades of the eighteenth century.

This was particularly true of the German territories, where many communities experienced family trials, as for example, in Amberg (1655), Menningen (1656), Reichertshofen (1661), Haidau-Straubing (1690, 1730), and Schwabmünchen-Augsburg (a wave lasting from 1728 to 1734). All of them started with children accusing members of their own families.

Most of the disturbances originated because an actual crime had been committed or was highly suspected. At the outset, the offense usually had nothing to do with heresy or witchery, but rather with such things as incest, concealed pregnancy, abortion, or infanticide. During the investigation these offenses were reinterpreted as *crimen magiae* (crime of black magic) and the culprits, usually parents and siblings, were accused of witchcraft.

The example of Haidau, a community in Lower Bavaria, illustrates the pattern. The town was the site of two witch-family trials, one running from 1689 to 1694 and the other from 1700 to 1702. Both involved a total of four families or twenty persons, all of whom were put to death.[1] The beginning of the first trial came about through the actions of a twelve-year-old girl, Katharina Gruber, who claimed that spirits regularly visited and informed her about the conditions of the souls of the departed. Soon she acquired the reputation of a medium; it didn't take her parents long to realize the commercial potential involved. They fixed up the servants' cottage for the public to consult the youngster, who never refused payment for her mediumship, and the whole affair gradually assumed the character of a busy pilgrimage center. However, the Catholic church took a dim view of the development. This displeasure was spearheaded by the Capuchin monks in nearby Regensburg, who would rather have had pilgrims give alms to bona fide shrines, such as their own. After a few months of selling other-worldly information Katharina was arrested. The initial charges had less to do with heresy and more with swindling the clientele.

The accusation changed abruptly once the girl found herself in prison: she reported to the jailer that she herself, her mother, and another woman were witches and had concluded a pact with the Devil and had regularly flown to the witches' dances. Apparently the girl offered this confession without having been pressured or provoked, and we can only guess at the underlying psychological process. The most likely explanation, as suggested by similar cases, deals with the impact of imprisonment driving the isolated person to align herself with the views and expectations of the authorities and "confessing" to anything that promises to alleviate deprivation.

As the authorities pursued the case, it began to engulf three families, of which all parents and eight out of ten children between the ages of twelve and nineteen were convicted of witchcraft and executed in short order. At the time of their arrest, the children, four boys and four girls, were between seven and sixteen years old. A girl of three years had joined the chorus in alleging to be a witch. Among other things she confessed to having had sex with the Devil; still, the court decided to spare her punishment. Katharina also implicated her sister, who, however, had an alibi and could prove that she had been working as a servant in a distant community during the implicated time; hence she was left alone.

Another witch-family trial took place in the German imperial city of Augsburg in 1625. The city council had long been reluctant to join the witch hysterias of neighboring jurisdictions, a reluctance typical of secular, imperial cities. Hence, the council initially doubted the claims of an eleven-year-old girl, Maria, that she had been seduced by relatives into the ranks of witches, danced at the witches' sabbath, and taken a demon lover. Yet Maria persisted in her story, despite suffering repeated thrashings by her parents, who wrongly assumed that beatings would improve the quality of her cerebration. Finally, at the urging of the parents, the council jailed the girl and began to examine her. This included a physical examination by two Augsburg midwives, who verified that the girl had never had sexual intercourse, let alone of the savage sort she had described in gross details.

Once in jail and her claim discredited, Maria changed her story. It wasn't the relatives who had persuaded her to become a witch, but her own mother. Maria volunteered the story without having been pressured or tortured. From all appearances she had no motive. It was precisely this apparent motivelessness that lent an appearance of truthfulness to her story. Consequently the mother was arrested and confirmed under torture what her daughter had said. The episode ended with the execution of the mother. Because she was thought too young to be punished, the treacherous daughter was allowed to go free, despite the court believing that she had participated in heretical crimes.[2]

Crisis of Confidence

Though not far from Trier, the town of Calw differed in its approach to the witch-hunts. Whereas Trier was one of the first jurisdictions involving significant numbers of children in its 1580s processes, Calw was the last European jurisdiction to do so during its 1680s trials. One town stands at the beginning of the period of children's processes, and the other at its end—a span of roughly a hundred years. Trier gave unlimited credence to the denouncing children; Calw hesitated to do so. Trier punished children by adult standards; Calw limited capital punishment to adults. Pressure to persecute in Trier came from above; in Calw from below, that is, from the ranks of the populace at large. Protestant Calw was less interested in prosecuting for theological crimes, such as heresy, and instead focused on *maleficia*; Catholic Trier, on the other hand, was very much attuned to the Inquisition's preoccupation with heresy.

The Calw panic never resulted in commensurate dimensions of prosecution, if we compare them to those seen in previous episodes. But the intensity of popular panic was as great as, if not greater than, that of the other episodes. This raises the question of why the usual correlation between degree of panic and degree of prosecution failed to ensue. The explanation is that a *crisis of confidence* had arisen during the late seventeenth century, a crisis of uncertainty concerning the identification of witches and the believability of testimonies, especially those offered by children. The Mora episode in Sweden of the 1660s was well known to the authorities throughout Europe, had been received with skepticism, and served as a warning against giving credence to children's allegations.

As a consequence, the Calw authorities hesitated to prosecute, and even threatened to punish those eager to denounce and start rumors. But the townspeople reacted quite differently: they clamored for prosecution, demanded it, and virtually initiated a series of trials that could easily have claimed more than fifty lives. Here then was a situation where persecution was encouraged from below, not from above, quite unlike the persecution in the Franconian prince-bishoprics.

In any case, the children of Calw persisted in the rampage of denunciations and mythomaniacal stories. Here is a sketch of the scenario according to H. Erik Midelfort's apt description.[3] The first ominous rumbling of trouble to come took place in 1673, when children ranging in age from nine to twelve accused a woman of having poisoned several neighbors. After the town magistrates had submitted the issue to the law faculty at the nearby University of Tübingen and received a negative judgment, the woman was set free. The consulted jurists deemed the children's testimony lacking in trustworthiness. Four years later, similar charges were leveled against a ten-year-old boy, Barthol Sieben. He was accused of having killed the schoolmaster's son, Johannes Crispen, with a poisoned cookie. When questioned, Barthol admitted having done so, but claimed that he had done it only after having been put up to it by his grandmother, Anna Hafnerin, who gave him the necessary poisonous powders for the express purpose of harming his classmates. Advice was again requested from the university, which ruled out harsh punishment because of mitigating circumstances such as the boy's age and the grandmother's weak condition. The boy got off with a public flogging. But the family remained suspect to the neighbors, who were convinced that sorcery and witchcraft were going on in that household, and in 1683 an eleven-year-old neighbor boy alleged that the old Hafnerin, now eighty years old, had initiated him into witchcraft and persuaded him to renounce God with words written in his own blood. He said that he had accompanied her to many a witches' dance and that at such occasions he had met many of his classmates. It could be proven that the boy had been sleeping in his bed during the time of his alleged demonic frolicking, but parents and neighbors concluded that the Devil was able to carry off the souls of the children while leaving their bodies behind. A wave of general unrest swept through the community. Parents began to keep their children awake during the night in order to prevent them from flying off to the witches' sabbath and to question them about their supernatural experiences. By doing so they inadvertently goaded the children on to tell ever taller stories of their demonic exploits. Finally the magistrates felt that something had to be done and in 1683 they began to examine nineteen of the more outspoken children, the youngest barely ten years old. The testimonies were nearly unanimous and concentrated on the witchery of the old Hafnerin and her grandson Berthol.

After the magistrates subjected the two to intense questioning, they confessed to being witches. Berthol admitted that he had indeed poisoned Johannes Crispen six years earlier and had served the Devil since. The grandmother admitted similar diabolic servitude, saying she did it for the promise of money, which, however, the Devil never paid her. The most damning part of the grandmother's confession was the admission that she had seduced a number of children into witchcraft. Grandmother and grandson pleaded for mercy on account of having never concluded a formal pact with the Devil and having been, respectively, too old and too young to have known better. This time the legal faculty at Tübingen regarded the evidence as damning enough and thought that the deeds alone signified voluntary alliance with the Devil, though no explicit pact may have been signed. The two were sentenced and executed in December 1683.

At this juncture no further trials might have followed had the townspeople been less aroused. But rumors and accusations chased each other in increasing numbers and more and more children stepped forth with fantastic stories, most of them dealing with whom they had seen at the witches' dance. The evaluation by the Tübingen jurists of over thirty children, ranging in age from three to twenty, concluded that the youngsters were either "dreaming or simple-minded." However, several of the children's voluntary confessions included some tangible offenses, such as blasphemies, and for that they were punished by being caned in front of their classmates. Otherwise the legal consultants warned against granting credence to the children's stories, reminded the magistrates of the Mora debacle, and advised a strict prohibition against rumors and accusations. Nonetheless, they added, a number of adults appeared guilty of serious infractions that would warrant examination under torture.

Rumors of such infractions prolonged the feverish tension in the town, pitting neighbor against neighbor and disguising such personal emotions as hatred and envy under the righteous cloak of reporting supernatural crimes. This served as convenient strategy to take revenge on an adversary or annoying neighbor in the absence of other legal means to do so. The harassed authorities saw it necessary to form a commission to interview the numerous claimants as well as suspects. By 1684 the number of denouncing children had increased to thirty-eight (fourteen boys and twenty-four girls). They accused seventy-seven adults of witchcraft. Again consensual clusters formed; for example, twenty-one youngsters all agreed that Wendel Kohler's wife was a witch.

But the commissioners were no longer easily convinced. On the contrary, they frowned on the way parents had instilled fears and hostilities in their offspring, causing them to develop paranoid attitudes, and especially on their method of keeping them sleepless at night, causing them to be chronically nervous and excitable. The commissioners also realized that the imagination of the children themselves played a significant and somewhat autonomous role. Among the youths they were able to identify as a ringleader, a "melancholy" twelve-year-old boy, Veit Zahn, who had been influencing his peers with wild imaginings.

The commissioners' main goal was to dispel a number of popular delusions. First, they disputed the assumption of the separation of mind and body of sleeping children, telling the townspeople that the Devil had no power to accomplish such a feat. Second, they particularly denied the children's ability to fly anywhere if they had been seen sleeping in their beds at the same time. Third, they defined the children's dreams and fantasies as delusions. Fourth, they disclaimed the entire idea of arriving at reliable evidence through spectral experiences. Finally, they found the children's stories varying so much from one another that no reliance could be placed on any one of them. This inability they ascribed to the clever deceptiveness of the Devil, who intended to confuse everyone. In conclusion they felt that it was not possible in any reliable way to condemn anyone of witchcraft.

The only action the commissioners took at this time was to banish three women: the mother of the executed Barthol, her sister, and the much-maligned Kohlerin. This was, however, less motivated by proof of any guilt than by the need to protect them from the wrath of the townspeople. The magistrates told them that lynch justice might endanger their lives if they stayed in Calw. Other suspects were admonished to lead quiet, inconspicuous lives and not to leave their homes for a while.

The effort to calm the populace was only partially successful. Tension persisted, and the authorities thought it necessary to move local militia to trouble spots. Even that proved insufficient, and finally the central government in Stuttgart dispatched soldiers under the command of a hand-picked captain to restore law and order in Calw. At the same time the authorities tried the educational approach to pacify the people, instituted special days of prayer, emphasized the deceitfulness of the Devil, and deemphasized the dangers of witchcraft. An eloquent preacher kept pointing out that this sort of frenzy and distrustfulness among human beings was nothing else than the doing of the Devil himself. Instead of constantly suspecting and denouncing neighbors, people should observe personal chastity and sobriety— these were the virtues best suited to combatting witchcraft and defeating the Devil. The educational approach at last showed results. The people gradually returned to their senses.

Children had played the central role in Calw's hysteria. They were responsible for two executions, the divisiveness in the community, the banishment of innocent persons, and the necessity of calling in the troops.

To reiterate: The authorities' valiant effort to suppress the witch panic did not grow out of their disbelief in witches or the Devil—they very much continued to adhere to these beliefs—but was a consequence of their inability to identify witches with any reliability during mass hysteria. The crisis of confidence in mass denunciations brought witch-hunting to an end not only in Calw but also in other regions, since the conditions of unreliability had ripened and become a prohibitive element in the judicial-demonological scenario as it stretched across the Holy Roman Empire.

How the machinery of the witch-persecuting industry slowly came to a halt can be illustrated even in cases of jurisdictions that had a record of the most ferocious witch-hunts. Whereas the authorities of Calw tried to suppress and control the population's witch fever, the Bamberg situation was characterized by the reverse. There, Prince-Bishop Johann Georg II confronted a population with ever-increasing demands to stop the persecution. As he unrelentingly persisted, the populace instinctively found a way to throw the proverbial monkey wrench into the machinery. The accused increasingly implicated the officials themselves and claimed to have seen one or the other participating at the witches' dance. The prince-bishop found himself in the unaccustomed position of having to defend himself on three fronts. First, there was growing evidence that many confessions and denunciations were confabulations and there was growing difficulty in telling true witches from false ones. The prelate responded to the problem by issuing repeated edicts warning the public of severe punishment in cases of false denunciations. After the second edict, issued in September 1628, proved ineffective, the tenacious prince-bishop resorted to draconian measures and erected a public *Wippen* to punish those giving false testimony. This was a torturing device consisting of a long beam see-sawing on a pivotal point, with the delinquent tied to one end so that he or she could be either dunked into water for near drowning or dropped on a bed of spikes.[4]

On a second front, the ruler of Bamberg had to defend the reputation and innocence of top officials who had been denounced as witches. For example, on November 3, 1628, Johann Georg found it necessary to write a letter to the emperor in which he assured him that his cathedral prior (the head of the cathedral clergy) and his suffragan (assistant) bishop had been defamed unjustly and were anything but witches. Ironically, Suffragan Bishop Fridrich Förner had been the prince's most loyal supporter in the witch-hunts.[5] Scores of his priests found themselves ever more frequently denounced as witches and as the Devil's fornicators. In one case, a Bamberg woman, Barbara Rött, denounced the priest Michael Kötzner of the prominent St. Martin's parish of having "tried to seduce her to fornication."[6]

Finally, Johann Georg had to respond to repeated admonitions by the emperor, who had been informed of the prince-bishop's disregard of due process in hunting witches.

Frivolous denunciations of clergy and officialdom were not limited to Bamberg but spread throughout Europe. In the Catholic principality of Ellwangen, bordering on Bamberg's jurisdiction, three priests and an organist were accused, found guilty of witchcraft, and executed in June 1615. The priests suffered the gruesome ritual of degradation from holy orders, commonly called defrocking. This consisted of cutting a hole into the right hand, the tonsure, and the forehead, then rubbing salt and vinegar into the wounds to expunge all traces of sacramental chrism. In this case the defrocking process went a step further: the priests' fingernails were ripped out, they were clothed in secular garments, and finally they were put to death.[7]

Such were among the more noticeable symptoms that revealed the crisis of confidence and heralded the debacle of the industry of the witch-hunts. But it took time to halt the industry completely. There were several more hysterical flare-ups of mass proportion. For example, the Inquisition prosecuted several dozen suspects, most of them children and teenagers, as late as the 1720s in the Bavarian bishopric of Freising. The majority of the accused were set free, but three beggar women and eight "witchboys," ranging in age from fourteen to twenty-three, were put to death.[8]

Apart from a few major regressions, only small, individual trials continued here and there, and the mass witch-hunts came to an end. And so, ultimately, also ended the deadly role of the little actors and actresses of evil.

End of an Era

By the mid-seventeenth century a crisis of confidence in witch-hunting had evolved, rendering identification of witches questionable. Adults accusing others, or themselves, had lost credibility to a significant extent. Some progress had been made in identifying mental cases. This was especially true for self-accusations. Johannes Weyer's explanation in *De Prestigiis Daemonum* (The Glitter of Demons) (1563) that many putative witches suffered from "melancholia" belatedly made an impact, despite vigorous opposition of the kind advanced by Jean Bodin in his *De la Demonomanie des Sorciers* (The Demonomania of Sorcerers) (1580).

The risks involved in accusing others had increased and people had gradually learned that to confess anything in detail was fraught with danger. Naming others as witches could backfire since the accusers could be named as accomplices by the very person just denounced. And torture could drive them to admit such complicity. Adults could assess these dangers and react with restraint; but children appeared unimpressed by the new conditions, or simply failed to take them seriously. Just as the furor of the hunt seemed to die down, children stepped to the forefront. There are many reasons for this, and some have already been mentioned. Here are some additional explanations.

1. Children were less imperiled. Under a certain age they could usually denounce with impunity, and at the same time harvest the rewards of feeling powerful, getting full attention, and being praised for their brave contribution to ridding the community of evil.

2. Children's emotional immaturity expressed itself in the lack of inhibition and compassion. They had not yet learned sufficient empathy for the suffering of others—a typical feature of their developmental stage.

3. The display of children's nonchalance became a major factor in prolonging the credence accorded children's testimonies. Inquisitors endorsed the timeless adage, "Fools and children never lie." The children's seemingly motiveless accusations especially impressed the inquisitors. Why else, they wondered, would children accuse anyone if it weren't true and if they had nothing personal to gain from it? The officials failed to realize that children indeed had motives and things to gain, usually deeply hidden and unconscious, not easy to

fathom by inquisitors trained in theology and untrained in any sort of child psychology. In her analysis of the Salem upheaval, historian Marion Starkey demonstrates that children took advantage of the impunity with which they could punish adults, but also in a sense the entire community for the restrictions, fears, and threats they suffered throughout their childhood under ascetic, punitive, and guilt-infusing Puritanism. Starkey speaks of Betty, the daughter of Calvinist Rev. Parris: "She had been exposed too long to the hellfire in her father's composition . . . [and] sickening from the inhuman strain of coping with an adult world that had been arranged without understanding of the needs and capacities of children."[9] In a similar vein, historian G. R. Quaife speaks of the anxieties that the younger generation suffers as it grows up under the harsh discipline of parents and other authority figures. Vengeance was the reaction—primarily unconscious and totally merciless. "To bring a flogging adult patriarch to his knees through an accusation of witchcraft was indeed juvenile vengeance."[10]

4. To reemphasize an earlier point, some historians have argued that parental oppression increased drastically during post-Reformation times, fueling resentment in the younger generation and promoting their inclination to retaliate with witch accusations, a weapon easily attainable.[11] Oppressive discipline was revived in the seventeenth century in a desperate struggle to reestablish order after a large part of the European continent had been racked by the Thirty Years' War.[12] The German territories were suffering the brunt of the devastation, enduring a holocaust that lasted almost the entire first half of the seventeenth century. In the war's wake, highway banditry, crime, and juvenile delinquency flourished; homeless and orphaned youth rallied in bands, adding to crime, disorder, and instability. It is a sociological principle that *anomie*—an absence of norms and a lapse of standards—stimulates an intense search for new order and predictability, and hence desperate authorities bore down, often savagely, on lawless youth.

5. It must never be overlooked that children, regardless of the era in which they happen to live, crave attention. What more attention can be had than in situations where one is the star witness, the prime accuser of such authority figures as parents or other adults? The experience meant a ride on the crest of power and the elation of

being in control. Being the kingpin of a situation must have been an experience of ecstasy for many of these children.

6. One further aspect explaining the longevity of children's involvement is that the Inquisition, or the authorities in general, took a dim view of marginal groups. Examples were beggars, vagrants, religious minorities, and to some extent even older persons, especially older widows and spinsters. The old-age group presents us with an interesting psychological issue. Older people tended to become a burden on the community, had to rely on handouts, on charity, or on other communally instituted forms of social security. As was the case in many communities, negligence in providing adequately for this marginal group created feelings of guilt, an emotion that has a vicious tendency to take dead aim at its source. The persons wronged will be seen in a negative light and construed as being undeserving. The psychological gyrations ensuing from such social circumstances tend to persecute the source so unpleasant and so degrading to ones's self-image. Hence, justification must be found first to legitimize the wrong-doing and second to try to eliminate the source of bad feelings. Accusations of witchcraft were an effective means to accomplish this. Researching the psychological underpinnings of English witch persecution, Alan Macfarlane has found these mental dynamics to have been a significant, albeit unconscious, incentive in persecuting older women. He makes a convincing case of the psychology of guilt-reaction to negligent care of indigents in the community and ultimately their vulnerability to witch accusations.[13]

The point here is that juvenile gangs also constituted marginal groups and that their activities were often interpreted in a heretical light. Delinquency, pranksterism, and the general nuisance created by urchins in gang format were certainly enough to draw attention and bring down the strong arm of law-enforcement agencies. The social-psychological dynamics of such situations include the role of mutual reinforcement of delinquent behavior among children, their own mythomaniacal interpretations of their experiences, and the resulting demonological perceptions of their world. When children initiated witch accusations—either in thoughtless play or as intentional malice against certain individuals—their unanimity in agreeing upon the identity of the witches must have been a persuasive spectacle to the inquisitors.

Notes

1. Wolfgang Behringer, *Hexenverfolgung in Bayern* (Munich, Germany: Oldenbourg, 1987), p. 351.

2. Ibid., p. 179.

3. H. Erik Midelfort, *Witch Hunting in Southwestern Germany, 1562–1684* (Stanford, Calif.: Stanford University Press, 1972), pp. 158–63.

4. Johann Looshorn, *Die Geschichte des Bisthums Bamberg,* vol. 6 (Bamberg, Germany: Handels-Druckerei, 1906), p. 40.

5. Ibid., p. 49.

6. Ibid., p. 65.

7. Midelfort, *Witch Hunting in Southwestern Germany,* pp. 104–105.

8. Behringer, *Hexenverfolgung in Bayern,* pp. 347–56.

9. Marion Starkey, *The Devil in Massachusetts* (New York: Time Inc., 1963), pp. 1–2.

10. G. R. Quaife, *Godly Zeal, Furious Rage: The Witch in Early Modern Europe* (New York: St. Martin's Press, 1987), p. 189.

11. Cf. Hartwig Weber, *Kinderhexenprozesse* (Frankfurt, Germany: Insel, 1991), passim.

12. Ibid., pp. 188–89.

13. Alan J. D. Macfarlane, *Witchcraft in Tudor and Stuart England* (New York: Harper, 1970).

Part 2
Witchboy—A Case Study

6

The Stage

The Prince-Bishopric of Bamberg

The story that is about to unfold is true. Its stage was a real place, its star a real person, and the supporting cast equally real and impressive. As the curtain rises we behold a scene that would beguile the heart of a romantic: the town of Bamberg, its Renaissance splendor sweeping up the hillside, decorating the bucolic landscape with old palaces, churches, and a fortress-like cathedral. At the foot of the hill lies the town proper, quaint with colorful beam-and-plaster houses gathered like a herd of sheep, looking up to the mighty shepherd residing in the palace on the hill—the mighty prince-bishop, ruler of ecclesiastical as well as secular affairs.

But the scene deceives. There is little romanticism, rarely a peaceful day, hardly a happy face behind the artful facade. Reality is a drama filled with more blood, gore, and human cruelty than conceived by Shakespeare when he wrote *Othello* or *Macbeth*.

This then is the stage of the case study: the town of Bamberg at the edge of the jagged Jura Mountains in the central German province of Franconia, ruled by fanatic princes of the church who perceived themselves as battling the ultimate evil of Christendom. The backdrop is formed by the tumultuous early seventeenth-century Holy Roman Empire with its endless wars, the plague, and the persecution of witches.

The star of the drama is suspected of witchcraft: a nine-year-old boy imprisoned and interrogated about the specifics of his diabolic crimes. He delivers a lengthy confession, the scribe filling twenty-

111

four handwritten pages, revealing not only personal intimacies of a young boy in a situation of life and death, but also the cultural and social characteristics of the day.

The significance of the confession and the world of ideas out of which it grew can only be understood if we take a glimpse at conditions that existed at the time. Before we turn to the confession as the central piece of information, a short introduction to the historical setting may prove helpful.

Witch persecution took on a particularly virulent character in Bamberg, where generations of prince-bishops held both secular and ecclesiastical power. One of them was noted for unusual zeal in the witch-hunt. According to his own bragging, Prince-Bishop Johann Georg II ordered the execution of over six hundred witches during his reign from 1623 to 1633.[1] He entered the annals of church history under the nickname of the *Hexenbischof,* the witch-burning bishop. He was responsible for the building of special witch prisons, complete with torture chambers,[2] and had many witches burned alive instead of first strangled or decapitated and then burned, as was often "mercifully" granted in other jurisdictions.[3] Numerous complaints against his judicial procedures, or the lack thereof, were lodged with the emperor, who then reprimanded the bishop, usually without effecting adequate compliance. The complaints included refusal to provide defense counsel, abhorrent torture, illegal renewal of torture, imprisonment and torture of pregnant women, hasty trials allowing merely a few days between accusation, conviction, and execution, and other violations of imperial law.

Why was the witch-hunt so extreme in Bamberg? A few background notes will help explain. The great historical upheavals of the sixteenth century took their toll on Bamberg's stability. As one of the oldest bishoprics in the German lands, it had been enjoying great powers, material as well as ideological. But the onslaught of the Protestant Reformation imperiled its existence as a sovereign religious entity. There were perils from within and without. Neighboring Protestant rulers began to nibble away at the old boundaries; independent aristocracies and Protestant knights carved out enclaves right in the middle of the diocese; Protestant and Reformed preachers invaded parishes and took over Catholic property, including the churches.[4]

Such takeovers were made easy by a Catholic clergy which had grown negligent and unreliable. For decades, the bishops had repeatedly sounded the same complaints and unsuccessfully commanded their priests and monks to uphold sacred duties. Continual problems included inappropriate attire, growing beards and long hair, considering un-allowable matrimony, living with concubines, and an affinity for wine outside of the Mass. In addition, choirs failed to show up in church, including the cathedral; priests didn't show up to say the Mass when they were scheduled to do so; and most priests and monks either had wives or concubines (one prince-bishop, overwhelmed by the ubiquity of their misconduct, finally acquiesced with the meek plea that they should at least avoid being seen publicly with their womenfolk).

Other denizens of the realm caused no lesser problems. Knights engaged in brawls; promiscuous women abounded and had to be banished from the diocese; numerous bigamists upset the bishop; the townspeople of Bamberg disputed fiscal matters with him; and premarital sex was so common that one bishop initiated punishment of such sinners by having them wear straw hats at their wedding ceremonies.[5] General lawlessness kept bailiffs, as long as they them-selves cared to obey the law, busy and the jails filled.

The symbol of degeneration of Catholic clergy of Bamberg was the filled *Pfaffengewölbe,* the nickname the townspeople gave the dungeon specifically reserved for errant priests and most of the time filled to capacity during the late sixteenth and early seventeenth centuries.[6]

And then there were such prince-bishops as Johann Philipp von Gebsattel, reigning 1599–1609, whose leaning toward Protestantism nearly matched his loyalty to Catholicism. This prince-bishop practiced pursuits that tended to divert his attention from bothersome eccle-siastical worries to more worldly joys: he was known throughout the empire as a womanizer, lecher, sybarite, and an imbiber of much more wine than was needed for celebrating the Holy Eucharist.[7] There were times when he cared very little whether it was a Catholic priest or a Protestant minister who used the churches of his diocese. Since Protestant ideologues could not be faulted with such theological non-chalance, it was not surprising that the erstwhile monolithically Catholic realm soon showed cracks in its political and religious structure. It has been estimated that at the turn of the seventeenth century about half of the population in the area had converted to Protestantism.[8]

Gebsattel's successor, Johann Gottfried von Aschhausen, who reigned from 1609 to 1622, was carved of a different wood. He tried to save what could be saved of the prince-bishopric by calling in the Jesuits. They wrested the cathedral's pulpit from unreliable clergy, founded a Jesuit college and a high school in 1611, and within a few more years opened the doors to thirteen *Stadtschulen* (basic schools).[9] Under his rule, Bamberg's heretofore minimal witch-hunting received new impetus: he was responsible for the execution of over one hundred witches.

The Jesuits played a weighty role in Bamberg's version of the Counter-Reformation, one divided between sacred rituals and educational functions. The first aspect dealt with assisting in the witch-hunt as father confessors, accompanying the condemned to the place of execution, and in performing exorcisms of presumably possessed persons. Prisoners who fell into this category were usually remanded to the Jesuits and liturgical penance may have spared them worldly punishment—but not always, for many did repent and *still* were put to death. As we shall later see, there is reason to assume that the fate of Witchboy was in the hands of the Jesuits, but it remains an open question whether they were custodians of his last moments or exorcists to rid him of demons. The second aspect of the Jesuit presence dealt with educational functions, such as running schools and teaching catechism.

These combined functions put the Jesuits in charge of *Kinderzucht,* the discipline of youth. They carried out most of the prince-bishop's orders concerning the rescue of Bamberg's deteriorated young generation. Not all measures amounted to punishment and repression. For example, when the horrors of the Thirty Years' War finally came to an end and peace was celebrated, the Jesuits did not forget to include the children: on St. Bartholomew's Day in 1650 a banquet for children was prepared in the garden of the Jesuit college and over one hundred boys and girls were treated to a generous meal.[10]

The *Hexenbischof*

When Johann George II ascended to the Bamberg throne in 1623 he brought along a fiery determination to halt further deterioration of the diocese and restore Bamberg to the true faith. He visualized his project as nothing short of reclaiming Bamberg for the kingdom of God. With this goal in mind he would pass one stringent edict after another. A major part of the prince-bishop's agenda was the eradication of witches.

People were almost daily reminded of the Great Conspiracy of the witches. Fear of the Great Threat incited mass hysteria, accusations, and executions. All communication media, including the word from the pulpit, the printed word, and grotesque pictorial descriptions, sustained the pitch of the excitement. For example, Suffragan Bishop Förner made raving antiwitchery sermons a regular part of Sunday Mass. To reach those who might have missed them, he had the sermons printed and distributed. Pictures showing the obscene escapades of the witches were accessible to all people. And so were arrests and executions, events that turned into spectacles resembling public festivals.

The prince-bishop authorized the printing of a special flyer, "Trudenzeitung," to describe the nature of the satanic conspiracy. Since its distribution threatened to spread beyond the diocese's boundary, and with it the hysteria, the neighbor city of Nürnberg officially banned it from its territory. When an overeager city printer reproduced it clandestinely, the city council threw him into the dungeon.[11]

The *Hexenbischof* was so determined to rehabilitate the religiously deteriorated youth of his realm that he initiated a number of draconian measures. Among them he ordered that each community prepare a list of all children and servants (most of the servants were in their teens) and to control their attendance at catechism, which was to be held every Sunday afternoon. He warned the family fathers to see to it that their dependents regularly attend catechism. Failure to do so would incur a fine of three *kronen* (German gold coins) on the head of the family for each neglect. The procedures were supervised by a special commissioner entitled to seek the assistance of secular officials to enforce the rule—an undisguised merging of the powers of church and state to carry out the prince-bishop's edict.[12]

Johann Georg was not about to let criticism of his edicts regarding supervising children and servants or of his policies eradicating witches interfere with his determination to reestablish order and the true faith. On October 28, 1626, he issued an order according to which, "No person may criticize or malign officials whose duties involve them in witch trials or witch executions," or, let alone, "interfere with officials carrying out [their] councilors' orders, especially at occasions of executions of witches."[13] Persons violating the edict were to be punished by public flogging and permanent banishment.

Another gag order was the *Urfede*. This order applied to all persons who had been subject to hearings, torture, and imprisonment and for some reason had been set free. This happened sometimes because a henchman's effort to extract a confession was unsuccessful (rarely), sometimes because a denunciation was retracted (more common), and sometimes because imperial pressure resulted in release (more common). Such lucky souls were bound by the *Urfede* to swear a solemn oath to reveal absolutely nothing of what they had experienced. It was an oath of "eternal silence" about treatment at the hands of the Inquisition.[14]

In sum, the regime of Prince-Bishop Johann Georg II pretty closely met the criteria set forth by George Orwell in his 1948 classic, *1984,* depicting a totalitarian society that enforces unanimity of thought, with a Big Brother watching over you and, if necessary, silencing you.

In the course of the new suppression, Bamberg renewed a medieval mentality and retained it markedly longer than most other jurisdictions in Europe. Symptomatic of the cultural lag were violations by Bamberg officials of the *Constitutio Criminalis Carolina* (the empire's code of laws, to which Bamberg's jurisdiction was presumably subordinated); consequent reprimands by the emperor; extreme and unlawful use of torture;[15] several deaths following torture; suicide by prisoners in the witch-prison; incarceration of pregnant women, who gave birth in prison cells; numerous refugees from Bamberg seeking asylum in other territories; violent takeovers by Catholic officials and clergy of parishes that had turned Protestant; conversion-or-banishment orders (encouraged by the pope) against all non-Catholic clergy and citizens;[16] suppression and extermination of Bamberg's intelligentsia by removal from office and execution of the prince-bishop's own vice chancellor, a number of town councilors, and several mayors. Of course, dissenting priests were not spared severe punishment; preachers and persons holding public office and professing Lutheran or Calvinistic creeds were to be banished as heretics.

An additional reason for Bamberg's extended medievalism has to do with a particular twist in its fiscal policy. Unlike secular jurisdictions where law sharply limited confiscation of private assets and property of the condemned, Bamberg's prince-bishops took advantage of their almost unlimited power in secular as well as religious matters. This explains why they could take what was not rightfully theirs, thereby making the witch persecution a lucrative enterprise. First of all, expenses arising from arrest, hearings, imprisonment, torture, and execution were the responsibility of the victim or his or her family. Even persons who had been friends with the condemned could be held responsible for reimbursing the authorities' expenses.[17] Hence the income of the various members of the industry of the witch-hunt, ranging from the bishop's jurist to the henchman, was usually safeguarded. Funds in excess of expenses went into the coffers of the prince-bishop. Sometimes the surplus was substantial.[18] Examples included:

1. auctioning off on October 30, 1625, the house and all belongings of Conrad Müller, who had fled the territory after being accused of witchcraft;

2. confiscation of the estate of a childless couple who had been executed as witch and warlock in 1628;

3. confiscation of the entire estate of Peter Fürst, executed as a witch on December 18, 1629, despite intercession by the emperor and a promise by the heirs that they would pay for the trial expenses;

4. Georg Elder, pointing out that he had been a loyal servant of the diocese for twenty-eight years, petitioned the prince-bishop for a waiver of the bill he was supposed to pay for the cost of the execution of his wife and son;

5. the abandoned children of parents who had been executed as witches in 1629 unsuccessfully petitioned the prince-bishop to let them have their rightful estate;

6. numerous petitions by heirs, who had fled the diocese, to receive the estates of their parents or relatives who had been executed as witches in Bamberg;

7. the execution as witches of all members of the Haan family (including husband, wife, son, daughter, daughter-in-law, mother-in-law) left no heirs in the diocese. Since the Haan patriarch, once the vice chancellor of the prince-bishop, was one of the wealthiest persons in the realm, his master's coffers experienced substantial enlargement.

Ultimately so many complaints accumulated at the court of the emperor of the Holy Roman Empire that in 1631 he sent a curt and clear order to the prince-bishop to refrain from unlawful confiscation. Undeterred, just as on previous occasions of reprimands, Johann George prevaricated, procrastinated with reforms, and continued his conduct.

The prince-bishop was merciless. Before anyone could be put to death, he had to give specific consent.[19] As far as my archival research has disclosed, he always gave it, although it would have been perfectly in his power to commute the sentence, set people free, or order a new trial. To be fair, it must be said that Johann Georg sometimes relented to the *Gnadenzettel*, a writ for mercy customarily accompanying the proposal for execution, by granting a milder form of execution. He might, for example, waive the *Zwicken mit glühenden Zangen*, the tearing of the victim's breasts with incandescent pliers moments before live burning (as was customary if the delinquent had confessed to child-killing or to the desecration of the Holy Host), or commute the sentence of live burning to strangulation before burning. But never have I found a commutation of a death sentence.

This then was the ominous stage on which unfolded the drama of Witchboy.

The Story of a Document

In years of studies of archival materials I have looked at dozens of witch trial transcripts. None has fascinated me more than that dealing with one little Bamberg boy imprisoned and investigated as a witch suspect. The manuscript recording his confession became separated from the Bamberg archives and found its way into Cornell University's Rare Books Department.[20] It was there that I translated it. It is one of the longer transcripts of its kind, twenty-four pages of handwriting on European seventeenth-century legal-size sheets, and it is evident that the Inquisition took the case very seriously and requestioned the boy over a period of several weeks. The telltale sign that the Inquisition ascribed great importance to the case can be seen in the fact that the boy was interrogated by prominent members of the prince-bishop's *Malefiz-Commission* (the commission made up of lawyers for the investigation of crimes) and that he had already been imprisoned for a while, though it is unclear precisely how long.[21]

The boy's life before and after imprisonment and interrogation is shrouded in mystery.[22] There is no explicit description of the immediate reasons for the boy's arrest, although, as we shall see in later chapters, we can make a pretty good guess at them. There is also no indication of the nature of the sentence that necessarily would have had to follow.

Even the boy's name is unknown. It is merely marked by the Latin substitute of N. N. Ironic as it may seem, the very fact that the name was withheld is a mark of importance. On September 19, 1616, the prince-bishop of Bamberg had initiated a rule, according to which prisoners confessing freely should be remanded to the Jesuits for doing penance; must identify all their accomplices, thereby signifying that they have told the truth; were then granted secrecy of protocol, which meant that their confessions were filed separately and could be copied only by the scribe of the criminal court and *not* by the scribe of any other office; and had their names omitted from transcripts.[23]

This rule was applied immediately in the September 1616 case of a fourteen-year-old Bamberg boy whose confession and denunciations are known, but not his identity.[24] It also applied to Witchboy thirteen years later.

Another interesting aspect of the transcript is that the victims of Witchboy's denunciations, which the boy gave quite freely and which referred to the boy's peers and conspirators, were similarly recorded as N. N. When the boy referred to ten of his friends, for example, the scribe in every case wrote N. N. instead of proper names. Similar opaqueness was observed in regard to the places they came from, although the description of the main locality makes it evident that the boy lived in Bamberg and that the bizarre events he describes took place there.

There are several reasons for the absence of the names of the denounced persons. First, they mostly were Witchboy's cronies, which means equally underage and temporarily exempt from being identified publicly, for it was hoped they could be rehabilitated. Second, anonymity protected them against the revenge by persons they had denounced. Third, the transcript is a rewrite of the original notes, with the names retained on the original. The sort of confessional document we find in archives was rarely written during the actual interrogation, but usually transcribed from a rough original jotted down during questioning and possibly torturing, then rewritten after the session. In this manner the final document would be in *Schönschrift,* a refined hand and style, and suitable for the official file. It is possible that the scribe expedited the procedure either by enclosing the original list of the denounced or a separate list prepared earlier with the cooperation of the accused.

In any case, the anonymity imposes several unfortunate limitations on the study. One is that we cannot be sure of the gender of the boy's friends. Were there girls involved? The best guess, based upon the various stories told by the boy, seems to suggest an exclusively male peer group. Another limitation is that in all probability we will never find out what the boy's sentence was. The expectation that his young age alone would identify him and make his continued record conspicuous so that we could recognize his identity in other archival material is optimistic, for it was not uncommon to find children of that age among the accused in Würzburg and Bamberg. The records show that scores of them were executed in these centers of witch mania.[25] It is possible that our boy, anonymously or otherwise, may have been included in the ranks of these youthful victims. To disappear in the machinery of the Inquisition in a totally anonymous fashion was a real possibility in Bamberg, where on some occasions the condemned were burned in groups and, instead of identifying the individuals by name, each was merely given a number and recorded as such.[26]

The document was written in May 1629 in Middle High German, with overtones of Franconian dialect. The translation of this type of writing poses a number of challenges. The translator is confronted with the decision to either translate as literally as possible and risk awkwardness and perhaps even unintelligibility, or translate liberally and risk obliterating the finer shades of meaning. I chose the second option, but occasionally modified it with a more literate translation in situations where the English idiom would obscure too much. For example, when the boy described the goings-on at the witches' sabbath he noted, among other things, that lights were "stuck into the ground" between participants. A smooth English rendition might be tempted to say "placed" or "set on the ground," thereby obscuring the nature of the lights, which apparently were torches or candles to be stuck into the ground and not lanterns to be put on it. As we shall see later, this difference bears on the definition of the situation—adults most likely would have lanterns, whereas children would be equipped with cheaper paraphernalia; the wording fits the context of a peer group gathering and not the type of adult meetings described as the witches' sabbath. In any case, it is hoped that the later chapters of analysis and interpretation will illuminate possible obscurities in the translated text.

The confession in its original form was written in the third person, that is, from the point of view of the inquisitors, or more specifically of the inquisitorial scribe, who not only recorded what the boy said, but also inserted observations about how the boy said things, what he didn't say, and in one situation even that the accused was being visited by his demon right in the presence of the inquisitors. In the chapter following the translated confession we will take a look at what these observations and opinions meant in the context of the early seventeenth-century world.

I decided to change the style of the narrative from the third to the first person. This means, for example, that when the scribe wrote "he said he broke into a wine cellar," it now reads "I broke into a wine cellar." The primary reason for the change is to confer to the confession a more personal and direct presence. The scribe's attentiveness to detail and hue leaves little uncertainty as to exactly how the boy said things and how he meant things. Hence the change in pronoun does not distort the meaning of what was going on, but, on the contrary, allows the reader to experience more vividly the events of which the boy spoke. Furthermore, speech in the first person pronoun avoids the often stilted and halting conjunctive mode typical of indirect speech.

I want to summarize why Witchboy's case deserves our attention and analysis:

1. The boy is a fierce protagonist, playing the role of the diabolic conspirator with at times incredible ferociousness. Every now and then the boy explodes with defiance, telling the Inquisition what fools they were believing they could keep witches away by scribbling the sign of the holy cross on their doors and windows, or telling the inquisitors to their faces that he'd rather burn in hell than be a servant of God. Witchboy was also a talented storyteller and a beautiful poet. He could create Kafkaesque episodes in one moment and compose haunting, poetic images in the next. For instance, witchboy included in his parade of phantasmagoria the only known traffic accident while riding a pitchfork to the witches' sabbath.[27] In spite of, or perhaps because of, his brilliance, the boy is anything but harmless and innocent, as we shall see.

2. The account of Witchboy is one of the most revealing documents about the nature of the cosmology to which the Inquisition adhered with so much vehemence. Specifically it describes the demonology of the time as shared by accusers and accused alike. Extraordinary as the content of the confession may sound, it nonetheless incorporates most of the common elements of demonological belief of the time, resulting in a drama highlighting the Zeitgeist of early-modern Europe and revealing the contemporary core concerns with the unabashed poignancy of a fearless child.

3. The document shows how the Inquisition misconstrued the nature of the boy's peer group, demonizing activities we would call juvenile delinquency today, interpreting them in the light of seventeenth-century anxiety about diabolic conspiracy.

4. The document allows us glimpses at both the elite and the popular culture of the time. While the confession was cast in the demonological-theological framework of the cultural elite, it simultaneously uncovers the boy's everyday life conditions and describes the activities of common street urchins. Hence we have the rare opportunity of listening to two parties speaking to us through the medium of the confession: the inquisitors as representatives of elite culture and the youngster as representative of the common folk.[28]

5. Finally, the document serves as a memorial to the uncounted multitudes of children who perished in the inquisitorial machinery, never to be known or remembered. Just as we mark the grave of the unknown soldier the world over with the phrase "Known only unto God," so, similarly, can we characterize this nameless case.

The material consists of twenty-four handwritten pages and is scant basis for an analytic reconstruction of what the character of the boy and the nature of his social involvements must have been. Thanks to the loquacity of the boy, there are, nonetheless, many interesting insights to be gleaned from his narrative. The method of the analysis then is to interpret subtle indicators for a broad understanding of what the reality must have been at the time.

Witchboy is presented with the general reader in mind, hoping that his account will serve as a picturesque introduction to a dark chapter of our civilization. A short glossary at the end of the book may prove helpful for review or clarification of some of the less common terms used throughout the pages. The endnotes are primarily for the perusal of the specialist. They are not essential for a general understanding of the text.

Notes

1. See estimations in Rossell H. Robbins, *Encyclopedia of Witchcraft and Demonology* (New York: Crown, 1959), pp. 35–37; and Graf von Lamberg, *Criminalverfahren vorzüglich bei Hexenprozessen im ehemaligen Bisthum Bamberg* (Nürnberg, Germany: Rieger & Wiessner, 1835), p. 21.

2. Pius Wittmann, "Das Bamberger Trudenhaus," *Zeitschrift des Münchener Alterthumsverein* 5 (December 1892): 21–26.

3. Up to 1624 it was Johann Georg's habit to burn all witches alive. After that it was possible to obtain a *Gnadenzettel,* a special writ of mercy by the bishop, to be decapitated or strangled before burning the body. See Herbert Pohl, "Hexenglaube und Hexenverfolgung im Kurfürstentum Mainz," *Geschichtliche Landeskunde* 32 (University of Mainz, 1988), p. 185.

4. Johannes Janssen and Ludwig Pastor, *Geschichte des deutschen Volkes,* vol. 8 (Freiburg, Germany: Herder, 1924), pp. 289, 432.

5. Johannes Looshorn, *Geschichte des Bisthums Bamberg* (Bamberg, Germany: Handels-Druckerei, 1906), pp. 29–32, 91ff., 163–73, 187, 264ff.

6. Ibid., pp. 91f.

7. Janssen and Pastor, *Geschichte des deutschen Volkes,* vol. 5, 243–44, and vol. 8, p. 170.

8. Ibid., vol. 8, pp. 289n, 432.

9. Ibid., vol. 5, p. 203.

10. Looshorn, *Geschichte des Bisthums Bamberg,* vol. 6, p. 402.

11. See Nürnberg Staatsarchive, S.I.L. 196, #9, pp. 2–9.

12. Michael V. Deinlein, "Zur Geschichte des Fürstbischofs Johann George II," *Bericht des Historischen Vereins Bambergs* 40 (1877): 1–41.

13. Looshorn, *Geschichte des Bisthums Bamberg,* vol. 6, p. 39.

14. Ibid., vol. 5, pp. 36, 40.

15. For example, the *Constitutio Criminalis Carolina* specified that torture may be applied only once and that the resultant confession or the lack thereof stands as the decisive juridical indication. Bamberg routinely violated the rule by defining repeated torture as "continued" torture. Such "continuations" frequently consisted of ten or more separate sessions. See ibid., vol. 6, pp. 37–38.

16. Ibid., vol. 5, pp. 252, 262, 334.

17. Ibid., vol. 6, p. 73.

18. Ibid., vol. 6, pp. 38, 48, 69, 70, 72, 79.

19. Ibid., vol. 6, p. 35.

20. *Witchcraft Documents from Bamberg*, Cornell University Library, Rare Books Dept. Mss. Bd. Wft. BF H63++.

21. Imprisonment (and execution) of children was not uncommon in Bamberg's history. For example, overlapping with the time of the Witchboy episode (1628–29) was the imprisonment of a little girl on suspicion of witchcraft. Sources show that in 1629 she had been in prison already for two years and that her shepherd father had repeatedly and unsuccessfully begged the bishop to set her free. See Looshorn, *Geschichte des Bisthums Bamberg*, vol. 6, p. 70.

22. There is a parallel between this study and Giovanni Levi's research into the trial of a man, the priest Giovan Battista Chiesa, brought before the Roman Inquisition in 1697. Levi's study also lacks documentation about the accused's life before and after the inquest. Similar to the method used in Witchboy, Levi extracts pertinent information from the trial transcript to project what reality and daily life must have been at the time. See Giovanni Levi, *Inheriting Power: The Story of an Exorcist* (Chicago: Chicago University Press, 1988).

23. Looshorn, *Geschichte des Bisthums Bamberg*, vol. 6, p. 35.

24. Ibid.

25. As indicated earlier, among the condemned in the prince-bishoprics of Bamberg and Würzburg were numerous boys and girls between the ages of five and twelve. See especially W. G. Soldan and H. Heppe, *Geschichte der Hexenprozesse*, vol. 2 (1880; reprint, Kettwig, Germany: Magnus Verlag, 1986), pp. 45–51.

26. Von Lamberg, *Criminalverfahren vorzüglich bei Hexenprozessen*, appendix, p. 27.

27. While the boy's claim refers to the actual experience of an accident, artist Michael Herr painted a strikingly similar scene circa 1650, a generation after Witchboy's invention. Herr's painting shows not only a boy flying on a pitchfork, but a neighbor craft losing its pilot.

28. A study with a similar goal and methodology—contrasting elite and popular cultures on the basis of documents reporting the interrogation and confession of a heretic—has been published by Carlo Ginzburg, *The Cheese and the Worms: The Cosmos of a Sixteenth-Century Miller* (New York: Penguin Books, 1982; Italian orig., 1976). Ginzburg's work is much more comprehensive, however, and he had the good fortune of being able to draw from a larger variety of documents. Furthermore, the star, Menocchio, is a much more protean character than Witchboy, engaged in relatively sophisticated heresy, proposing an alternative cosmogony. Nonetheless, there are some parallels, the most striking of which is the protagonists' verbal and imaginative skill, something that is not often encountered in trial documents.

7

The Confession

The Cast

The normal complement of persons present at an inquisitorial hearing included two interrogators. In the case of Bamberg they were two jurists belonging to the *Malefiz-Commission,* the prince-bishop's counselors on crimes, particularly crimes of sorcery and witchcraft. Additional persons present were the court scribe, one or more henchmen ready to carry out torture, and of course the accused. In some instances additional persons were called into the room, such as a priest, a defense counsel, and witnesses to testify against the accused. The interrogation room was identical to the torture chamber and usually located within the witch prison where the accused was kept until he or she would confess and until final sentence was passed. This, then, was the setting in which the confession of Witchboy was obtained.

Some technical remarks: The italics type in the following text indicates observations made by the interrogators or the scribe; the rest of the text is statements made by the boy, as written down by the scribe. All twenty-four pages of the statement are translated here. Some remarks by the scribe were made in Latin; several of them were exclamations written in the margin of the transcript to call attention to particularly important points, such as *nota bene!,* meaning "take note!" or "attention!" Other Latin phrases served to exculpate the writer for repeating a profane expression used by the accused, such as *sit venia verbo,* meaning "excuse the expression." To achieve fluidity throughout the confession, Latin phrases have been translated. Readers curious as to what the original Latin phrase may have been can find brief explanations in the endnotes.

The Hearings

Tuesday, April 3rd in the year of 1629.
The boy, approximately nine years old, is brought before the inter-rogators and declares himself willing to confess, after having been encouraged to do so in goodness [i.e., without the application of torture]. He confesses:

About two years before I was locked up in prison, something woke me up one night between eleven o'clock and midnight. As I looked around, I saw that it was my friend George who stood beside my bed and started to talk to me. He tried to persuade me to learn the art of witchcraft. While George was talking to me, a number of additional people suddenly appeared in the room and I got scared. I told them that I didn't want to get involved in witchcraft and that I wanted them to leave me alone. George got very angry at that and wouldn't leave me alone. Finally I called on Jesus—first I wanted to make the sign of the holy cross, but at my age at that time I didn't know how. Anyway, when I called out the name of Jesus, George and the other persons disappeared.

It was George who later became my little demon-lover. He grew horns and had two goat's feet. He was usually in the company of three friends and flew on a pitchfork on which there was room enough for all of them. George's fork was made of silver that we had stolen from a goldsmith's shop where bells were also cast, and where gold and silver could be found lying around everywhere. My own pitchfork, however, was made only of brass, which we had also stolen from the goldsmith's shop.

Take note! The boy reports that his demon would usually ride a silver pitchfork and that one of named friends would always wear silver shoes to their get-togethers.

I knew from the very beginning that one of my playmates had already learned how to do witchcraft and that it was George who had taught him. But at one of the witches' dances George told me that he had already taught witchcraft to two other playmates before that and that these two now demanded to have their own demon-lovers.

These, by the way, were the friends who had accompanied George that first night. As far as I know, they didn't play any particular pranks that night.

However, the very next day a number of my friends travelled with George to the fields outside of town and cut down crops. Later that day I went to join them. As I approached the fields, I saw lots of mice scurrying around, and a number of them came running up to me and suddenly changed into my friends. As George changed back into a human body, he scolded me and demanded to know why I had not listened to them the night before. Finally I gave in and told him I would learn black magic.

All this happened on the Monday during the last week in September,[1] the day after George and his friends tried to talk me into learning witchcraft.

Take note! The boy joined the others in doing a lot of damage and in gathering up the crops they had cut before the farmer could come to harvest.

After we were through cutting down the crops and collecting the grain, we all went to a small creek next to the fields, where my demon produced a white sheet. One of the boys quickly jumped on his hay fork and took off to fetch a pillow.

As soon as he returned, the pillow was placed on my demon's [George's] sheet to serve as a baptismal bed. Creek water was poured over me and I was baptized in the name of the demon and of the demon's lord [the Devil]. One of the fellows became my godfather. His name was Jacob; and so, of course, I was baptized with that name. From then on, I went by the name of Jacob. My godfather's gift was a gold coin tied into a piece of cloth. But I couldn't keep it; I had to hand it over to George, who said he would save it for me.

Take note! The conspirators offered the Devil the boy's real name as a sacrifice.

Wednesday, April 4th of 1629.
The interrogation of the boy is being continued and he confesses further:

After the baptism was over, my demon George tried to stab me in the left arm and in both eyes. But since I was scared that it would hurt, I didn't want him to do it. That made my demon quite mad and he threatened to break my neck. Anyway, finally he got the upper hand and stabbed me in the arm and in the eyes with a tiny spear that was very sharp. The blood was then used to write my name into a secret book.

After that, George commanded me to stop calling on God or praying to Him. Instead, from then on, I was to regard my demon as my God and pray to him—just as all other witches were supposed to pray to their demons. Whenever I made the sign of the cross, I had to do so in the name of my demon.

The boy hesitates to respond to the repeated questions as to what the special prayer was that his demon taught him; he only admits that it had something to do with "threads" and "pears."

Suddenly there is a strange change coming over the boy; he turns obstinate. It is quite obvious that he is presently possessed by his demon, who must be telling him to keep quiet and to stop giving further information.[2]

Then, finally, the boy continues to confess:

I have been to three different witches' dances, which took place on a pasture not far from town, and on those occasions four of my friends played music for the witches to dance by. I flew to these celebrations on my brass pitchfork, always taking along my bride and usually giving a ride to one of my other friends. One time my friend happened to fall off the pitchfork while over the River Main.[3] As the poor fellow splashed into the water, he changed into a mouse and scurried over the water toward a row boat that happened to be there. After he climbed on board, the boat headed straight for the river's bank, although no one seemed to be rowing it. Upon reaching the bank, the mouse jumped from the boat and instantly changed back into a human being. My bride and I piloted the fork to the ground and picked him up; he was perfectly fine. Then the three of us flew to the witches' dance.

At the witches' dances each witch-person had behind or beside him or her a light, which was stuck in the ground and burned a bright red. One of the fellows, the son of the well-known burgher X, was charged with the responsibility to keep the lights burning. He had to clean them constantly. His effort was frustrated twice when two of the lights went out because the witches caused a fierce wind.

The witches feasted at their meetings. The meals were served on a white sheet spread on the ground, and the witches sat around it in a circle. But before we were allowed to sit down to eat, we had to dance around the circle three times. This we had to do before and after eating, instead of saying prayers. After dancing three times, we sat down, with the lights between us, and began to eat. Once, during lenten, we had fish. After we finished our meals, we again danced three times, and then we (*pardon the expression*) kissed each other, and everybody flew home.

One night, within a year of my baptism, I went with my witch-god-father to the cemetery to dig up the grave of a child. We pulverized [burned to ashes] the body to make a powder that we mixed into the food or drink of people to make them sick or to even kill them.

During the second year after my baptism, I was one of the gang that blinded an ox in a nearby village. We received the order from our god, who also told us how to do it. To start with, we had to collect (*pardon the expression*) droppings from the ox, boil it until it was dry, grind what was left into a fine powder and stir it into the ox's (*pardon the expression*) urine.[4] We then sprayed this mixture into the eyes of the ox while saying: "Perish in the name of the Devil. He will never make you well again."

Two weeks after we had dug up the grave in the cemetery, three of my friends and I went to a nearby town to steal wine. We took along two spigots that my friends had whittled from wood, a bucket, and several leather flasks. We bought the flasks, but we stole the money to buy them. During the trip to town we used ropes to tie these things to our pitchforks. In the wine cellar we inserted the spigots into the barrels and let the wine run into the bucket and flasks. After they were full, we filled the empty barrels with water. Then we tied things back on the pitchforks—and we took off.

One year after my baptism, several of my friends and I flew to another town where we wanted to do the same thing. We again broke into a wine cellar and dined and wined on what we found. Besides drinking as much as we pleased on the spot, we took along enough wine to have a party later.

During the same season, we broke into still another wine cellar. This time it was the cellar of a monastery located in the middle of a neighbor town, where we not only drank wine on the spot, but again took lots of it along with us.

He reports this with a certain amount of pride.[5]

I know for a fact that it is entirely useless for people to write the sign of the holy cross on the bedroom windows or on the doors so that witches can't enter, because witches can get into houses by flying in through the chimney or through the smallest opening; even through a hole as small as a pea.

Sometimes the whole gang or just one of us would fly out to scare people by pinching or smothering them when they were asleep. However, I swear I did this only once, and that I did it to a woman living here in town. I pinched her while she was lying in bed with her husband. She had one arm curled over her head, and looked very pretty.

Another time I went along on a night flight with one of my friends who wanted to pinch a person. The tweaking really hurt badly, because the person screamed and yelled; but my friend just laughed about it; and then we both jumped on a pitchfork and flew off.

Take note! The boy adds that they pinch people hard enough to leave blue bruises.

The person whose name I didn't want to tell you yesterday evening was burgher X. He is a man who, instead of doing an honest day's work, gossips like a washer woman.

I also have to admit that when my friends and I seemed to say the rosary, we just pretended because we were only allowed to count the beads. We weren't allowed to even mention the Lord's Prayer, the Ave Maria, or the Confessional Prayer.

Our power to spoil the growth of grain and other fruits of the field depended on doing a certain ritual just the right way. We needed a wagon with its hitching pole sticking straight out. Then one of us would have to crawl underneath the pole three times. At the same time, the friends would have to step across him just as many times.

Afternoon of the same day.

I must first of all report that a certain person is a scoundrel and a thief (*pardon the expression*) because he initiated one of my friends to witchery; and it was this friend who in turn initiated me later.

One half year after having been baptized, two of my friends gave me a ride on their pitchfork and took me to a wine cellar, where a bunch of other friends were waiting for us. There we stole a load of wine,[6] then went to a well from which we fetched four cats, spotted black and white. While three of my friends were busy refilling the empty wine barrels with well water, the four cats were busy for more than two hours flying the wine to a hideaway in the countryside, far from town. We hid the wine there for future parties. My job in the cellar was to sit on top of the wine barrels and whip them with a leather strap, which my demon had given me for exactly this purpose. At the next witches' dance, which took place in that secret pasture, we all guzzled as much wine as we wanted.

My demon George would come flying to all the witches' dances on a he-goat as big as a horse, with the grooming duty assigned to one of my friends; this fellow had to fetch the goat whenever the demon wanted to fly somewhere. The demon's wife would always fly on a she-goat.

Last night around two o'clock, and again today right after the morning session, my demon visited me and cussed me out fiercely because I had confessed so much. He threatened to break my neck if I reported anything more. The demon was unhappy not only with me, but also mentioned how mad he was at two other friends, whom he called thieves (*pardon the expression*). Because I was writing down everything the demon said, he grew furious and called me a cowardly traitor, and then he left.

One of the first things George and my friends taught me was how to make fleas. I tested the recipe several times at home. You had to extract the black stuff from the grease used for pitchforks and smear it into a skillet while saying: "In the Devil's name I am able to create fleas." As soon as I would say this, the grease changed into fleas. One night I tossed a skilletful of them into the house of a woman. They jumped on her and tormented her soundly. At the next nightly meeting of our circle, which the woman attended, we teased her about this and made up a guessing game: she had to guess who had played the prank on her. After she tried several times and finally guessed right, she was furious and cussed me out to no end.

The white part of the pitchfork grease was used in a more dangerous way and used on those we meant to punish the most. We would rinse the drinking glasses of these people with it, and after drinking from them, people would get sick or even die. Quite a few people had already died from that. Just to mention one of them—Mrs. X who lived here in town.

Besides making fleas, we had also learned how to make rabbits. My demon had explained to me how to make a special lotion with which I could do that. For making the lotion I first had to beat to death a dog, take some of its flesh and blood, mix it up with a secret dye given to me by my demon, and then smear this mixture all over the dog's body. When I did this, I was supposed to dedicate the sacrificed dog to my demon by saying certain words. I tried it and when I finished, a rabbit jumped out of the dog's carcass and hopped away.

I must admit that I have denied God and turned my back on Him; therefore I will never go to heaven.

Now I wish to receive the Holy Eucharist[7] to be safe from the demon; so that the demon cannot reach me anymore.

I must also admit that the demon fetched me from prison to take me along to a wedding feast; I am talking about the wedding at the X family.

The demon got into my prison cell by taking the key from the wall and opening the lock with it—then out and away we flew on the demon's pitchfork through a tiny crack in the wall. Later the demon returned me to the cell through the same crack.

Here finally are the words with which the boy has been told to pray to his false God, and which he didn't want to tell us during the morning session:

Black thread,
White thread,
Pahrles pears,
It takes off in the Devil's name.

The boy starts to cry and can't speak anymore.[8] *After he recovers, he revises the wording and assures us that now he tells the truth and remembers the exact prayer with which he had to pray to his false God:*

> It takes off in the Devil's name,
> Green thread,
> And white thread,
> Black thread,
> And Pahrleins pears.[9]

Now the boy makes a statement of renunciation of God, and says verbatim:

"I never want to belong to God anymore; and in the name of the Devil I spit three times into His face. My star shall burn in hellfire, and I want to belong to the Devil for all eternity. I renounce God in heaven, the most holy Virgin Mary, and four angels, St. Andrew, St. Michael, St. George, and St. Jacob."

Thursday, April 5th, 1629:
Today the above confession was read to the boy word for word. He ratifies it and says it is the truth.

Monday, May 7th, 1629:
The boy has requested an additional hearing and says that he wishes to add a number of points to his confession:

1. I forgot to report two other persons who dabble with witchery; they are X and X.
2. And there is still another person: the woman X, who once visited me after I had been arrested and was locked up. She came one night between eleven and midnight and urged me not to tell the authorities about my own witchery or of my baptism, but rather to obey my demon George and to carry out all his commands. She even offered to help me escape from prison by inviting me to join her on her pitchfork. But I made the sign of the holy cross, and she immediately disappeared through a crack in the wall.
3. I once saw how a certain woman stopped the strongest hail

storm by placing a saucer on top of a heap of dung (*pardon the expression*). Right away the sky darkened and the hail stopped.

4. I have also seen the same person stopping the heaviest rain by shaking empty flour sacks in her attic. Immediately a sharp wind began to blow and chase the rain clouds away.

5. If a person—regardless whether a man or a woman—went to the Great Fiend and learned witchcraft, he or she would be given a small glass jar with a salve that could make people sick or even kill them. I must confess a personal experience and admit that I received such a jar with salve and hid it in my father's house. Once I chanced upon a place where the Great Fiend gave a woman, the daughter of the burgher X, one of these jars. I happened to see this in the forest on X Mountain where I was busy gathering wood for my father to make barrel staves.

6. Two weeks after my initiation, our god called the friends together to plan special revenge on a couple of beggars who lived in the town of X, because they had stolen a blue-striped scarf from us, a scarf we used to wear when we went to church. So the whole gang of us—I named everyone before— flew to the place where the beggars lived and torched their house, which burned clear to the ground. Three of the gang, X, X, and X, carried the fire on their pitchfork—they flew together on one fork. As soon as we were done with the prank, we all mounted our pitchforks and flew home.

7. My demon George came to me one night and threatened to break my neck. It was the night following the day you [the interrogators] had me confront the X woman and testify to her face that she had not only been present at my initiation but even helped with the celebration. I heard that the woman was then executed.

8. I and my friends had two gods. One was black, and I accepted him as my god; he was kinder and nicer than the other one, who was reddish like a fox and always appeared at our get-togethers; this one was evil and malicious.

9. A year after my initiation the two gods commanded me and my friends to fetch a crucifix from a certain church. Five

of us carried it to a secret place and stuck it into the ground. Then we flew out to steal food and drink; when we returned we took turns making fun of the crucifix and spit at it. We also used it in a guessing game and in a card game; we laid it on the ground and sat around it in a circle and played. Whoever won a game had to pick up the crucifix and poke the others in the belly with it. After we had dined and wined and played, the same friends who fetched the crucifix flew off with it and returned it to the church.

10. The Great Fiend and the witches have extraordinary cats and dogs that can be recognized by their eyes.[10] However, people who have small children at home usually have normal and natural cats and dogs. Anyway, the fiendish cats and animals can be recognized by their strange eyes.

11. Whenever I and my friends settled down to enjoy a meal and needed something, there were always two dogs who waited on us and fetched us whatever we wanted. One dog was black and white, the other red-spotted.

12. Our god visits the imprisoned witches, comforts them, and again and again commands them not to confess anything. Sometimes during the interrogations the demon has actually grabbed their tongues to keep them from being able to speak.

13. If I would be one of the inquisitors and had to deal with witches who refused to confess, I would put them on the rack and stretch them until the sun could shine through their hides.

14. Now that I have finally renounced my demon god, I am able to confess that he visited me in prison the very night after the day I renounced him, cussing me out for telling on the gang and turning my back on him. I wasn't the only one to be cussed out; my friends were told off just as much. The demon god said that he would punish us horribly if we turned our backs on him. He promised to make us miserable forever.

15. I now remember four more persons that I've seen at the witches' dances. They were N, N, N, and N.

16. It will be exactly two years at the next church festival [*Kirchweih*] in N. village that my demon god George had

changed himself into a red star, flew out through the window, and disappeared.

17. I confess that I have been in cahoots with the Veiled Women. Since they were always totally wrapped in white veils, I really couldn't tell who they were. But they knew how to make a deadly powder by taking some hair of the person to be killed, putting it into a mortar, adding a special powder that their god had given them, and grinding it up. As soon as the women threw a dose of this stuff into the house from which the hair came, one of the persons living there would have to die. This happened once about a year after my initiation; it was I who brought the hair to the Veiled Women.

18. At one of our meetings I was told by five of my friends that they had conjured up a rain shower to spoil a church festival [*Kirchweih*] in N. village. They reported that while they were returning from the festival, two of them stepped behind two large boulders along the road and used coals to draw two magical signs, which they dedicated to their god.[11] As soon as they did this, a heavy rain shower broke loose and drenched the village. When these friends reported this at one of our meetings, all the others and especially our god praised them highly for the prank.

19. Finally I wish to report that St. Joseph in heaven actually is the patron saint of the witches, and that all witches are very fond of him and adore him.

17th of May 1629:
The boy ratifies all these points and swears they are true.

Notes

1. The boy refers to one of the four seasons of penance, specified in the liturgical calender of the Catholic church. Here he means the week after the third Sunday in September.

2. The inquisitors' belief in the visitation by the demon to command the witch to be silent was nothing out of the ordinary. Such instances have been reported from many jurisdictions. See an interesting example where

Weather witches brew a magic elixir to create a storm. From
Ulrich Molitor, *Von den Unholden und Hexen* (1489).

Milk magic: Kneeling on a pentagram, the witch steals milk while the milkmaid comes up empty. From Hans Vintler, *Tugendspiegel* (1486).

Torture scene depicting burning, stretching, and cutting off a hand.
From Ulrich Tengler, *Layenspiegel* (1508).

Witchburning in Derneburg in the Harz Mountains (1555). Sensational reports of executions and other terrible events were promulgated by means of such printed images distributed as flyers.

an interrogated woman begged the inquisitors to get her demon-lover out of her so that she could speak and confess: Herbert Pohl, "Hexenglaube und Hexenverfolgung im Kurfürstentum Mainz," *Geschichtliche Landeskunde* 32 (University of Mainz, 1988), p. 171. As a principle, the interrogators observed and recorded not only what the delinquent said during a hearing, but also his or her body language, including tone of voice, crying, gestures, and so on. This applied to the accusers as well as to the denounced in a face-to-face confrontation. The reactions of the denounced were interpreted and often used as additional *indicia*. Hence a person's paling, blushing, shedding tears, becoming restless, embarrassed, angry, timid, vociferous, ad infinitum, became significant indicators and could be taken as evidence of guilt. Since there were no objective norms of evaluation, the biases of the interrogators had free license. Negative attitudes toward the interrogated person tended to see *any* form of body language as confirming guilt. Cf. Herbert Pohl, "Hexenglaube und Hexenverfolgung im Kurfürstentum Mainz," *Geschichtliche Landeskunde* 32 (University of Mainz, 1988), p. 168.

3. The Main River is one of the major rivers of Germany, with Bamberg located on its southern banks.

4. Here the scribe inserted a Latin phrase, clarifying—and sterilizing, as it were—the boy's slang express, *Saich,* delicately putting it as *id est urina.*

5. To report the interrogators' observation, the scribe used the Latin phrase *Narravit cum quadam admiratione.*

6. The boy used the technical term *Fuder,* a wholesale measure of wine consisting of between 800 and 1,800 liters, depending on the region. If Witchboy spoke truthfully, this would mean the gang stole an amount of anywhere between 200 and 420 gallons.

7. The *Agnum Dei,* as the scribe put it.

8. The scribe used the Latin phrase *Incipit flere A nihil ulterius loquitur* to indicate that the boy broke down and started to cry.

9. With the exception of the first line referring to the Devil, the original version in Middle High German rhymes:

Hebt sich an, in des Teüfels Nahmb,
grüenen Zwiern,
undt weissen Zwiern,
Schwartzen Zwiern,
und Pahrleinsbiern.

10. The boy is referring here to the so-called familiars, demons disguised as domestic pets or farm animals. The inquisitors took this matter very seriously and were quite interested in knowing the exact appearance of the telltale eyes of the familiars. They asked the boy for a description, and

the scribe dutifully tried to reproduce it by inserting a crude design of a staring eye into the text.

11. The boy tried to demonstrate the signs to the inquisitors by drawing a cross resembling a simple addition sign followed by a design with a long horizontal line from which a number of shorter vertical lines extended downward, resembling a comb.

8

Leitmotif and the Scripts of the Drama

Today's readers are undoubtedly tempted to project their own incredulity onto the inquisitors and assume that these learned men could not possibly have believed in the factuality of the boy's statements, could not possibly have taken him seriously. After all, these men were presumably experienced, educated, erudite.

It is here that the modern, empirical-scientific Zeitgeist falls short of understanding the cosmology of the inquisitors. There is no doubt that seventeenth-century authorities accepted the boy's confession as deadly serious and true. The few exceptions among the inquisitors, such as the Jesuit Friedrich von Spee[1] or the Spanish inquisitor Alfonso de Salazar y Dias,[2] who raised questions about the truth and factuality of confessions, especially if obtained through torture, largely went unheard or unheeded. Historians concur that when it came to demoniacal views the blind faith of the inquisitors, as well as that of the general population, was nearly unlimited.

There are a number of specific indications throughout the interrogation that testify to this type of unreserved credulity and characterize Bamberg's Inquisition.

First, the most telling sign of the inquisitors' belief consisted of their perception of the boy being possessed by his demon *while* they tried to interrogate him. To them this was firsthand evidence of the boy's actual relationship with evil spirits.

Second, the boy was called before the interrogators a total of

139

six times. Measured against the usual Bamberg procedures, this exceeded the normal number of sessions in witch trials. The importance ascribed to the case is also reflected in the unusually long transcript of twenty-four pages. The boy's seemingly unending loquacity may have contributed to the length of the hearings.

Third, the inquisitors considered the boy truthful enough to arrange a face-to-face confrontation with a person he had denounced and who was later executed, although it may not have been exclusively the boy's denunciation that brought the accused to the stake. Such personal confrontations were staged by the Inquisition less for reasons of testing the trustworthiness of the denouncer than for breaking the resistance and self-confidence of the denounced. Bamberg's prosecutors accepted testimony and confirmatory confrontations by unusually young witnesses. For example, five-year-old Andreas, to whom we will refer repeatedly, was called before Bamberg's Inquisition to testify.

Fourth, the inquisitors kept asking the boy about the specific prayer he used to offer his demon, insisting on an answer, although the boy initially could not or was not willing to recite the idolatrous verse. Alone this insistence shows that the questioners seriously believed in the boy's relationship with the demon. Their insistence was possibly reinforced by hearing about the gang's "two gods." Some sort of serious heresy may have been suspected.

Fifth, as reported in the first part of this book, there is documentary evidence that children were prosecuted and sometimes executed as witches, particularly in the prince-bishoprics of Bamberg and neighboring Würzburg.

An illustration adding to the last point parallels the Witchboy case. It deals with little Andreas Förster, who was brought in from the outlying community of Oberscheinfeld and arraigned before the prince-bishop's all-powerful *Malefiz-Commission* on May 8, 1629, a date within the span of Witchboy's imprisonment and interrogation.[3] This five-year-old boy was denounced by a neighbor after he had bragged that he was flying on his pitchfork to church towers to attend witches' dances there. The boy did not hesitate to admit to these lofty ventures when the Inquisition had him arraigned before two prominent members of the commission, lawyers M. Herrnberger and Jakob Schwartzconz. The commissioners took Andreas's confession (including his denunciations) seriously and subjected him to a number of questions:

Who were the accomplices accompanying him on the flights?
How often had he flown to the church towers?
Who had been the musicians playing at the witches' dances?
How did he get involved with the Devil?
How and with whom did he engage in devilish fornication?

Little Andreas, similar to Witchboy, responded loquaciously and colorfully, and we will have reason to come back to his report later.

What today would appear to us as totally unbelievable, even absurd, or at times hilarious, was an article of firm belief to the people of the time. Of course, our modern scientific-empirical attitudes would cast a different light on the evidence. We would want to look behind the personae to learn what energized the performance. Our penchant for analysis would lead to an exploration of the dynamics of the drama of the witch-hunt—what it was that motivated the stars of the show, the inquisitors and the accused.

The leitmotif of the drama was the most obvious element—the theological assumption that the Devil was at work. Since it was thought that Satan could personify himself, it was only logical to think that he was able to interact and communicate with human beings and recruit allies among them. The most contemptible sort of ally was the witch, regardless whether it was man, woman, or child, who accepted the Devil as master. This, incidentally, was the demarcation between sorcerer and witch: the witch *served* the Devil; the sorcerer or sorceress *used* the Devil and other evil spirits, commanding them to do certain things. Hence the first character obeyed the Devil, the second character manipulated him. This distinction made the witch a heretic, the sorcerer or sorceress merely sinfully opportunistic. During the early phase of the witch-hunt the Inquisition took this distinction into consideration and adjusted punishment accordingly, but the hunting fever gradually obscured the difference.

Trial transcripts reflect a striking regularity in the type and sequence of questions asked.[4] A recurrent structure of roughly ten elements can be recognized, and they are reflected in Witchboy's confession.

First Encounter and Demonic Sexuality

The inquisitors' initial question invariably focused on the circumstances under which the accused first met the Devil. Witchboy was very specific about this and reported time and place; it was between eleven and midnight and took place in his bedroom. On this occasion the demon tried to persuade him to join the ranks of his allies.

In most cases, the Devil's attempt to win the person for his evil purpose was coupled with a sexual encounter. This was stereotypical fare of the confessions—culturally known, believed, and adhered to. Every witch accusation simultaneously was an accusation of sexual misbehavior; the witches' nature was thought to involve deviant sexuality, mainly sexual relations with the Devil. Witches were thought to be the Devil's paramours, or, as Luther indelicately put it, the Devil's whores. The Inquisition generally, and the *Malleus Malefi-carum* specifically, concentrated with misogynistic obsession on the witches' alleged sexual transgressions. Great detail was given in the explanation as to how sexual intercourse between human beings and spirits can take place, and "doctors of the church" devoted lengthy cerebrations to the topic.

It is of social-psychological significance that the answers of most confessing persons were somehow related to episodes in their actual sex lives, which means that real activities were interpreted within a demonic worldview. Often the interpretive process was energized by a number of powerful human emotions, such as guilt, revenge, and a complex mixture of the two, usually resulting in the portrayal of the sex partner as a demon.

The pattern is reflected in the confession of an accused even as young as our nine-year-old boy. Although there is no record of sexual activities, the stereotypical form is preserved during the first part of the interrogation. The awareness of the typical expectation is reflected by the boy himself as he used "little lover," the appropriate nomenclature concerning his personal demon. This is a rare version among confessional documents. While transcripts commonly used the terms *Puhle* (masculine) or *Puhlin* (feminine) when referring to adult-age illicit sex partners, it was rare to use the term *Puhlein,* the diminutive and neuter, as used by Witchboy. (A subsequent discussion will try to understand the choice of this term in the context of the boy's peer group.) For the moment it is important only insofar as it demonstrates the retention of the sexual-transgression model of a witch suspect even in the case of a child, despite total absence of indication that sexual activities of any sort had taken place. We may be certain of such absence, for the inquisitors were in the habit of spelling out the smallest indication with voyeuristic meticulousness and would undoubtedly have done so in this case if there had been the slightest reason. Rather, they merely retained the form without any content, as the boy failed to give any specific sexual accounts, indicative of his indifference or inexperience with sexual issues. Indicative of the nonproductiveness of the the issue was the gradual disappearance of the term "little lover" as the interrogation progressed. The inquisitors turned to other aspects of witches' behavior that yielded more fruitful information.

Not all children failed to give sexual information. On the contrary, some children dwelled on it with great eagerness. There were significant individual differences among the children of the Inquisition, as would be true among children of other historical eras. Some of them dwelled on lavish details of sexual involvements. This might have been due to actual sexual or erotic experiences, be it through childlike exploration of their own bodies, through relatively harmless experimentation with peers, or through serious sexual involvements. Mostly it was probably due to that fascinating mythomaniacal tendency of children—as much affliction as talent—to fabricate fantastic stories. The claim of a three-year-old girl that she had sex with the Devil is a blatant instance of such confabulated sexual activity.[5]

On the other hand, the above-mentioned interrogation of five-year-old Andreas Förster yielded responses that are in the range of credibility, at least partially so. In response to leading questions he reported that, "One night he danced with a little girl under the linden tree in town, drank beer and shared a fine dinner with her." Later that night, "The girl visited him in his bedroom, grabbed his naked penis, and they hugged and petted each other."[6] While having had a "fine dinner" stretches credibility, considering the conditions of hunger and squalor under which children had to live during the Thirty Years' War, the description of petting appears quite plausible.

Diabolic Death Threat

After an accused person had described the Devil's play at seduction, the next question was, did the accused cooperate? This obviously was a rhetorical question, because as far as the Inquisition was concerned an accusation usually equalled a conviction. But the answer allowed the accused a small measure of excuse with which he or she could introduce mitigating circumstances: "The demon threatened to kill me if I had refused cooperation."

In the Bamberg region the demon's favorite threat was death by wringing the neck of the uncooperative. The boy's response followed this general pattern.

Little Andreas was afraid of a sound beating. His "little companion" [*Genösslein*] thusly threatened should he betray him or refuse to go along with his wishes.[7]

Diabolic Baptism

All witch trials centered on the pact with the Devil as it was concluded through the ritual of satanic baptism. Witchboy delved into the matter in great detail and his imagery invoked an infant's baptism: a white sheet was spread out and a pillow was fetched to serve as his "baptismal bed." This was an unusual rendition of demonic baptism and an interesting illustration of children play-acting. Stereotypical, on the other hand, was that one of the heretical conspirators would step forward as his "godfather" and confer his name, Jacob, on him.

The power of the cultural imagery of the time manifested itself in a similar way in the confession of little Andreas, who, already at the age of five, was able to convey detail and hue of the black baptism. His description included his grandmother [*Babel*] functioning as his devilish godmother: "She baptized me to the name of 'Treebranch' [*Bauma asten*], took a bowl of water and poured it over me." To round out the scenario, Andreas noted the demonic appearance of his grandmother: "She had ugly hands, like a chimney sweep, also ugly clubfeet, and a freakish head full of lice, [and] her nose had been cut off."[8]

Baptismal Gift

As in all sacrilegious baptisms of this sort, the initiated were entitled to a gift, either from the officiating Devil or from the newly acquired godfather or godmother. Stereotypically, this gift, in most cases a coin or piece of gold, would come to naught as it later turned into a worthless piece of broken pottery, a piece of coal, a rock, or a clump of feces. Witchboy reported a different experience; he claimed that he was asked to hand over his gold piece to his demon for safekeeping. This version of the fate of the gift mirrors the custom of the time according to which it was thought improper for children to keep money or other valuables; they were expected to hand such things over to their parents.

The Collectivity of Demons and Conspirators

From the very beginning of the confessions, demons and human conspirators demonstrated gregariousness. They came in twos, threes, or entire flocks. The boy made references to their sociability in many situations, starting with the first nocturnal visit by his demon when he came flying in tandem with a number of conspirators, continuing with the entourage at the baptism, and ending with various group-centered thieveries. It was at these occasions that names were mentioned—sometimes with lethal consequences to those named. The main gathering was the witches' sabbath, where plots of *maleficia* were worked out and a lavish festival took place. The boy describes details of mostly stereotypical character. For example, the three dance rounds, to be performed before and after dinner, were commonly understood as the blasphemous substitute for prayers of thanks.[9] The boy left out, however, the perverse customs commonly thought to accompany the sabbath, such as dancing back to back, the *osculum infame* (the witches reverently kissing the Devil's posterior), hetero- as well as homosexual fornication, and other abominations. The closest the Witchboy came to referring to anything sensual was that before taking leave from the witches' sabbath the participants kissed each other. Even this reference to the mildest of carnalities elicited a shocked "*s.v.*" ("pardon the expression") on the part of the scribe. The absence of any more involved sensual, let alone sexual, activities at the sabbaths or at other conspiratorial get-togethers again is testimony to the boy's disinterest in the genre. This is a radical departure from the usual adults' descriptions of the sabbath and other demonic encounters.

Why did the Inquisition insist so fervently on the reality of the witches' sabbath? It seems that the credibility in the reality of the Great Conspiracy required proof of a patently simple precondition, namely that the accused had gatherings during which they concocted their evil plans. In other words, a conspiracy without some sort of committee meeting was unthinkable and would have rendered their alleged nefarious deeds infeasible. Hence the assumption that such conspiratorial meetings took place formed an intrinsic part of the theological-judicial underpinnings of inquisitorial thinking. Lacking such assumption and lacking subsequent evidence would have put in question the rationality of denunciations and could have brought the witch industry to a halt. Since this would have been an inconceivable turn of events to the hierarchy of the church, the reality of the inter-linked sabbath, conspiracy, and night flight had to be maintained.

Night Flight

The locations of the get-togethers played an important role in the confessions. The boy's report is no exception; he names a number of places, such as wine cellars and other romantic and pastoral settings. Irrelevant as they may initially sound, the location and distance of these places played significant roles in the assessment of the witches' capabilities. Since some of the locations were a considerable distance from the homes of the accused and a measure of alibi had been established for the suspects, the question arose: how did they get there in an often limited time frame? The answer by the demonologists as well as the answer of the confessing witches confirmed the witches' ability to fly swiftly over the lands.

This conception established the necessary logical link between attendance at the sabbath and the means to get there. The descriptions by Witchboy are exquisite on this matter. His demon's vehicle, in the form of a pitchfork, was forged of silver, whereas his own was forged from the more lowly brass, as was appropriate to his subservient status.

Transforming the common witches' broom into an aeronautical craft made of metal, even of precious metal, constitutes a uniquely extravagant description of the witches' vehicle. Such technology has never occurred to the numerous artists depicting the witches' night flight, exemplified by such painters as Hieronymus Bosch, Salvator Rosa, Hans Baldung-Grien, Michael Herr, and the many anonymous artists who created woodcuts, paintings, or drawings on the topic during the Middle Ages and the Renaissance. They all depicted the witches' vehicle as the unrefined agricultural tool, the common household broom, or some kind of plain farm animal. This leaves our Witchboy with an outstanding imagination. The basic idea of the witches' flight was of course an old cultural image,[10] and the boy may well have seen this in pictorial forms; for example, a number of the pictures included in this book had been around before (and were available during) the boy's time.

Witchboy's most vivid imagination, however, was reserved for the stunning description of a passenger falling off his pitchfork. This undoubtedly stands as a unique claim by Witchboy and represents the only known report of a traffic accident while en route to the witches' dance, excepting Michael Heer's woodcut a generation later. That the fallen passenger's life was saved by instantaneous metamorphosis into a mouse deftly scurrying over the surface of the water sounds like a vignette out of an amusing fairy tale, were it not for the deadly seriousness with which the inquisitors received it.

The description of the accident scene included the boy's casual aside, in which he referred to an additional passenger as his "bride." Witchboy never elaborated on this figure, and the scribe failed to clarify the gender of the "bride." It definitely was not George, to whom he only *initially* referred to as his "little demon-lover," because it seems that after the interrogators obtained a merely perfunctory reference to a "lover" lacking any sexual connotation, George was never again referred to as such, but rather as "his demon," "his spirit," or "his god." But who else was this "bride" then? Perhaps just a random remark popping out of the boy's fantasy? A chance remembrance that the inquisitors had a special appetite for intimate references and might be pleased to hear something of the sort?

Little Andreas's penchant for flying to church towers equally gratified the expectations of the inquisitors. He reported that his grandmother invited him to fly along on her pitchfork and that they visited the town's church tower to attend the witches' dance. It apparently occurred to the little boy that flights to such heights were dangerous and might result in accidents; so he advised the interrogators that he didn't fall down because he held on to the pitchfork "very tightly" and that the descent on the return flight was "very fast."

Both boys agreed that the pitchforks needed to be lubricated (*geschmiert*) for the flights. Witchboy went into detail and explained the properties of the different ingredients of the lubricant (some could be used to sicken or even kill people). Andreas, probably after he had been asked about the whereabouts of the lubricant, informed the inquisitors that his grandmother took it with her when she died.

While the boys' stories about the lubricant for the night-flight vehicles may touch us as amusing, it nonetheless has a serious background. It was widely believed that witches used mysterious salves to anoint their bodies and their flight vehicles before they took off for the sabbath. Some modern interpretations of this cultural stereotype connect the lubricant to psychedelic drugs with which certain women presumably experimented and consequently only *imagined* night flight. The idea of the witches' grease must be seen in the larger frame of the pharmaceutical dabbling, ranging from herbal knowledge to poisons and the uncanny witches' broth, conjuring up images of the bubbling cauldron. In fact, the boy may very well have seen pictures of scenes showing the witches' predilection for wicked pharmacopeia.

Destructive Magic

To render an acceptable confession, the accused had to include admission to a number of destructive deeds. Admitting alliance with the Devil in abstracto was not sufficient; actual harmful *maleficia* had to be added.

The vast majority of the suspects who initially had hesitated to admit *maleficia* quickly succumbed to torture and offered acceptable confessions. Of course, the mere knowledge that torture could be applied at any time sufficed in many cases to yield confessions right at the beginning of the interrogation.[11] And then there were a few persons who for one or another reason, perhaps including serious psychopathologies, stepped forward and volunteered confessions of the most incredible *maleficia*—usually quite credible to the inquisitors.[12]

In the case of Witchboy we seem to have a free-flowing confession offered without physical coercion, though one could argue that the terror of imprisonment and the intimidation of having to stand before stern interrogators were torture enough to prompt a confession. Moreover, the obviously streetwise youngster was certain to know all about the means of torture and execution. Without doubt he had plenty of opportunities to witness public executions in Bamberg. Considering that the time of this interrogation was 1629, that about six hundred witch executions (plus countless executions for other crimes) reportedly took place in Bamberg between 1623 and 1633, and that almost all of them were performed publicly, we may assume that our boy was well informed of what happened to criminals, secular as well as ecclesiastical.

But there are reasons to believe that it was not fear of torture or of death that prompted Witchboy to offer a detailed confession with such zeal and vigor. Other, or at least additional, reasons seem to exist, which we shall consider when we come to the discussion of the psychological background of the confession and try to penetrate Witchboy's persona.

In the meantime we observe a wide variety of claims or admissions to *maleficia*. Some of them are totally incredible, but some are credible, at least in the sense that they are feasible. We must keep in mind, however, that both categories were believable to the inquisitors, and that our distinction between credible and incredible events is based on biases that are part of our modern worldview.

First among the reported offenses that we would categorize as pure fantasy was the stealing of silver and brass to cast the aeronautic pitchforks. The prankish pouring of a potful of fleas into somebody's house is equally unbelievable, since the method of creating them, getting them into the pot, and then getting them into the house without the pests immediately seeking refuge on the nearest body, that is, the deliverer's, defies all scientific principles. The congregation of witches at the so-called sabbath lacks historical evidence, and the boy was reciting cultural images that had captured the imagination of the masses of the time.

Totally lacking credibility within today's scientific framework is the boy's claim that witches could cause deep freezes that would ruin every kind of fruit and grain. We may recall the boy's report that these freezes were carefully planned at the witches' sabbath.

The credulity of the authorities on this point may astound us today; nonetheless, a diary written at the time by Maria Anna Junius, a nun in a Bamberg convent, conveys an example. She wrote that on St. Urban Day (May 25) of 1626 an "unnatural" night frost killed all growing grain, fruit, and grapevine. She described the severity of the frost by saying that in the morning everything was frozen as hard as stone.[13] "A loud cry went up in the city," she continued in her diary, "and the people were frightened to death." Indeed, the consequences for the population were catastrophic; a famine set in, and during the following months scores of people dropped dead of starvation. The Inquisition immediately went to work; scores of suspects were arrested, interrogated, and tortured; and, as was foreseeable, confessions showed that the freeze had been caused by witches' malice. The inquest and the trials dealing with this particular misdeed stretched over a full year, and still in 1627 scores of people were being burned at the stake for the crime, because, as Maria Junius innocuously wrote, "Our prince was furious about this crime."[14]

Other parts of Witchboy's confession concerned rather indelicate pharmacological escapades and reported the poisoning of people by four different methods. One alleged method used the ashes of a burned corpse of a child. Ingestion of the ashes might cause some degree of constipation, if anything, but not death. The second method dealt with the extract from the lubricant used to keep the pitchforks flying. The third method used a poisonous salve given to witches by the Devil. Since the boy generalized on this point, the claim could only be true if there was indeed a personified Devil and a multitude of witches to receive the salve. Finally Witchboy talked about the mysterious Veiled Women, whose manufacture of poison, with the main ingredient being human hair, is equally incredible scientifically, but most interesting from an anthropological point of view: it represents an example of the practice of "contagious magic," i.e., the power of curse (or healing, for that matter) can be achieved when a personal item of the targeted person is obtained and hexed through powerful ritual or formula.[15]

The rather unhygienic concoction prepared for the blinding of an ox might cause some annoyance on the part of the beast but no loss of sight. Nonetheless, the preparation of the substance and the attempt to apply it with the intent to blind may indeed have been factual. Finally, the boy confessed that through magical powers he and his conspirators stunted the growth of grain and other fruits of the fields. This relates to the stereotypical image the people held of the powers of witches and again finds no counterpart in the perspectives of modern worldview.

On the other hand, the boy recites a long list of delinquencies that he and his peers could actually have carried out. It is possible that they stole precious metals from a goldsmith, though what they did with it is another story. Cutting down crops, most likely consisting of rye or wheat, was certainly something they could have done either out of prankishness or for the utilitarian purpose of getting grain for baking bread. Most likely it had something to do with the latter motive, for the transcript makes it a point (*take note!*) that the group "gathered up all the ears." Still, in most recent history, during wars and famines crop stealing in this fashion was common practice. A customary way of legally gathering grain used to be (and still is in some parts of the world) the collecting of wasted grain *after* the farmer had harvested; sometimes he allowed children to drive a gaggle of geese across the emptied field.

One of the more serious confessed crimes was arson. The motive seemed to be revenge for the theft of a scarf, possibly belonging to a member of one of the boys' families. The thieves were beggars who lived in the "beggars house," probably meaning the poor house of the community. The gang burned it to the ground, and the boy named the specific peers who had started the fire. (Starting a fire at that time was not as simple as today's striking a match or snapping a lighter; some of the boys may have had to literally carry some form of open fire, such as hot coals.) One of the reasons why this report may be factual is the likelihood of the interrogators knowing whether such a major fire had actually occurred in their community at the time. The boy, obviously clever throughout the interrogation, would have realized that he could not fabricate such a major event.

Finally, three of the boy's reported offenses are of dubious nature. They might have occurred, but it is unlikely. One dealt with the alleged exhumation of a child's corpse in a graveyard to "pulverize" it and use it as poisonous substance. This again was mainly the lore of stereotypical witch behavior, and the boy may have listed it because it fitted the role he was expected to play.[16]

A similar cultural image existed about witches sneaking into bed chambers at night and tweaking, smothering, and terrorizing people. Though Renaissance houses lacked alarm systems, they were equipped with sturdy doors and window shutters, and an intruder would hardly have gotten as far as bedside. Moreover, the reported entry by a narrow crack in the wall or by a sooty chimney is simply beyond modern credulity. Nonetheless, it is possible that Witchboy and his peers engaged in some nocturnal disturbances that he exaggerated and demonized. It is possible that a degree of voyeuristic curiosity—natural to children— played a role in the boys' nocturnal window gazing.

In addition, there existed the cultural image of the witch sneaking into bedrooms—through the narrowest crack in the wall or through the keyhole, if necessary—to enact the role of the incubus, the seductress. Still today in the Bamberg region, or in Franconia generally, some of the older peasants believe in the reality of a form of the witch incubus and call it *Hexendrücken,* the witch's smothering.[17] Obviously, Witchboy and his peers were familiar with such cultural imagery and convincingly incorporated it into confessions.

Then there was the killing of the dog in order to make a rabbit out of it. While the killing of the dog may indeed have taken place and may not have been considered a particularly serious offense— animal rights did not flourish during past centuries—the rest of the story is chimerical.

The discussion of *maleficia* is usually lengthier than the other segments of the confession because it also constituted a significant aspect of the secular law. In most parts of the empire, a person could be legally convicted only if harmful deeds could be proven. This was one of the tenets emphasized in the *Constitutio Criminalis Carolina,* but was often disregarded in such jurisdictions as a prince-bishopric, where the prince-bishop held secular as well as ecclesiastical power.

To conclude the discussion on *maleficia,* a definitional aspect of *maleficia* must be addressed. This type of wrongdoing was thought to serve no purpose other than to harm—malicious deeds that did not gain the witch anything useful for herself or for anybody else. Most of the boy's pranks and offenses consisted of this type of useless harm, for example, the reported *maleficia* of inflicting the pest of fleas, blinding an ox, and torching a house. Other offenses, however, were utilitarian, such as stealing wine, food, grain, and metal for forging the alleged flying pitchforks. Strictly speaking, this would not be defined as *maleficia,* but as common crimes with utilitarian motives. It was the truly malicious act, devoid of any other motive, that the Inquisition rated most abominable and considered a reflection of diabolic conspiracy. They called this category of crimes *crimen exceptum* (exceptional crimes) and were prepared to punish them most harshly.

Blasphemy

All witch suspects were expected to confess to specific acts of blasphemy. Considering the demonological framework, this was a logical expectation, for it was based on the broad premise that witches had denounced God and substituted the Devil as their master. Blasphemy represented the most serious crime of the time; it was considered abhorrent under both secular and ecclesiastical laws. Perhaps the most astounding moment in the boy's confession was his outburst renouncing God and declaring loyalty to the Devil. That instance would normally have sealed a death sentence. What is puzzling is that the boy must have known that. Later, when we discuss the psychological aspects of his confession, we will have to grapple with this question.

Strictly speaking, blasphemy was not thought of as *maleficia,* i.e., it was not considered harm directed against persons and the community; rather it was seen as offending God directly and personally and hence constituted the category of the worst offenses conceivable in Christendom. While no human being has the power to *harm* God, he or she can *offend* God. The boy freely confessed to a number of blasphemous actions. Besides renouncing God, Witchboy rebuked a number of His angels, mocked the Virgin Mary, even spit into her face, "borrowed" a crucifix from a church for blasphemous play, and prayed to Satan. There was only one blasphemy left that would have topped the others: the desecration of the Holy Host— the most abhorrent crime the church could imagine. Witchboy did not include this offense, the witches' crime par excellence, in his report.

There was another instance of theological derailment in the boy's confession. It concerns his claim that the peer group had two different gods, one black and the other one reddish. He said that he preferred the black one because he was nicer than the other. This statement reflects as much blasphemy as outright heresy. Witchboy cast the metaphysical thought into a group context, signifying that it was not he as an individual who stood in some sort of relationship with the two gods but his peer group as a collectivity. (Because of the emphasis on the group, we'll defer discussion of the issue to chapter 10, "Family and Demonized Peer Group.")

Before we leave the issue of blasphemy we should point out that revilement of the sacred is facilitated in a belief system that places a premium on dualism. Christianity's sharp dualisms between good and evil, God and the Devil, the saved and the condemned, heaven and hell, and so forth, promote blasphemy by providing the logical possibility of reversals between poles. Linguist Mikhail Bakhtin chose the term "dialogic inversion" to describe this type of reversal.[18] Witchboy's mindset was filled with such inversions. Examples include the mock baptism, the false god, using the crucifix in a secular if not immoral game, using a heretical prayer, and having the most coveted festival, the *Kirchweih,* rained out—the annual festival cherished by the common folk for gorging, dancing, gaming, and merry-making. Even the boy's *maleficia* can be defined as a form of "dialogic inversion," as the boy chose the exact opposite of good behavior.

Denunciations

No confession was complete without disclosing who else was a member of the diabolic conspiracy. This insistence was what kept the inquisitorial machinery moving. In order to substantiate the actual Great Conspiracy, ever more and newer conspirators had to be discovered. Any method was considered justified to drag into the light of inquisitorial justice those who were in collaboration with the Devil and gnawed at the foundation of the Christian community.

Being coerced by irresistible torture to denounce others in the community, including neighbors, friends, even relatives and close family members, caused most of the accused to suffer additional mental agonies, knowing what awaited those they named.

Witchboy suffered no such compunction. The profuseness with which he reported third parties fails to make the impression that he suffered any mental anguish at drawing others into the deadly machinery. His willingness to supply the Inquisition with denunciations was particularly explicit when, on May 7, 1629, one month after his confession had been technically completed and he had ratified it word for word, he asked to be allowed to add additional points. These points mostly consisted of denunciations of persons in the community who allegedly had committed crimes of witchery or other offenses. This adjunct was entirely voluntary and, as it were, beyond the call of duty.

We can only speculate on the emotional reasons for the boy's eagerness. His despair and loneliness must certainly have been aggravated by an imprisonment that continued despite lengthy confession and unreserved ratification. Witchboy's request for an additional hearing to have the opportunity to offer further confessions and denunciations may have been motivated by the hope of finally achieving a merciful consideration by the investigators.

On the other hand there may have been something quite idiosyncratic, even pathological, in the boy's personality that compelled him to continue talking—a personal talent for mythomania. Perhaps unbridled confabulation created a colorful world of his own and compensated for the dreary life of prison.

In the meantime the cold facts were that the young prisoner added name after name of accomplices and suspects whom he described as practitioners of witchcraft. The line between peers with whom he engaged in diabolic *maleficia* and blasphemy, on one side, and other members of the community whom he accused of acts of witchery, on the other, is not clear. This unclarity is mainly due to the fact that the scribe withheld the names.

There is no reason to assume, however, that the absence of the list of names from the transcript is any indication that the Inquisition failed to take the boy's denunciations seriously. On the contrary, the interrogators showed serious interest in the boy's denunciations as indicated, among other things, by the reference to the fate of a woman who, since the time the boy had denounced her, had been executed as a witch.

Little Andreas likewise satisfied the inquisitors' voracity for denunciations. He named a certain man in the community who allegedly had introduced him to a "lover" (*bule*); and in that connection he talked about a "little girl" with whom he had danced, feasted, and petted.

Ratification

According to imperial law every confession had to be ratified at the end, without applying or renewing torture to obtain such ratification. This meant that the accused was expected to swear before the judge that the confession was nothing but the truth and the entire truth. Thereupon the judge would pass sentence, and the trial was technically over. A convicted criminal would then be turned over to the executioner.

At times there were deviations from these procedures. Many local jurisdictions, Bamberg very prominently among them, had a reputation for violating numerous tenets of the law. For example, Bamberg inquisitors forced ratifications by "continuing" torture, and through this semantic trick got around the law forbidding "renewed" torture.[19]

In the case of our boy there were no such complications. He ratified not only once, but twice, and did so without the threat of torture. In fact the second ratification became necessary because he had asked to give additional testimony. This is unusual behavior warranting a psychological examination, to which we now turn.

Notes

1. Von Spee was the father confessor of numerous condemned witches and recorded clandestinely his observations about them. His book *Cautio criminalis* (Frankfurt, Germany: 1632) was to be published after his death to spare him the disapproval of the Inquisition. He felt strongly that the condemned were totally innocent of the accusations and were victims of a mass mania.

2. Salazar was an influential Spanish inquisitor who during the early seventeenth century carefully checked confessions, among them self-accusations by young girls, and came to the conclusion that they lacked credibility. See discussion in Julio C. Baroja, *The World of Witches* (Chicago: Chicago University Press, 1965), pp. 184–87.

3. The case of Andreas Förster, Staatsbibliothek Bamberg, R. B. Msc. 148 (pp. 452–54). Cf. Johann Looshorn, *Die Geschichte des Bisthums Bamberg,* vol. 6 (Bamberg, Germany: Handels-Druckerei, 1906), p. 64.

4. See research based on documents from Bamberg archives: Hans Sebald, "Witches' Confessions: Stereotypical Structure and Local Color," *Southern Humanities Review* 24 (Fall 1990): 301–19; or a German version, "Hexengeständnisse: Stereotype Struktur und lokale Farbe," *Spirita—Zeitschrift für Religionswissenschaft* 4 (May 1990): 27–38.

5. Wolfgang Behringer, *Die Hexenverfolgung in Bayern* (Munich, Germany: dtv, 1987), p. 352.

6. The case of Andreas Förster, Staatisbibliothek Bamberg, R. B. Msc. 148, p. 454: "Seie dieses Mädlein Zue ihme in sein Cämmerlein kommen, habe ihm beim schwanzt nackerten genommen, vnnd einander geschmeisselt." In the process of translating this phrase, interesting serendipitous information was obtained, showing how the meaning of words can change over time. It began by noticing that the scribe had made what I thought was a startling omission when he failed to insert the phrase *sit venia verbo* ("pardon the expression") after using the word *schwantz* (literally "tail") to refer to penis. (Scribes usually showed a sanctimonious compulsion for apologizing for words having a direct visceral or obscene connotation.) This word, in *today's* German colloquial parlance, would be considered quite obscene and certainly never used in an official transcript, unless immediately and apologetically identified as bad language used by the interrogated and repeated merely for the sake of protocol. The question arose: why did the scribe's usual allergy against gutter language fail to show when he used *schwantz*? Checking the historical background of the word explained things. At the time of Witchboy, the expression was entirely proper and chaste, analogous to today's sterilized expression of "member" in the English-speaking world. Over time, however, the connotation changed and *schwantz* became street language. See Jakob and Wilhelm Grimm, *Deutsches Wörterbuch,* vol. 9 (Leipzig, Germany: Hirzel, 1899), p. 2262.

7. There is, however, a question whether the "little friend" was meant to be a demon. He can also be understood as a simple friend who would get into trouble at home, should Andreas name him, for he had, as Andreas put it, a very strict father.

8. The case of A. Förster: "Habe ihn Bauma asten gehaissen . . . seie ein schüssela mit wasser dorten gewesen, Babel habs über ihn abgegossen," p. 456; "Seine Babel habe wüste händt gehabt, wie ein schlothfeger, auch wüste Stockfüeß undt einen schandtlichen lawsigen Kopf, seie ihr die Nasen abgeschnitten gewest," p. 455.

9. Dancing as such did not have the sexual or erotic connotation during

the seventeenth century that it later acquired. It was considered more a play or game than anything else. See Philippe Ariès, *Centuries of Childhood: A Social History of Family Life* (New York: Vintage, 1962), pp. 85–86.

10. Certain versions of the night-flying woman predate the Christian image of the flying witch. In fact earlier pagan forms may have inspired Christian interpretation of flying demons. The image of the goddess Diana, for example, was a pagan view that early Christianization had to cope with during the conversion of the pagan tribes in Europe. The pagan image was conveniently redefined as evil, diabolic, and ultimately served as one of the major characteristics of the witch. See interesting discussions on this topic in Hans Peter Duerr, *Traumzeit—über die Grenze zwischen Wildnis und Zivilisation* (Frankfurt, Germany: Syndikat, 1978), and Margaret A. Murray, *The Witch-Cult in Western Europe* (Oxford, England: Oxford University Press, 1921), and *The God of the Witches* (London: 1933). Murray's work, however, necessitates a *caveat emptor* insofar as her ideas lack sufficient empirical verification and are accepted by few historians. More recent studies revived the idea of the pagan connection on the basis of more careful investigation and connected it to the age-old image of the "wild hunt," the raging horde of hunters flying through the night sky: Carlo Ginzburg, *Storia notturna. Una decifrazione del sabba* (Turin, Italy: Giulio Einaudi editore, 1989). I have noted the lingering belief in the nightly hordes, the *Wütenker* (derived from the pre-Christian Germanic notion of *Wotans Heer*—Wotan's Horde), among Franconian peasants still in this century. See Hans Sebald, *Hexen damals—und Heute?* (Frankfurt, Germany: Gondrom, 1993).

11. After approximately 1625, the futility of resisting to give a confession became so obvious and widely known in the German territories that most of the arrested admitted to anything the Inquisition wanted to hear at the very first interrogation. See Herbert Pohl, "Hexenglaube und Hexenverfolgung im Kurfürstentum Mainz," *Geschichtliche Landeskunde* 32 (University of Mainz, 1988), pp. 167, 169.

12. See examples of obvious mental disorders of confessing witches in Gregory Zilboorg, *A History of Medical Psychology* (New York: Norton, 1941); Judith S. Neaman, *Suggestions of the Devil: Insanity in the Middle Ages and the Twentieth Century* (New York: Octagon Books, 1978); Otto Snell, M.D., *Hexenprozesse und Geistesstörung* (Munich, Germany: Lehmann, 1891); Hans Sebald, "Fire for the Female, Medicine for the Male: Medical Science and Demonology during the Era of the Witch-Hunt," in Rudolf Käser and Vera Pohland, *Disease and Medicine in Modern German Culture* (Ithaca, N.Y.: Cornell University Western Societies Program, 1990), pp. 13–35.

13. K. Hümmer, *Bamberg im Schwedenkriege* (Bamberg, Germany: Buchner Verlag, 1890), p. 12.

14. Ibid.

15. See the classic treatment of this topic in Sir James Frazier, *The New Golden Bough* (New York: New American Library, 1964), pp. 62–70.

16. The belief in the magical properties of parts of children's corpses was widespread and apparently occasionally encouraged grave robbery. See discussion in R. Po-Chia Hsia, *The Myth of Ritual Murder: Jews and Magic in Reformation Germany* (New Haven, Conn.: Yale University Press, 1988).

17. See ethnological details in Sebald, *Hexen damals—und heute?*

18. Mikhail Bakhtin, *The Dialogic Inversion* (Cambridge, Mass.: Harvard University Press, 1968).

19. The Bamberg authorities got around the imperial prohibition of "repeated" torture by calling it "continued" torture. They based their reasoning on the *Malleus Maleficarum,* which excused "continued" torture if new evidence was found in the case. Of course, what exactly qualified as "new evidence" was largely left to interpretation and gave henchmen undue license. Cf. Johannes Janssen and Ludwig Pastor, *Geschichte des deutschen Volkes,* vol. 8 (Freiburg, Germany: Herder, 1924), p. 565.

9

Lifting the Boy's Persona

What was the hidden agenda behind Witchboy's persona that propelled him to play his role in the drama so convincingly and with such virtuosity? Here was a delinquent turning into the inquisitor's delight. No messy torture, no urging was necessary. The accused confessed profusely and provided ample denunciations. In other words, he was a marvel of cooperation. And yet at times there were unexpected eruptions of defiance in which Witchboy spoke as if hoisting the banner for the Devil and turning his back on God.

Talent and Malice

Rather than seeing these contrasting expressions—one moment cooperative, the next rebellious—as a logical contradiction they must be viewed as integral parts of the boy's role: the accused was assuring the accusers that they were indeed fighting heroically against the ultimate evil, that they were the heroes in a struggle between primordial powers. Such a battle can be confirmed only if sufficient resistance is encountered. And the boy provided confirmation by superbly playing the required counterrole, goading the inquisitors' zeal to fight and giving them a chance to win the battle. The height of the drama was reached when the boy shouted into the face of the inquisitors that he would rather be with the Devil and burn in hell for eternity than belong to God. Here was a dramatist at work, hewing his script to perfection.

161

The boy's blasphemous outbursts netted him a hidden victory: by using the Devil as his shield, he grabbed the opportunity to hurl the ultimate insult at the authorities, whom he could not possibly attack any other way. It was an impressive empowerment, temporary as it might be, for an imprisoned boy. The opportunity was usually safeguarded by the camouflage of "possession" because thereby the accused could establish his lack of culpability and claim in one way or another that, "The Devil made me do it."[1]

The most conspicuous quality running throughout the entire confession is the boy's rich imagination. He flaunts a flair for the fantastic and verbalizes splendidly. The elaborations and details offered by the boy were in excess of what the inquisitors normally expected; they would have settled for plainer statements, though, to be sure, they must have been gratified by the richness of the boy's report.

The concept central to the boy's character was mythomania—obsessive-compulsive myth-creating, classified as a psychopathology when occurring in adults.[2] When occurring in children, it is usually defined as a deviant talent, an artful mind with a loquacious tongue able to spin the most unreal stories with expressiveness, great detail, and color. The uniqueness of the boy's report is not so much in *what* he says but in *how* he says it, for the content is culturally grounded and he uses popular symbols as building blocks to construct imaginative edifices.

The situation into which the boy was forced tended to strongly reinforce his mythomaniacal talent. Fantasy and storytelling were rewarded; reticence and refusal to confess were punished. The situation included both rewarding and aversive stimuli and thus created a persuasive psychological climate to encourage the boy to keep talking. It was a situation with the core elements of so-called brainwashing.

This brings us to another powerful element that must be figured into the boy's situation: the immense pressure by the inquisitors to reprogram the boy and have him perceive his life prior to arrest as having been demonized. In effect, the situation consisted of the convergence of two persuasive conditions, one psychological and the other social. First, the boy brought along a natural talent for storytelling; second, the inquisitors added the social conditions for brainwashing. Let's look at these conditions one at a time.

Until very recently the pioneer work by E. Dupré concerning

mythomania[3] has received little attention by psychologists, a surprising lacuna when one realizes the concept's explanatory potential in a variety of investigations, particularly in situations of witch-children trials. In a majority of such trials, children played the accusers and displayed the splendors of mythomania. Examples, some already mentioned, include the Salem trials,[4] the mania of Mora,[5] various Bamberg trials,[6] numerous hysterias in other German territories, such as Bavaria,[7] and the Rhineland,[8] and in such countries as Spain, England, France, and many others. In all these episodes the concept of mythomania has the potential to shed light on the decisive dynamics.

Witchboy pursued the victimizing role with a vengeance, denouncing more than seemed necessary to fulfill the expected quota. And he did so without being tortured and without being exposed to the *territio*—the threat of torture with display of the instruments. Under such contingencies a majority of the interrogated denounced, but usually named only those alleged conspirators already executed. The boy didn't even try this diversion, although he could have found plenty of opportunity in persecution-racked Bamberg. Rather, he freely pointed to townspeople alive in the community, accusing them of witchery and describing their *maleficia*, all the time having enough street wisdom to realize the lethal consequences that might befall the denounced. The deadliness of such denunciations was quite clear to the children of the time; executions were carried out publicly to teach a moral lesson.[9] Scarcely anyone, old or young, "could fail to witness one at least once in a lifetime."[10]

One of the persons the boy denounced was a girl he claimed he had chanced upon in the woods while she received a jar of poison from the Devil. Another was a tradesman he accused of malevolent slander and gossip: "A man having nothing else to do but gossiping like a washer woman." Dozens of additional denunciations involved what appears to have been Witchboy's peers. He accused them of stealing, flying on pitchforks, participating in the witches' sabbaths, molesting sleepers, torching a house, conjuring up rain, manufacturing fleas, robbing a grave, poisoning people, and other pranks and crimes.

The only offenders of witchery and poisoning Witchboy left unidentified or unidentifiable were the mysterious Veiled Women. They may very well have been figments of his imagination, although it is possible that the depiction of women all wrapped up and veiled

may have corresponded to some sort of mythological figures understood in local lore. At this time the description matches no known
folkloric or demonological image of the region.

Witchboy's malevolence waxed ferociously when he boasted that
if he were an inquisitor he would put witches on the rack and stretch
them until the sun could shine through their hides. This utterance,
again manifesting his uncanny flair for imagery, is not only in grotesque
discordance with his position, but also demonstrates a lack of compassion and readiness to hurt others.

It seems incongruent, and quite ironic, that a person admitting
to witchcraft would fling condemnation at other persons committing
it. At least two points must be examined if we want to understand
the boy's mind. First, the boy harbored a nearly uncontrollable, blind
rage, most probably in reaction to the brutalization of imprisonment.[11]
Second, he had internalized the new demonized reality and accepted
the point of view of the inquisitors—an often observed consequence
of the interaction between powerless captive and powerful captor.

Prison, Privation, and Brainwashing

The latter ingredient deserves elaboration because it deals with an
important social-psychological phenomenon: brainwashing. The
generic process by which this can be accomplished falls into eleven
phases:[12] (1) assault upon the identity; (2) establishment of guilt; (3)
self-betrayal; (4) reaching the breaking-point by inflicting conflict and
profound anxiety; (5) assurances of leniency and the opportunity of
redeeming oneself; (6) compulsion to confess; (7) channeling of guilt;
(8) reeducation or redemption and the logical devaluation of the
previous identity and of all those persons associated with that identity;
(9) progress toward a new harmony whereby a Gestalt integrates along
new *prägnanz lines,* which are major structural dimensions assigning
meaningful places to details; (10) summing up: the final confession;
(11) the completion of a new identity.

Persons processed by the industry of the Inquisition are subject
to the above elements, or at least to enough of them to cause essential
changes in their perceptions of the world and of themselves. The
process has a good chance to work if the accused is exposed long

enough to the brainwashers and is isolated from interfering influences. Considering the age of the boy, the isolation of imprisonment and the intense exposure to the inquisitors, it is more than likely that the boy significantly changed his view of reality. Besides, mythomanes tend to believe in their own stories if they tell them often enough and find believing ears. The absolute glory for them is when they find a credulous audience. This the boy had to the utmost degree. The audience furthermore was the only human connection he had. He used it to the fullest, extended it as long as he could, and so escaped, at least temporarily, from the isolation of the prison cell. In the process Witchboy's consistent role-playing performed a sort of self-brainwashing—demonstrating the ultimate power of role-playing. Social psychologist Erving Goffman sums it up:

> One finds that the performer can be fully taken in by his own act; he can be sincerely convinced that the impression of reality which he stages is the real reality. When his audience is also convinced in this way about the show he puts on—and this seems to be the typical case—then for the moment at least, only the sociologist or socially disgruntled will have any doubt about the "realness" of what is presented.[13]

There is no need to point out that at the time there weren't any sociologists around to make a "reality assessment." And as to the "socially disgruntled" deviating from the authorities' reality view, they most likely were called heretics.

By sharing a common cosmology with the boy the inquisitors had already won half the battle. The belief in the ability of supernatural powers to intervene in human affairs was a firmly entrenched article of faith in the boy's as well as in the inquisitors' minds; hence it must have taken little leverage to convince the boy of the supernatural implications of everyday life. We have to be aware, however, that the boy did far more than merely explain happenings: he created them, or at least many of them. He engaged in a mixture of inventing and reinterpreting events.

A number of causes can underlie a person's habit of recounting events that have not occurred and yet the person can firmly believe that they have. In some cases this is the telltale sign of mental illness as accompanied by various forms of hallucinations. However, the restructuring of experiences and the making up of new ones is not necessarily the product of an impaired or diseased brain. It can be elicited in persons with perfectly normal brains; in fact one could argue that it works all the better in those with superior brains. The effect of brainwashing is another illustration of the working of an unimpaired brain. Through isolation, prolonged indoctrination, and the manipulation of emotions it is possible to achieve astounding feats of reprogramming. Indeed, one can argue that an impaired mind, such as an autistic one, cannot be reprogrammed.

Consider the situation of Witchboy. His circumstances included major elements for achieving success in brainwashing. Here is a summary of them, showing how they correspond with the generic model.

1. The boy's identity was assaulted right at the onset of the inquest by not asking whether he was a witch, but by immediately asking how he got involved in witchcraft. The authoritative assumption foisted upon the boy was that he was a witch.

2. The boy's guilt was established by mere accusation or repeated rumor. The matter at hand was to get him to admit it. The mere guessing at *indicia*, the proof of wrongdoing, was considered sufficient evidence. In Saxony this was codified by the zealous witch-hunter Benedict Carpsov, who coined the oxymoron *Vermutungsbeweis*, "evidence by surmise."[14] Accusers and implicating witnesses did not have to be identified, and they did not have to confront the accused.

3. By all appearances the boy was willing, if not eager, to go along with the tenor of the accusation.

4. The seriousness of the procedure and of the alleged crime must have inflicted profound anxiety in the boy. How serious the inquisitors took his report and how much they believed in it is indicated by the fact that they arraigned the boy five times over a period of seven weeks.

5. As in almost all witch trials, the inquisitors promised forgiveness in the name of God if a full and honest confession would be made. Several psychological functions followed from this promise, including a readiness to confess and the dissipation of guilt and anxiety. The promise was particularly meaningful for the accused in witch trials since it presumably also meant avoidance of torture. Torture was of course a possibility never far remote, because of the *crimen*

exceptum, the special crimes, those on trial were accused of. Because of the crime's exceptional nature, most inquisitors from the very beginning felt that they were not bound to live up to their promises. Their deviousness harmonized with their manual, the *Malleus Maleficarum,* which encouraged interrogators to make false promises and fake consolations.[15]

6. Frequently the displacement of guilt drew into the inquisitorial machinery illicit lovers, hated neighbors, disliked relatives, and envied peers. The boy profusely denounced his peers, describing them as having coerced him to join the conspiracy, having put him through a mock christening, and having made him a member of the group. Furthermore, he blamed the cunning and menacing demon for his wrongdoings.

7. In conjunction with the demonological interpretation by the inquisitors, the identities of the peers are devaluated and cast into a demonized frame. They are the Devil's and are intent on harming God's creation, as it includes human beings, animals, and the fruits of the field.

8. A new identity emerged in the boy. He now saw himself as the recruit of the Devil.

9. This was the time the full confession was forthcoming.

10. The confession and its ratification (in the case of the boy there were two of the latter) sealed the identity; these acts functioned as rites of passage with all the emotional persuasiveness that such ceremonies exert on the human mind.

In most instances of "normal" brainwashing, the end goal of the brainwashers is conversion; in the case of the Inquisition it was more often liquidation. On some occasions the inquisitors' goal was indeed rehabilitation, that is, guiding the misguided back to the correct religious attitude, but Christian dualistic theology made this difficult and added a lethal twist to the concept of rehabilitation. An absolutistic attitude derived from a body/soul dualism, whereby it was possible to punish and liquidate one in order to save the other. In its starkest terms this might mean to burn the body while trying to save the soul.

Another element deals with the aforementioned factor of isolation, whereby the accused is cut off from his or her social background and deprived of peer or family support. This creates a condition of psychological disorientation, the mental equivalent of sensory deprivation. Human beings are creatures highly dependent on their social environment. Manipulation of the social support system—whether through solitary confinement in prison, dehumanization in concentration camps, or separation of soldiers from their buddies—is often enough to disorganize the firmest of identities.

Although the length of time Witchboy had spent in prison between his arrest and interrogation is not known, the time spent in prison during the inquest alone, seven weeks, can be considered long enough to break a nine-year-old child.

Before we leave the subject of brainwashing, a modification must be added. We are obviously dealing with the hypothesis that witch suspects suffering an inquest do in fact restructure their view of reality, especially their self-views. The only certain way of verifying the hypothesis would be to proceed with psychoanalyzing the persons in question. Since the clients can no longer be interviewed, and reliance on historiographic material is speculative, we cannot safely generalize. Some of the condemned may have come to believe their own stories; on the other hand, we know that some retained a clear vision of the nature of their forced fabrications. This was demonstrated in 1628 by Johannes Junius, the denounced mayor of Bamberg. After having suffered through the total hierarchy of tortures and facing the prospect of repetition, he finally admitted to the stereotypical fare of witchery. But before his execution, he succeeded in smuggling a letter out of his prison addressed to his daughter in which he assured her that he was not guilty of any of the items in the confession, that he was going to die an innocent man, and that he made the fabrications only to stop the horrendous torture.[16]

On the other hand, such clear-mindedness can be juxtaposed with accounts leaving little doubt that brainwashing had succeeded. In the case of one late-seventeenth-century Scottish witch trial, a woman confessed to a long list of misdeeds, including metamorphosis into beasts, and argued that "she deserved to be stretched upon the iron rack and that her crimes could never be atoned for, even if she were to be drawn asunder by wild horses."[17] The Inquisition more or less accommodated her wish. Another case concerned a nun who voluntarily informed the authorities that for many years she had maintained a sexual relationship with a fallen angel; in remorse, she claimed, she tried to crucify herself.[18]

While we will never know with absolute certainty what was going on in Witchboy's mind, there are strong indications that he believed in his own stories—a belief forged out of the elements of mythomania, brainwashing, isolation, and the demonology embedded in Christian cosmology.

Notes

1. Cf. similar cases: Hartwig Weber, *Kinderhexenprozesse* (Frankfurt, Germany: Insel, 1991), pp. 98–99.

2. The issue of mental illness in connection with the witch phenomenon has often been sensationalized. A common misconception is that a large proportion of the accused, if not the majority of them, were afflicted with mental disorders that the Inquisition interpreted as diabolic possession or as a sign of being in cahoots with the Devil. Still today at occasions of lecturing on the subject many members of the audience come with preconceived images of what the persecution was all about and offer such opinions as "at that time they burned the mentally ill; today we put them into institutions." This is a vastly exaggerated view. Mentally ill persons made up an insignificant proportion of the accused and of the convicted during the witch-hunt. But the myth is perpetuated. Gregory Zilboorg's widely cited work on the history of medical psychology has contributed little to dispelling the myth; on the contrary, it has reinforced it. Zilboorg sees the witch-hunt in the context of early modern psychiatry surrendering to demonological theology, causing "hundreds of thousands of mentally sick [to fall] victim to this violent reaction [of witch-hunting]," *A History of Medical Psychiatry* (New York: Norton, 1941), p. 153.

3. E. Dupré, *Pathologie de l'imagination et de l'émotion* (Paris: 1925).

4. The catalytic role of children in episodes of witch hysterias was mentioned by John P. Demos, *Entertaining Satan* (New York: Oxford University Press, 1982); Marion L. Starkey, *The Devil in Massachusetts* (New York: Time Books, 1963); Sigmund von Riezler, *Geschichte der Hexenprozesse in Bayern* (Aalen, Germany: Scientia Verlag, 1968); and Rossell H. Robbins, "Mora Witches," in *The Encyclopedia of Witchcraft and Demonology* (New York: Crown, 1959), pp. 348–50.

5. Robbins, "Mora Witches," pp. 348–50.

6. Bamberg Witchcraft Manuscripts, Cornell University Library, Rare Books Dept., Mss. Bd. Wft. BF H63++. See also references to denouncing children in Franconia in Friedrich Merzbacher, *Die Hexenprozesse in Franken* (Munich, Germany: Beck, 1970), pp. 50n, 114, 162, 173, 190–92.

7. Riezler, *Geschichte der Hexenprozesse in Bayern,* pp. 270ff.

8. See W. G. Soldan and H. Heppe, *Geschichte der Hexenprozesse,* vol. 2 (Kettwig, Germany: Magnus Verlag, 1986), p. 83.

9. Merzbacher, *Die Hexenprozesse in Franken,* p. 173 (see Merzbacher's references to Hans Fehr, *Massenkunst im 16. Jahrhundert,* Berlin: 1924). Eberhard Freiherr von Künssberg, *Rechtsbrauch und Kinderspiel,* Sitzungsbericht der Heidelberger Akademie der Wissenschaften, vol. 3 of *Philosophische-Historische Klasse* (Abhandlung, Heidelberg, Germany: 1952).

10. Richard van Dülmen, *Theatre of Horror: Crime and Punishment in Early Modern Germany* (Cambridge, England: Polity Press, 1990), p. 1.

11. The rage of the imprisoned was similarly expressed in the case of Menocchio, the heretic in Carlo Ginzburg's *The Cheese and the Worms: The Cosmos of a Sixteenth-Century Miller,* trans. John Tedeschi (New York: Penguin, 1982), p. 81: "His impulse grown out of powerless desperation, isolation . . . [drove him] to revenge himself on his persecutors, lash out against the symbols of the oppression, and become the outlaw."

12. Based on the model suggested by Robert J. Lifton, *Thought Reform and the Psychology of Totalism: A Study of Brainwashing in China* (New York: Norton, 1961).

13. Erving Goffman, *The Presentation of Self in Everyday Life* (New York: Doubleday, 1959), p. 17.

14. Benedict Carpsov, *Practica rerum criminalium* (Wittenberg, Germany: 1635).

15. Promises of mercy and forgiveness have an abominable record in the history of the Inquisition. Already the *Malleus Maleficarum* suggested that such promises could be used as means for getting a confession but did not have to be kept. For example, the *Malleus* describes maneuvers that can be used by an inquisitor to get around his promise of reducing the death sentence to lesser punishment without appearing to have lied. It also suggests that a judge may make promises, get a desired confession, then resign from the case and have another judge mete out any punishment he sees fit. See Montague Summers, ed. and trans., *Malleus Maleficarum* (New York: Dover, 1971), pp. 226f.

16. See a copy of Junius's original letter in Robbins, p. 291.

17. Charles Mackay, *Extraordinary Popular Delusions and the Madness of Crowds* (1841; reprint, New York: Noonday Press, 1974), pp. 501–502.

18. Otto Snell, *Hexenprozesse und Geistesstörung* (Munich, Germany: Lehmann, 1891), p. 87.

10

Family and Demonized Peer Group

Who played the supporting roles behind the scenes, outside the spotlight in which we have seen the star presenting his dramatic persona? Although they were invisible, they had a real presence, and knowing something about them will further illuminate the nature of the main character.

The question calls for the reconstruction of Witchboy's social background—not so much of the broader cultural background, which has been sketched in preceding chapters, but more of the immediate and intimate social involvements, such as Witchboy's family and peer group. Regrettably, a good deal of such analysis is speculative, due to the sparseness of the boy's comments about such matters. Furthermore, whatever comments he made must be filtered as to their credibility. As has often been said: we possess mountains of assertions, anthills of proof.

Seventeenth-Century Childhood

The sparse information about the life conditions of children is typical not only of the region but just about everywhere during the sixteenth and seventeenth centuries. Research literature is surprisingly incomplete on the topic. Historian Philippe Ariès's *Centuries of Childhood,* generally thought of as the standard work on the history of childhood, is no help at all; it deals neither with the children of common people nor with the Franconian region. Historian Klaus Arnold echoes the common consent among his reputable colleagues when he says that Ariès's limited research misleadingly suggests that "the child did not exist prior to the seventeenth century" and that he saw social change when actually there was continuity.[1] Johannes Janssen and Ludwig Pastor's *Geschichte des deutschen Volkes* (History of the German People) contains a plethora of information on nearly every subject, except children. Johann Looshorn's multivolume *Die Geschichte des Bisthums Bamberg* (The History of the Diocese of Bamberg), ostensibly by far the most pertinent reference work for the region under investigation, has very little to say about Bamberg's children. Looshorn, a Catholic priest of the Bamberg diocese, was mainly interested in the vicissitudes of Bamberg's clerical hierarchy and its political ramifications. (Nonetheless, he presents data about the witch persecutions in the diocese by illustrating the policies of the various ecclesiarchs.[2]) Karl-Sigismund Kramer's research, *Volksleben im Hochstift Bamberg und im Fürstentum Coburg* (Life of the Common People in the Diocese of Bamberg and the Principality of Coburg) (1967), which delves into the folkways of the prince-bishopric of Bamberg and the neighboring county of Coburg from 1500 to 1800, resulted in information about nearly every tradition, but presents next to nothing about the lives of children.

It often was through children's involvement in the witch persecution that information about children *in general* has trickled through to us and provided a base for plausible inferences.[3] Hence vignettes such as that of Witchboy have far wider implications than merely presenting us with narrow records of extraordinary episodes; their significance lies in opening vistas upon children's life conditions in general.

The fact that chroniclers of the sixteenth and seventeenth centuries have paid so little attention to children is a telling commentary about the contemporary perception of children's nonimportance, which radically contrasts with the importance we accord children in modern society. Elin McCoy sums up his research findings on the matter when he writes: "As late as the seventeenth century, children were not seen as individuals with their own identities. They were considered interchangeable, and frequently given the same name as an older sibling who had died. . . . [They] were important only insofar as they could benefit their parents. Considered possessions with no individual rights, they were used to further adult aims."[4]

This view has been contested. Klaus Arnold, for example, holds that children were cared for and loved as individuals just as much as today. He cites numerous sources that have recorded deep parental affection toward children and profound mourning at their loss. His examples include the story about a Nürnberg butcher who was so distraught upon the accidental death of his two children that he committed suicide.[5]

Many scholars agree with McCoy, believing that parents gave little affection or love to their children.[6] One of the main reasons mentioned by scholars is that life was too precarious and the mortality of infants and children too staggering for parents to dare invest emotions that they knew might come abruptly to naught.

Historian Edward Shorter carries this pessimistic portrayal a step further. He agrees that parents lacked emotional involvement, but thinks that the high mortality rate of the young was the *consequence* of lack of maternal care, not the other way around.[7]

Family Background

Witchboy's confession includes only two direct references to his home. In one instance it was the casual backdrop of hiding a jar of poison that he claims he had received from his demon. He hid it "in his father's house." In another instance Witchboy reported that his father sent him into the woods for gathering what appears to have been building material for barrel staves, suggesting that his father was a cooper. This specialization gains significance in the light of Bamberg's (since then abandoned) role as a wine-producing area. As late as the seventeenth century grapes were grown all around the town,[8] and the prince-bishop used it as a major trading item with other regions (for example, as payment for salt from the Salzburg duchy[9]). The boy's repeated references to breaking into wine cellars thus becomes plausible—there simply were plenty of them around. This also explains why nearly a dozen wine merchants were among the accused and executed witches in Bamberg between 1623 and 1630: they simply were numerous; this should warn against assuming that the prosecutors singled them out for some specific reasons.

Both references to his family suggest that Witchboy had a home, lived in the house of an artisan, and therefore did not live in poverty. So we know that the boy was not an orphan or a homeless street urchin.[10]

The boy makes no direct reference to his mother. Was she deceased? If so, could this, at least partly, explain parental neglect and lack of supervision and thus involvement with a delinquent gang? There are two instances in the confession that warrant special attention in this connection. They concern the boy's reaction to the inquisitors' insistence on knowing the idolatrous prayer that the demon allegedly taught him and with which he was supposed to pay homage.

When first confronted with the request, the boy stalled and broke down crying—a reaction of despair that the inquisitors defined as demon-inspired noncooperation. It was the only time during the entire confession, stretching over seven weeks, that the boy showed despondency. He tried to recite the prayer, but was able to do so only in fragments. The reaction must have been so strong as to lead the inquisitors to note that, "It is evident that he is presently possessed by the demon, who tells him to keep quiet and stop giving further information."

Even more vehement sentiments overcame the boy when, during the subsequent session, the inquisitors pursued the question of the "heretical prayer." (The inquisitors' interest is understandable, for such prayers formed the central idea of heresy, which, after all, was the Inquisition's core concern.) Immediately after Witchboy had at last given in to the pressure of the interrogators and recited the alleged prayer he burst out in what appears to be a blind, savage rage. He renounced God in a way that would prompt a dedicated inquisitor to want him burned on the spot. He shouted into the face of his tormentors, "I never want to belong to God anymore. And in the name of the Devil I have spit three times into His face. My star [soul] shall burn in hellfire, and I want to belong to the Devil for all eternity." This was evil blasphemy at its highest, erupting from the depth of some emotional agony.

What was this special prayer that caused such extreme dismay to a boy who otherwise showed insolence and nervy willingness to report any and all nefarious deeds the inquisitors wanted to hear? It was basically a nursery rhyme, including some words in Franconian dialect, which a mother would sing or hum, describing threads of different colors and pears on a tree. The boy demonized the verse by adding one line, which failed to rhyme with the rest and thereby shows its extraneousness: "It starts in the name of the Devil." The boy chose a phraseology with the connotation of "lifting off," hence making the "prayer" a suitable exclamation at the time of mounting the pitchfork and taking off to the witches' sabbath. The boy's talent for mythomaniacal brainstorming apparently fused an element of family life with an element of demonology.

We can only speculate about the reasons for the extreme emotionality the boy exhibited whenever he was confronted with the demand to disclose the "prayer." Could it have been due to memories of family life, the warmth of a hearth, the security of a home, the care of a mother? Or was it simply a reaction of helplessness to the inquisitors' pressure?

It is noteworthy that in all other instances the boy volunteered information, in fact he showed great eagerness to inform the interrogators about a mass of details. And all the details more or less followed stereotypical expectations; hence the boy was never at a loss about what to say and how to describe things. But the demand to report the blasphemous prayer presented a hurdle that Witchboy had difficulty clearing. He suddenly found himself at a loss about what to say.

It appears a weak explanation that the boy's vehemence was merely the result of frustration at his temporary inability to remember the "prayer." If that were the case, why would his vehemence reappear when he finally responded to the interrogator? It seems more convincing to argue for a deeper reason, one having something to do with the origin of the rhyme and its emotional meaning to the boy.

There was another instance in the confession that seemed to echo experiences normally embedded in family life. Not one single confession among the many examined in the Bamberg archives elaborates the mock baptism to the extent that Witchboy's did. He talked about the large white sheet and the pillow into which he was bundled as if an infant. The realistic counterparts would be the swaddling cloth and the elongated pillow, the latter to be folded lengthwise over the infant's body and then tied together crosswise, which used to be a custom in Franconia and other parts of Germany. The boy resorted to an element in family tradition and presented it in a demonized light. It obviously wouldn't have been his own infant baptism that he remembered, but perhaps he had younger siblings whose christening he had witnessed; or Witchboy had observed a christening in church, because this, like many other rituals of Christian liturgy, had always been a public ceremony.

From the references to his family background we may venture additional hypotheses. First, the boy most likely lived in Bamberg proper (which, at that time, had a population between thirty and forty thousand), for his artisan father would not be located in the village. Villages were for peasants, not artisans.

The boy claimed writing skills when he said, "The demon cussed me out for writing down what he said." But in the description of his lifestyle Witchboy never mentioned schooling, which was available in the diocese, though not mandatory. Although not free (there was a tuition to be paid to support a schoolmaster), the cost was minimal. Poor families paid merely pennies a year, and after 1630 school was free for all children, with the bishop paying for the deficit.[11] There are three possible explanations for the statement: (1) The boy did in fact attend enough schooling to learn the rudimentaries. (2) He was home-taught, perhaps by his father, for it was common for literate burghers to teach their children at home.[12] (3) He lied and made his claim a part of the overall fabrication, meaning to create the impression that his writing skill was a magical gift obtained by his demon.

To argue that the third explanation is implausible—because the inquisitors would have known the boy's actual literate ability and would have confronted the lying boy—ignores the fact that the inquisitors shared the boy's magical belief. It was quite common to believe that the Devil or his demons could bestow—and remove—special skills upon dedicated followers. In any case, we lack confirmatory evidence.

There is another ambiguous issue. If the boy's home was indeed an artisan's home, which normally would have been relatively secure in the material respect, why did he engage in stealing grain? Could it be that he had joined a peer group that included children from poorer homes? There is at least one indication that that might have been the case. We must recall that Witchboy was not one of the gang when they went to the fields to steal, but that he joined them there when they had already cut the grain. He encountered them at the field where, disguised as mice, they were busy stealing grain. From this may be concluded that Witchboy personally had no great interest in the illicit harvest.

Demonizing a Delinquent Gang

Need is not always the motive for stealing; the bravado and thrill inherent in the act may provide sufficient impetus to engage in it. This seems to be particularly true of children.

Daring and natural playfulness often causes children to choose certain activities. But the inquisitors had no understanding of the playful nature of the gang's behavior; they were educated in a strictly theological paradigm and quick to interpret the gang's pranks in a demonic light. For instance, when Witchboy reported that on the occasion of one of the gang's wine heists he sat on a barrel and beat it with a leather belt, he described nothing else than an imitation of riding a horse. Witchboy sat on his fantasy horse, spurring it on and riding over hills and valleys. Perhaps for a moment Witchboy saw himself as one of the knights he had seen on many occasions riding up the hill to the castle. The inquisitors, on the other hand, saw nothing playful in this, asked him where he got the leather belt, and were satisfied with the answer: "My demon gave it to me."

This brings into focus the colorful category of children's games definable as imitation play. During past centuries this type of play made up a much larger percentage of children's play activities than today. Children entertained themselves primarily by reenacting adult behavior and making a game of it. This included card and gambling games, which children learned by watching adults. The diary of the aforementioned Maria Anna Junius, a nun in a Bamberg convent, dolefully reports that children's morals had deteriorated and one could see them gambling for money in the streets and alleys.[13]

Of great significance are those imitations that dealt with events children found fascinating and could observe at home, in the street, or in various public places. Examples included the children's reenactment of the election of a king; the procession of the bishop;[14] baptism; confession; weddings; delivering a sermon; swearing oaths; robbery;

knight and servant; driving out witches; public executions, particularly hangings; rituals and formulas to ask for asylum, protection, or to impose a ban; and other social or ceremonial events that fascinated them.[15]

Probably the most impressive of public events were pillorying and the execution of witches and other criminals. Children were not only allowed to view them, but often ordered by the priest, the teacher, or the judge to attend. The intention was to teach them an early lesson. So children were sometimes ordered to mock and molest prisoners chained in public pillory and throw garbage at them. (One boy was punished, however, because he threw a rock.) At other times they were required to sing pious dirges at executions. At the same time, children with a record of disobedience received a solid spanking in full view of the execution so that they wouldn't forget what sort of punishment awaited evildoers.[16]

The intended function of having people witness public execution was the learning of three lessons in one jolt: that the Devil was at work, threatening the welfare of the community; that the government was waging a brave war to keep him at bay; and that deviants would suffer the ultimate punishment if they sided with the Devil.

However, some children learned a different lesson from the experience. Probing into the background of some of the defendants, judges discovered that the accused had made a pact with the Devil right at or soon after viewing an execution. One boy reported that he was so overcome at the moment of execution that the Devil was able to "seduce" him. A girl reported that she collapsed after viewing two men being put to death, and a few days later began to hear "the voice of the Devil."[17] In sum, the trauma of watching the executions was anything but prophylactic.

The mock baptism of Witchboy was a parody of another important public event. It may never have taken place and may only have been invented by the boy in response to a leading question; initiation into the Devil's conspiracy was thought to proceed in such manner. But it may really have taken place, perhaps as harmless play. In any case, the inquisitors accepted the report and believed that an act of heresy had been committed.

Another item of the confession dealt with the scene where George, Witchboy's demon, tried to pierce Witchboy's eyes. To understand this act, we must reiterate what the societal setting was. It was the time of the Thirty Years' War, a time of inhumanity and unspeakable cruelty, of homelessness, banditry, and lawlessness. Many people may have been spared personal mayhem, but none the horrifying rumors. One of the rumors told of roaming bands that kidnapped children, cutting out their tongues and gouging out their eyes. It is possible that the Bamberg gang playfully, or even seriously, tried to enact the rumor. There is hardly any deed, including the most grotesque, that has not been imitated by past or present youth.[18] In fact, there is status to be gained among one's peers for daring to do the outrageous.

Another of Witchboy's declared activities was acquiring the magical power to destroy crops. We were told in the confession that a number of children were required to perform the ritual; one boy, in this case Witchboy, had to crawl three times underneath a wagon pole, and the others had to step three times over him. This performance resembles a children's game that used to be played during that era and was called "Emperor or King?" It was a method by which a group of children could be divided into teams. On one side of the wagon pole stood two leaders, the "emperor" and the "king"; on the other side stood the rest of the children. The choice as to which leader they wanted to join was decided by each child as he or she crossed below the pole, while the rest of the gang chanted, "Emperor or king?" The youngster shouted his choice as he approached his leader. According to historian Eberhard Künssberg, sometimes this procedure was not a method for team-forming, but a game of status, whereby the leader with the most followers won.[19]

The resemblance between the alleged magical ritual and the age-old children's game, especially the aspect of having to crawl underneath a wagon pole, suggests that the boy reformulated a form of play to fit the demonic meaning pursued by his interrogators.

By examining these details of the confession, we obtain some insight into peer group involvement and the power of collective cohesion. Hardly any prank or crime was reported as an individual act; rather it was always depicted as peer conspiracy or peer-centered spontaneity. In modern jargon we might understand the boy's peer involvement as delinquent gang behavior. It is almost certain that the reason the authorities arrested the boy in the first place was his involvement in delinquent acts. In the modern setting, Witchboy and his peers might be defined as "incorrigible"; the Inquisition saw their behavior as symptomatic of diabolic alliance.

It is possible, though unlikely, that the gang perceived itself as a demonic conspiracy. If so, it would cast the boy's vehement renunciation of God and his endorsement of the Devil into a truly demonological mold. In that case the boy's stance would be nothing short of classical heresy, knowingly and intentionally deviating from orthodoxy. We have no evidence for this, however. Considering their usually reality-based lifestyle and such practical motives as appeasement of empty stomachs and the thrill of adventure and daring, gang members probably had more visceral and concrete goals in mind than exploring heretical ideas. It is far more plausible to assume that quite normal motives were at the core of their agenda. Most probably it was inquisitorial cosmology that cast the gang's mischief into demonized behavior and inspired the boy to render a compatible confession.

Nonetheless, Witchboy made the astounding statement that he and his peers had "two gods—one nice and the other fierce." Contrary to popular conception, the nice one was black and the nasty one red. Another rebellious inversion of popular modes? In any case, this is a theological statement, and a heretical one at that. What are we to make of it? Was it merely a childlike adaptation of the dualistic theology of Christianity with God and the Devil at its core, or does it signify a philosophy of some degree of autonomy, hence a heresy?

In order that the answers make sense, we must reiterate that the decades preceding the Witchboy episode characterized Bamberg's nadir in religious and social cohesion. The diocese suffered greatly in the aftermath of the Reformation and the confusion accompanying the vying and warring between Catholics, Lutherans, and Calvinists. Governance and religious affiliation fluctuated within the prince-bishopric according to the principle of *cujus regio, ejus religio,* the forcing of subjects to adopt the religion of the ruler. Accordingly, some localities within the bishop's territory changed religious affiliation every ten to fifteen years.[20] In some parishes Catholic and Protestant clergymen literally chased each other out of town. Catholicism declined quantitatively as well as qualitatively.

The religious instability may be reflected by the boys' metaphysical ruminations. It may mean that the gang was influenced by religious pluralism and stimulated enough to playfully recreate a peer version of a supernatural pantheon, albeit not very much different from dualistic Christian cosmology, save for the surprising color coordination of the good god being black and the bad god being red.

If indeed the story was a form of heresy, we face the fascinating question of its origin. Was it a spontaneous creation of the group, where group dynamics recreated a dualistic minicosmos, inadvertently mocking the larger Christian dualistic cosmos? Were there group needs that prompted the allegorization of the elements of good and evil and their final apotheosis in the form of divergent deities? In other words, did group impulses set up a minipantheon with the essential figures of God and Devil?

Or have we perchance glimpsed folklore independent of official Christian culture, a residue of pagan tradition—a reflection of ancient tradition that had survived in the play of children? This question brings to mind the claim made by historian Carlo Ginzburg in his research of the peasants of Friuli in northeastern, alpine Italy, where presumably the ancient tradition of the *Benandanti* (literally meaning "good walkers"; a secret organization within a folk society during the sixteenth and seventeenth centuries) was redefined by the Inquisition as heretical behavior.[21] In another research report, dealing with a heretical miller of 1600, Ginzburg suggests that "the fact that many of Menocchio's utterances cannot be reduced to familiar themes permits us to perceive a previously untapped level of popular beliefs, of obscure peasant mythologies."[22]

A totally different type of interpretation could resort to Jungian psychology and portray the gang's religiosity as an atavistic emergence of primordial ritual. A fictionalized version of such an event was presented by William Golding in *Lord of the Flies,* where a group of English schoolboys, stranded and isolated on an island, gradually evolved awe for the supernatural and implemented that awe in idolatry and ritual. Jungians would see this as a manifestation of archetypal propensity. There is similarity between the isolation experienced by Golding's boys and the Bamberg gang: both were without adult guidance and isolated on islands, the English boys on a geographic island and the Bamberg boys on a social island, separated from adult society as a marginal group, left to their own devices, and dependent on their own deliverance, material as well as spiritual.

Another explanation could use Emile Durkheim's famous sociological theory concerning the origin of religiosity. His assumption is that certain mesmerizing group activities—dancing, using alcohol or drugs—create sensations of ecstasy, which, when collectively reinforced, produce such powerful feelings that a supernatural explanation is derived from it.

Unfortunately, these are merely titillating attempts to explain the gang's notions. Perhaps promising hypotheses can be formulated from them. In any case we must not lose sight of the limitless imagination of children. A ubiquitous characteristic of children's mindscapes is the blurring of boundaries between worldly and otherworldly affairs, making interpenetration possible, so that the living can glimpse into the world beyond and the dead can return. Incidentally, this notion is not at all rendered impermissible by church dogma and tradition. Quite the contrary is true, as exemplified by the church's often ambiguous stance on the nature of purgatory. It was common belief during the early-modern age that "poor souls" could temporarily leave purgatory to visit the living at opportune or inopportune times. However, there was a thin and dangerous line between acceptable belief in the poor souls and the heresy of necromancy, which would have prompted church condemnation.[23]

How ideas about the transitory line between life and death can influence childlike thinking is quaintly illustrated by little Andreas, who reported several instances where persons died more than once and visited him in between. In this vein he told the interrogators that his grandmother died, came back, and then died again (and on the latter occasion took along the witches' ointment). Andreas sadly added that his mother and father also died but failed to return. And concerning the little girl with whom he apparently had shared erotic moments, he reported that she also died but returned a number of times to visit.

To a modern psychologist the interpretation of these statements is close at hand: five-year-old children are often incapable of understanding the permanency of death. This inability may have been accentuated by wishful thinking in the case of Andreas, for he was an orphan suffering dismay and confusion from the lack of warmth and security of a family. Wishful fantasy may have been a form of compensation. The inquisitors had anything but understanding for the conditions of an orphan's psyche and instead seriously pondered the supernatural—and possibly heretical—meaning of all this.

Beliefs originally based on permissible dogma could derail into situations which, in the eyes of the church, took on the appearance of demonic events. Recent research by the German anthropologist Karin Baumann explores this process: the church's eagerness to combat popular superstition actually heightened it for at least two main reasons. First, because the fervor with which the church criticized the supernatural created the impression among the masses that there might, after all, be something credible about so-called superstitious attitudes. Second, the formulation of certain criticisms actually suggested the authenticity of the targeted heretical approaches, as, for instance, in the case of the First Commandment: Thou shalt not have other gods before me. The not entirely illogical implication for some people was that you cannot prohibit something that doesn't exist; ergo: other deities do exist. The heretical implication was that, ipso facto, you could turn to them, if you wished. Baumann presents a list of major catechetical items and points to their popularized equivalents and their tendencies to turn into heretical liabilities.[24]

The *Hexenbischof* may have been aware of this danger and saw its significance in relation to the vulnerability of children. In a 1631 letter to the emperor he worried about the increasing practice of witchery and how increasing numbers of children were being introduced into it: "You can hear children tell in the street how they have been seduced [into witchcraft] and to which places they have been taken at night."[25]

Johann Georg's goal was to create a community dominated by the Christian spirit. To achieve this, his methods included: (1) establishing "thought police" to control the personal lives of his subjects; (2) enforcing religious indoctrination to gain thought control and unithink; (3) engaging in far-reaching disregard of civil liberties; (4) demanding absolute obedience; and (5) exterminating deviates. In short, the prince-bishop put in place the essential ingredients of despotism.

There is a parallel between the government's increased authoritarian measures toward children and the increase in the proportion of children featured in witch trials. Among the hypotheses as to what caused this correlation is the psychoanalytic argument made by historian G. R. Quaife, who saw in the children's greater aggressiveness a revenge reaction against an increasingly repressive social order.

Ironically the increased strictness was in part a function of the gradually emerging philosophy of protectionism toward children. With the advancement of industrialism so many destructive side effects came to bear on children's lives that society became aware of children's vulnerabilities. The first European mandatory school-attendance laws were passed less out of an abstract love for knowledge per se than out of the necessity to protect children, to get them off the street and turn them away from crime.[26]

Questions of Feat or Fable

Now let us turn to some of the major events Witchboy claimed he had experienced, and ask what they meant in the context of his time.

Making Mice

One of the first gang-related scenes was set in the fields, where the boys cut down crops and stole grain. Except for the offense of stealing, there is nothing necessarily demonic or malicious about this act. Grain was a dietary necessity for humans as well as animals. (During the Thirty Years' War, starvation was one of the scourges decimating the population.[27]) Grain could be ground into precious flour and also fed to small livestock kept by many townspeople, such as geese, chickens, pigeons. According to Witchboy's confession, his peers had already been at work when he joined them. He demonizes the situation in the imaginative and colorful style that seems to be his trademark by having his peers metamorphosed into mice.

It is interesting that mice, notorious thieves of grain, were the vermin most dreaded by peasants. The boy's mythomania created a simple and yet quite appropriate allegory. For the Inquisition it was anything but an allegory; it was sufficient evidence of the diabolic *corporum mutatio in bestias,* a transformation into the bodies of beasts, accomplished through the Devil's magical powers.

The small field mouse often played a big role in the demonic scenarios of the Middle Ages and early modern era. As a perennial thief, the little rodent was unequivocally placed in the category of evil. The boy twice referred to the role of mice in relation to witches' conduct: in the grain-theft incident and when one of his companions fell from the pitchfork and saved himself by changing into a mouse scurrying over the water.

Witchboy's idea to choose the mouse metamorphosis was no accident. Neither was it unique. For example, approximately forty years after the Bamberg episode, mice and rats caused epidemic decimation in the fields belonging to the Salzburg bishops. An investigation by the Inquisition resulted in defining the devastation as witch-caused *maleficia*, and scores were arrested and interrogated and inevitably confessed to witchery. The prosecutors' conclusion was clear: they were witches, Satan's collaborators, who had, by black magic, "created" the vermin, or, even worse, engaged in condemnable *mutatio* (metamorphosis) to accomplish the destruction themselves, pushing the Christian community to the brink of famine and the coffers of the bishop to the brink of bankruptcy. No mercy could be shown to such fiends, and the Inquisition condemned roughly a hundred people to be burned at the stake. A majority of the executed *Malefiz-Personen* (criminals) were boys between the ages of ten and fourteen.[28] The reason for the preponderance of boys in this trial was its focus on delinquent gangs, which were composed mainly of boys. Identical perceptions of the supernaturalism of mice infestations prevailed in the adjacent Bavarian territories, where such epidemics were considered the most compelling proof of the real existence of witches and where the law of the land retained penalties against the crime of "mice making" well into the 1700s.[29]

The hysterias involving the black-magic definition of the mouse were amazingly widespread. A coven of sorcerers in Switzerland was accused of practicing *mutatio* by transforming people into mice; the prosecutions stretched from 1392 to 1404.[30] The cases of witch-children during the early 1600s included numerous magical-mice instances. The epicenters of such disturbances were usually located in schools, as, for example, in the Jesuit college of Hildesheim, where in 1604 scores of children were accused of using "magical poetry" (incantations) to create mice and other creatures.[31] As late as 1769 the Bavarian *Malefiz-Ordnung* (criminal law) advised that suspect children should be firmly interrogated in order to find out "against whom they loosed mice."[32]

The little field mouse was a creature with whom no one wanted to be identified. The Saxon clergyman Thomasius, initially himself active in the witch persecutions, reportedly said that during witch panics a child merely shaping her or his handkerchief into a mouse ran the risk of being accused of black magic, with possibly serious consequences.[33] It seems that the tiny mouse should be added to the list of the Inquisition's most frightful phobias, joining the likes of women's sexuality, blaspheming the Holy Eucharist, and raiding ecclesiastical wine cellars.

The report of mouse *mutatio* occurred during the traffic accident while traveling via pitchfork to the witches' sabbath. This would of course be considered pure fiction from the modern point of view. But what seems to us a fairy tale was considered a real possibility during that era. The dialogue between the boy and his interrogators created scenarios that made perfect sense to both parties.

Stealing Wine

The gang had a steady affinity for wine cellars, and its most frequent offense dealt with raiding them. (It would be interesting to have reliable statistics on alcoholism among minors. We do know that custom allowed the young to drink in public; indeed, at folk festivals, including religious holidays and public executions, children were often treated to a jug of wine or a stein of beer. Sometimes an event was sufficiently out of the ordinary that, besides free drink, children were given specially minted commemorative coins.[34])

This specialized thievery was probably motivated by more than one factor. It may have had something to do with alcoholism afflicting some of the boys; it may have been a food substitute for hungry street kids; it may have been the prankish, playful bravado of a gang of boys; and quite simply it may have been just one of the ever-present commodities that could be stolen.

The food motive may very well have been of overriding importance, because from the description of the gang's actions we may conclude that they were hungry street urchins and not the well-fed children of the better-off families. Several instances of breaking into wine cellars were described as virtual banquets. The reports were explicit: they drank *and* ate there. Wine cellars at the time were not just storage for liquids, they were cool places also serving as larders, especially for such perishables as meats, sausages, and dairy products.

Though we don't know the details, the admission of having stolen money, with which the gang bought leather flasks to carry off wine, may have been based on fact; that they took along as much as they could carry sounds equally believable. But that they loaded it on pitchforks or brooms to transport it to hideouts is of course another story. In one instance of raiding a wine cellar, youthful fantasy had the gang recruit the help of cats (familiars) to ship the booty to secret places in the countryside.

Familiars

It was widely believed possible to employ familiars (demons in the form of felines, canines, or any other creature) to commit crimes. For example, the airlifting of stolen wine was reported two years earlier by Linhard, also a nine-year-old boy, in the Protestant county of Henneberg, a mere forty miles northwest of Bamberg. The Henneberg magistrates had lured Linhard to confess various delinquencies and ascribed the customary demonological meaning to them. Remarkable similarities in the confessions of Witchboy and of the Henneberg boy emerge: (1) stealing wine from the cellars of monasteries or hospitals; (2) using cats for the transport of the wine, with Linhard specifying that it required fourteen cats to transport a thousand liters; (3) a youngster was designated to keep the lights clean and burning at the witches' dance; (4) witches' salve was made from children's corpses, with Linhard claiming the corpses were gotten from grave diggers at Schweinfurt; (5) planning of *maleficia* as part of the agenda at the witches' sabbath; (6) enjoying lavish banquets with many fine meat courses at the witches' dances; and (7) making deadly powder from the ashes of unbaptized children.[35]

The similarities in magical practices of Witchboy and his Henneberg counterpart reflect widely shared views about the nature of supernatural events of their time. While adults and children held the same metaphysical views, children more than adults were prone to enact them.

Hideouts

It is quite believable that the boy and his cronies had secret hideouts where they stored food and other stolen items and held their get-togethers. It seems to be a universal and timeless propensity of children to create such nests and minifortresses. Perhaps Stanley Hall, the "father of the social psychology of adolescence," may after all have had a point when he proposed that children *naturally* go through a stage where they crave such shelters.

The feasts celebrated at the hideouts were projected by Witchboy into the scenario of the stereotypical witches' sabbath, including meticulous details—a circle, in the center a linen on the ground, the celebrants sitting around it drinking and eating. The arrangement reflects the way a gang of boys would accommodate itself in the countryside. It included lights placed between each participant. To be exact, the lights were "stuck" into the ground. This alludes not to lanterns, which adults might have carried, but to cheaper torches or candles more easily available to children.

There is no evidence that the gang members gave their activities a demonized meaning at the time they engaged in them. Again the demonologists forced the issue and gave peer celebration a demonic ambience.

Arson

Children seem to be just as fascinated by fire as they are by hideouts. It is therefore quite possible that the boy's report about his peers torching a house is factual. It probably was this type of serious crime that ultimately brought the heavy arm of the authorities down on the gang.

Teasing and Terrorizing

Another reprehensible behavior was the boys' frightening of sleepers in their bedchambers. While the boy obviously parroted the stereotype of the witch entering a room through a crack in the wall or through the chimney in order to "pinch and smother" people, he and his friends may indeed have practiced some type of intrusion into people's privacy. The behavior may have been part of the boys' arsenal of mischief and prankishness, and, underlying it, a vying for status.

A related interpretation deals with a form of peeping-tomism. Undoubtedly, human nature throughout the ages has included voyeurism, the thrill of glimpsing persons in intimate and erotic situations, and the boys' behavior may have been influenced by this natural inclination. A clue to warrant this interpretation was Witchboy's remark that he enjoyed watching the lovely posture of a woman in bed with her arm curled around her head.

Defaming Adults

The boy and his peers may have accrued quite a reputation in the community and may have been known as a delinquent and mischievous bunch of street urchins. Their reputation was mirrored in one of the boy's final denunciations when he talks of a man who "spends his time gossiping like a washer woman instead of sticking to his work." Here the boy may have counterattacked, reacting to a citizen's complaint about the gang's mischief.

Dabbling in Magic

When members of such bands got caught in the machinery of the Inquisition, they were flogged or tortured and usually confessed to sorcery and witchcraft. The significance of such confessions is that they sometimes were *true*: youngsters indeed had attempted to manipulate their fates by recourse to magical ritual.[36] This is not at all surprising if we realize that the basic premises of this view were held by common people as well as by high officials and princes. It would indeed be surprising had the children and their fantasies *not* been affected by a tradition that included a wide range of magical images, from the witches' flight to mice making. Witchboy's report of the *mutatio* into mice and the "making of fleas" may have sprung from the entirely honest belief that these were possibilities.

To these activities and rituals belonged what today we would carelessly dispose of as children's preoccupation with unhygienic and unappetizing things. Witchboy's confession abounds with things of gore, filth, and grime. To consider this merely a commentary on the contemporary lack of hygiene is to see only one side. The gang members' wallowing in filth and handling of blood, feces, and dead animals were rituals belonging to *their* liturgy. One could argue that there are intriguing, perhaps even amusing, parallels between a Catholic priest's eucharistic ritual, including the handling of the blood and the flesh of his god in order to create a supernatural presence, and the street urchin's handling of the blood and flesh of an animal to perform magic. There are significant differences: what we call religion is acceptable, what we call magic is unacceptable; the priest practices better hygiene, the child is indifferent to filth; the priest proceeds on the basis of cultural acceptability, the experimenting child cannot claim the protection of a tradition; the priest has the backing of a powerful church, the child has only the vulnerable peer group; the priest earns money for his rituals, the child merely earns status among peers.

In the more mundane context, the boys' activities also reflected the limitations of their world and the scarcity of toys and plays. Taking into consideration that children usually lack adult abhorrence of feces and dead animals, it should come as no surprise that their repertory of acceptable experiments includes such things as the attempt to blind an ox with cooked feces, create a rabbit out of a killed dog, concoct fleas, and prepare magical potions from corpses.

Today's children are fascinated by the magic they can perform on the screen of the computer or through other electronic devices; in 1600 children were fascinated by the magic they, and everybody else, believed they could perform by mixing powders and brewing witches' potions. Common elements underlying both include the children's flair for experimentation; their early attempts at personal power; their longing to see the magical formula at work. We all know that this desire for power can be trained onto a lattice to grow in the sun, or left to crawl on the ground like a poisonous nightshade.

Potions and Poisons

Folk pharmacopeia assumed a significant meaning in this connection. Widespread use of salves, greases, lotions, and unguents—those of presumed medicinal quality as well as those used in demonic ritual—became a serious concern to the authorities of the early seventeenth century. Bamberg's prince-bishops were sufficiently disturbed by superstitious pharmacopeia to issue formal edicts demanding that people abandon such practices. A 1610 edict had apparently little effect;[37] it was repeated in 1617 in sharper terms. Almost all potentates of the German jurisdictions passed similar edicts, usually with similar ineffectiveness. The infamous "Sorcerer Jackl" trials from 1675 to 1690 in Salzburg still lingered on witchery crimes committed through black-magic salves and ointments. Over half of the imprisoned or executed victims were members of juvenile gangs, with "Jackl" being the major ring leader. Once more the local prince-bishop forbade such evil pharmacological pursuits as making "grey powder to make storms and a black one to kill people and livestock" or concocting "a salve to rub into one's body before flight."[38]

Records show that some of the accusations concerning pharmaceutical dabbling were based on facts and ultimately resulted in proving that harm had indeed been done. For example, a woman was convicted in Bamberg's neighbor diocese of having used a salve to maliciously poison the roots of fruit trees. However, most accusations appear rather unrealistic. For example, a conviction was based on the allegation that "an evil lotion smeared on the old miller's feet caused him to limp and walk crookedly for the rest of his life." Other allegations included the preparation of "Devil's powder," which was used to poison sheep, make fields infertile, and, when blown in the air, conjure up bad weather.[39]

Ignorance and fear of the plague, repeatedly ravishing European countries during the early 1600s, added a particularly abhorrent significance to witches' salves and powders. Many people, in agreement with the officials, believed that the origin or the spread of the Black Death was the doing of witches. A fascinating diary written by Rev. Christian Lehmann, a Protestant minister in a province adjacent to Franconia, himself a believer in demonology, recorded a lynching and several official executions prompted by *indicia* that the victims had prepared devilish lotions or powders to spread plague in the home community, which was being decimated by the disease. In 1614 a grave digger was burned at the stake; he had been accused of using parts of corpses—victims of the plague—to prepare a magic lotion, which he ritually dripped onto a skull, with each drop causing another person in the community to die. In 1623 another grave digger was lynched by the townspeople, who claimed they saw him scatter a black-magic powder in the town square that would bring down the plague on everyone. In 1633 a thirteen-year-old girl and her mother were executed for similar reasons; they had confessed (under torture) that they had hexed the cemetery so that everyone in town would die of the Black Death. The authorities made them undo their curse and out of mercy had the mother strangled and the girl decapitated before being burned.[40]

It was this widespread abuse of pharmacopeia with its quack and black-magic lotions, lubricants, and powders that prompted Bamberg's exasperated Prince-Bishop Johann Gottfried von Aschhausen to reissue an edict against their use in 1617,[41] declaring a seventeenth-century war against drugs.[42]

Both delinquent youth and the authorities believed in the effectiveness of the prohibited pharmaceuticals. Not surprisingly, entire groups of youngsters were implicated in their use and were subsequently liquidated by the Inquisition. Gangs of "sorcerer-boys" were imprisoned or executed in Styria (1678), Tyrol (1679, 1679–80), Salzburg (1678–90), and Bavaria (1690, 1698, 1700, 1705, 1707, and 1712).[43] After 1715 the wave of prosecutions of juvenile bands spread westward and engulfed the prince-bishopric of Freising, where between 1715 and 1717 fifty-six boys, almost all under the age of twenty, were prosecuted for the crime of sorcery or witchcraft, usually involving the role of evil pharmacopeia. Again, the preponderance of boys engulfed in these trials can be explained by their affiliation with gangs primarily consisting of male members.

The Gang as Marginal Population

It is characteristic of the government's preoccupation with juveniles during the final decades of the witch persecutions that the last witch to be executed in Bavaria was a youngster, a girl of about thirteen years. A vagrant orphan who had been abused by her stepfather, she ultimately ended up on the street in need of the basic necessities of life.[44] In 1756, Veronica Zerritsch offered one of those confessions that may indeed reflect her serious attempt to invoke spirits and demons to help her in her need. In other words, she was observed practicing black-magic rituals.

Life in the juvenile gang was separated from adult life; it displayed a style of its own, was marginal to the established order, and can thus be defined as a type of youth subculture that provided a peer haven for many otherwise homeless, neglected, and castaway adolescents. But, of course, the youth subculture of modern times differs radically from that of the early modern era. Today's teenage subculture thrives on a segregation of the young created for entirely different reasons. The young stand apart from adult social structures because of the highly specialized division of labor, the prolonged custody of formal education, and the clever machinations of profitable commercialism cultivating and manipulating a "youth market." In contrast, the youth subculture of previous centuries evolved from basic survival needs. These needs manifested themselves in often lawless actions. They also manifested themselves in the young's own supernatural views; Witchboy's report on his peer group's visualization of "two gods" and his descriptions of various occult practices may be entirely truthful reports of a peer group's religious and magical orientation and the accompanying liturgical rituals.

One of the exotic mischiefs reported concerned several peers who supposedly had been at some village for the purpose of joining the festivities occasioned by the village's *Kirchweih,* the annual church festival. Every town and village, small and large, claimed this annual festivity, which nominally celebrated the anniversary of the church's inauguration. (This custom, in Franconia and in other German territories, is still being exuberantly observed today.) The sacred connotation, however, had long since been abandoned by the time of the Witchboy episode. The celebration, then as now, had the character of a carnival. In fact villages and hamlets not even having their own church had, and still have, *Kirchweih.* The preoccupation was decidedly secular, frankly epicurean, focusing on food and drink, dance and merrymaking. Entertaining sources of information concerning the character of the festival are the paintings and woodcuts of contemporary artists who recorded the robust and often vulgar behavior of the celebrants.[45] It was the day, weekend, or an entire week when special baking would provide pastries not available at any other time of the year, for example, the Franconian *Krapfen,* a sort of butter-baked donut. There were shooting booths and lotteries, jugglers and musicians, dancers and drinkers, and the ubiquitous fried sausages. There were games for old and young.[46] The place of least celebration remained the church, if there even was one.

For children this was the most exciting event of the year, equalled perhaps only by Christmas. Most of the celebration took place outdoors. The *Dorflinde,* the village linden tree, played an important role by providing shade and a roof under which the musicians and dancers would rally. The weather was of greatest importance. The worst thing that could happen at *Kirchweih* was that it would be rained out. It would be a disappointment for everyone involved, including merchants hoping to sell their wares; innkeepers set on emptying barrels and larder; and children eager to play games, rally around musicians, compete in apple bobbing, and gorge themselves on tasty *Kirchweih* food.

This was the ruination on the minds of the boys when they conjured up a rainstorm as claimed by Witchboy. His confession specified the procedure and the diabolic signs used to create the rain and havoc. Although no particular motive is given for the mischief, it is a manifestation of intense hatred, whether the report was factual or confabulated.

If it is indeed true that the boys attempted to spoil the celebration by black magic, they may have been motivated by revenge. Thieving and rowdy behavior were not uncommon at *Kirchweih*; it is possible that such behavior got the boys chased out of the village. This would also fit the description of the location of the black-magic ritual: they were outside of the village on their way home. It is also possible that the motive was the sort of rivalry traditionally found and belligerently cultivated between villages or towns, a rivalry not unlike those we find associated with sporting events today.

There could be an alternative explanation for Witchboy's report. Probably both parties, the boy and the interrogators, knew that a particular *Kirchweih* had been rained out. Misfortunes like that were important to the community and their memories lingered a long time. By reporting the cause of a well-known event, Witchboy might have been attempting to establish credibility.

Bamberg at Witchboy's time had suffered a long history of juvenile crime and social disorganization. Already in the latter part of the sixteenth century the various Bamberg ecclesiarchs had passed edicts trying to control unruly youths. Institutional measures were taken to get homeless children off the streets; and Bamberg, as was the case in almost all cities in the German territories, had its poorhouse, orphanage, and workhouse, the latter two being more or less identical places. Orphans had to work for their keep.[47]

Similar edicts in neighboring jurisdictions give forceful testimony to the widespread disturbance caused by juvenile bands, with their behavior ranging from mere nuisance to serious crime. The 1600 Schaumburg edict, for example, tried to control the excesses of hordes of begging children who became particularly troublesome at occasions of weddings, baptisms, and funerals, where tradition had allowed them to expect some modest alms, food, and drink. Now, "when their demands weren't met willingly, they enforced them by threats and even violence. Hordes of them entered towns and villages and, under the guise of begging, broke into houses, became a danger on the street, and committed robberies, murders, and arson."[48]

While most gangs were made up of young males, there were some special bands consisting of homeless women and girls, who roamed the countryside and whose "hysterical" behavior bordered on violence. "They declared themselves possessed by the Devil, displayed grotesque distortions of their bodies, accused scores of people to be witches or warlocks, and spread dread wherever they went."[49] The government tried to stem the tide of these hysterias and responded by public flogging, branding with the mark of the outcast, banishment from their territories, and even the occasional execution. Instead of succeeding in eradicating the behavior by such draconian measures, the publicity stimulated imitation and spread the hysteria even further. And the more the hysteria spread, the more it convinced the populace that it was the doing of the Devil. Here again is an example of the power of collective behavior and its ability to spread infection in ever wider circles. The typical style of the vagrant juvenile bands included a mélange of harmless begging, performance of carnival-type tricks to entertain and earn enough to survive, delinquency and crime, and practicing sorcery and witchcraft and believing in the effectiveness of magical formulas and rituals.

So now exits the star of the drama, stepping out of the spotlight and disappearing into the unknown. Witchboy was a fierce actor, knew his role, even overperformed. Nonetheless, he was a small protagonist among the hundreds of thousands who were caught in the inquisitorial machinery to be punished and eliminated. The difference between Witchboy and these unknown multitudes is that he will not be forgotten. Presenting his case to the reader immortalizes him. Never mind what his real name was; it is Witchboy now.

Notes

1. Klaus Arnold, *Kind und Gesellschaft in Mittelalter und Renaissance* (Paderborn, Germany: Ferdinand Schönigh, 1980), p. 11.

2. Looshorn condemned Bamberg's witch persecution and called it a terrible mistake. As a consequence he suffered the disapproval of the archbishop, successor of prince-bishops since about 1800, who in 1906 refused to grant his books the church's imprimatur, Catholicism's official seal of approval.

3. Valuable contributions were made by Hartwig Weber, *Kinderhexenprozesse* (Frankfurt, Germany: Insel, 1991); Wolfgang Behringer, *Hexenverfolgung in Bayern* (Munich, Germany: Oldenbourg, 1987); Wolfgang Behringer, ed., *Hexen und Hexenprozesse* (Munich, Germany: dtv, 1988); Wolfgang Behringer, "Kinderhexenprozesse," *Zeitschrift für historische Forschung* 16 (1989): 31–47; Sigmund v. Riezler, *Geschichte der Hexenprozesse in Bayern* (Aalen, Germany: Scientia Verlag, 1968); and Rossell Robbins, *Encyclopedia of Witchcraft and Demonology* (New York: Crown, 1959), passim.

4. Elin McCoy, "Childhood through the Ages," *Parents,* January 1981, p. 61.

5. Arnold, *Kind und Gesellschaft in Mittelalter und Renaissance,* p. 37.

6. See prominent examples in Lloyd deMause, ed., *The History of Childhood* (New York: Psychohistory Press, 1975).

7. Edward Shorter, "Der Wandel der Mutter-Kind Beziehungen zu Beginn der Moderne," *Geschichte und Gesellschaft. Zeitschrift für historische Sozialwissenschaft* 1 (1975): 256–87.

8. Hartmut Kugler, "Gelobtes Bamberg," in *Literatur in der Stadt,* ed. Horst Brunner (Göppingen, Germany: Kümmerle, 1982), p. 103.

9. Max Spindler, *Handbuch der Bayerischen Geschichte* (Munich, Germany: Beck'sche Verlagsbuchhandlung, 1966), p. 698.

10. Johann Looshorn, *Das Bisthum Bamberg von 1623–1729,* vol. 6 (Bamberg, Germany: Handels-Druckerei, 1906), passim.

11. Friedrich Wachter, *Pottenstein* (Bamberg, Germany: Kollerer, 1895), pp. 138–39.

12. Philippe Ariès claims that for the majority of youth, reading and writing, if taught at all, "was acquired at home or in apprenticeship to a trade," *Centuries of Childhood: A Social History of Family Life* (New York: Vintage, 1962), p. 141. However, Ariès's account is heavily slanted toward families of means or nobility. He reveals his bias when he says that sometimes a youngster would find a scholarly adult, for example a priest, who might

assume the responsibility of educating the youth. It certainly was a rare day when a common child, let alone a street urchin, would receive this type of dedication.

13. K. Hümmer, *Bamberg im Schweden-Kriege* (Bamberg, Germany: Buchner, 1890), p. 8. That such games were very popular among youngsters during the early modern era is suggested by Bamberg's neighbor city, Nürnberg, whose city fathers tried to limit their excesses in 1525 by forbidding all card and dice games. See Harold Grimm, "The Role of Nuremberg [Nürnberg] in the Reformation," in *Continuity and Discontinuity in Church History*, eds. F. F. Church and T. George (Leiden, the Netherlands: Brill, 1979), p. 192.

14. The pageantry of the "child-bishop" was well known and widespread in German territories. It started with a procession of school children, usually with the schoolmaster at the head, and ended with the children going from house to house asking for donations, usually food and drink. Bamberg prohibited the parody, perhaps out of piety, but perhaps also because schoolmasters used to exploit the occasion by hoarding the collected food for themselves "so that they could feast on it for three months." See Karl-Sigismund Kramer, *Volksleben im Hochstift Bamberg und im Fürstentum Coburg* (Würzburg, Germany: Schöningh, 1967), pp. 96–97.

15. Eberhard Freiherr von Künssberg, "Rechtsbrauch und Kinderspiel," *Sitzungsbericht der Heidelberger Akademie der Wissenschaften*, vol. 3, 1952, pp. 40ff.

16. Ibid., pp. 11, 16–18, 24.

17. C. Ernst, *Teufelsaustreibungen. Die Praxis der katholischen Kirche im 16. und 17. Jahrhundert* (Bern, Switzerland: 1972), p. 59.

18. See "imitation file" in Hans Sebald, *Adolescence—A Social-Psychological Analysis* (Englewood Cliffs, N.J.: Prentice-Hall, 1992), pp. 205–13.

19. Künssberg, "Rechtsbrauch und Kinderspiel," p. 51.

20. Looshorn, *Das Bisthum Bamberg von 1623–1729*, vol. 6, p. 98.

21. Carlo Ginzburg, *The Night Battles: Witchcraft and Agrarian Cults in the Sixteenth and Seventeenth Centuries* (New York: Penguin Books, 1985).

22. Carlo Ginzburg, *The Cheese and the Worms: The Cosmos of a Sixteenth-Century Miller*, trans. John Tedeschi (New York: Penguin, 1982).

23. Cf. Philip M. Soergel, *Wondrous in His Saints: Propaganda for the Catholic Reformation in Bavaria* (Berkeley: University of California Press, 1993).

24. Karin Baumann, *Aberglaube für Laien. Zur Programmatik und Überlieferung mittelalterlicher Superstitionskritik*, vols. 1 and 2 (Würzburg, Germany: Königshausen & Neumann, 1989).

25. Pius Wittmann, "Die Bamberger Hexenjustiz (1595–1631)," *Archiv für katholisches Kirchenrecht* 50 (Mainze, 1883), p. 195.

26. Sebald, *Adolescence*, pp. 15–16.

27. Looshorn, *Das Bisthum Bamberg von 1623–1729*, vol. 6, pp. 129–33.

28. Gerald Mülleder, "Neuere Forschungen zur Geschichte der Hexenverfolgung," Abstracts: *Fachtagung der Akademie der Diözese Rottenburg-Stuttgart mit dem Arbeitskreis Interdisziplinäre Hexenforschung*, Stuttgart-Hohenheim, March 1990, p. 3.

29. Riezler, *Geschichte der Hexenprozesse in Bayern*, pp. 272–73.

30. Weber, *Kinderhexenprozesse*, p. 120.

31. Ibid., p. 244.

32. Ibid., pp. 230–31.

33. Von Künssberg, "Rechtsbrauch und Kinderspiel," p. 71.

34. Ibid., p. 28.

35. Details about the Henneberg boy come from Ludwig Bechstein, *Hexengeschichten* (Rostock, Germany: Historff Verlag, 1986), pp. 229–40. While Bechstein took literary license and told "stories," data and detail come from reliable archival records.

36. Behringer, *Hexenverfolgung in Bayern*, p. 353.

37. Looshorn, *Das Bisthums Bamberg*, vol. 6, p. 30.

38. Behringer, *Hexen und Hexenprozesse*, p. 426.

39. P. Beck, "Hexenprozesse aus dem Fränkischen," *Bericht des Historischen Vereins für das Württembergische Franken* 84 (1883–84), p. 79.

40. Christian Lehmann, *Erzgebirgsannalen des 17. Jahrhunderts* (Berlin: Union Verlag, 1986), pp. 106–11.

41. See Pius Wittmann, "Die Bamberger Hexenjustiz (1595–1631)," p. 180.

42. The pervasiveness of the belief in nefarious pharmaceuticals can be illustrated by the fact that it knew no confessional boundaries. Both Catholic and Protestant authorities accused witches of using evil potions. But that wasn't all. Religious comedy at its funniest had Protestant and Catholic polemics accuse each other of using magical potions to secure believers and snare converts. For example, in a pamphlet printed in 1566, a Lutheran minister "explained that the Jesuits were able to work their numerous conversions through the aid of magical salves which they smeared on their pulpits to attract the young and simple." See Philip M. Soergel, *Wondrous in His Saints*, p. 152.

43. Behringer, *Hexenverfolgung in Bayern*, pp. 353–63.

44. Ibid., p. 361.

45. See a picturesque discussion of *Kirchweih* using the iconography of several woodcut artists and painters of the late Middle Ages and early

modern era in Alison G. Stewart, *The First Peasant Festivals: Eleven Wood-cuts Produced in Reformation Nuremberg,* Ph.D. dissertation, Columbia University, 1986.

46. It is interesting to note that games at that time did not observe the modern distinction between children's and adults' games. Rather they were unitary and brought old and young together. See Ariès, *Centuries of Childhood,* pp. 72–73, 79.

47. Johannes Janssen and Ludwig Pastor, *Geschichte des deutschen Volkes,* vol. 8 (Freiburg, Germany: Herder, 1924), p. 319.

48. Ibid., vol. 8, p. 371.

49. W. G. Soldan and H. Heppe, *Geschichte der Hexenprozesse,* vol. 2 (Kettwig, Germany: Magnus-Verlag, 1986), p. 83.

Part 3
Probing the Persona

11

Masks of Myth and Mania

Mythomania

What sort of personality dynamics propelled the children to act as they did during the witch trials and when they faced the Inquisition? This analytic question has been much neglected in the historiography of the witch persecutions, and is best approached by focusing on the most formidable element in children's testimonies: their indulgence in mythomania, or, in modern psychiatric parlance, *Pseudologia phantastica.*

    Dr. E. Dupré, an early-twentieth-century Parisian physician, is credited for his pioneering work in the field. While working in forensic medicine he frequently had occasion to observe children giving false testimony, and he found it necessary to conceptualize the pathological tendency of children to lie and invent stories.[1] In the course of his professional work, he discovered that a mythomane may initially lie deliberately and consciously, but gradually come to believe in what he or she was saying. The vast majority of persons engaging in such confabulation were children or the mentally retarded. Interestingly, he found that lying by children does not necessarily indicate a chronic pathology, hence in their case it is not classifiable as mental illness, whereas for adults it is. He found that children telling mythomaniacal stories were usually motivated to do so by unmitigated maliciousness, the need for attention, or precocious sexual appetites. In situations where mythomanes are motivated by attention-seeking or by malice, they are particularly susceptible to suggestions. With a flair for figuring out what is expected to be heard, they set out on their mythomaniacal journeys. During their courses, compelling auto-suggestions evolve, wherein the storytellers program their brains to confer reality on their stories.

Dupré also noticed that the substance with which children built their imaginative structures most often consisted of things gleaned from adult conversations. Mythomaniacal children are not merely passively suggestible but actively seeking suggestions; their radar, as it were, is constantly scanning the social horizon for cues to spin stories netting them fame and laudation. Theirs is the skill to evaluate quickly what they overhear and recognize how they can use it to their advantage.

This skill, in addition to verbal expressivity, enables mythomanes to tune into a theme with persuasive loquaciousness. Through confabulation and strategic gossiping they can humor the biases and expectations of other people with such effectiveness that their utterances are accepted as true revelations.

For some children these skills are character attributes and never stop with one story; there is a basic need to go on and on, and ever new and more fantastic stories are told, rendering the mythomaniacal child into a steady and inexhaustible source of fantastic stories. These were the little, harmless-looking snowballs that waxed into deadly avalanches during the time of the witch persecutions.[2]

Whether the mythomaniacal propensity of certain children is learned or of genetic origin is still a matter of research. An insight supporting the learning theory was derived from research and observations by Gordon Deckert, a psychiatrist at the University of Oklahoma College of Medicine:

> Some of these people were so terrified while they were growing up that they would be abandoned or shamed or physically abused that they began lying as a means of protecting themselves against assault and blame. Down deep, these people really don't believe they're worth anything. They're constantly trying to buttress their image of themselves by telling these grandiose stories.[3]

Modern situations in which this type of child can wreak tragedy include court proceedings where children tune into a theme and harmonize with it. They often derive cues about how to harmonize from leading questions—questions that aren't meant to be leading but cannot withstand the intuitive exploitation by perceptive children. Chapter 12 will elaborate on and exemplify this point.

Demonopathy

The ultimate escalation of mythomania is not only telling stories and believing them, but acting them out. This can be exemplified by "the state of being possessed" and signifies the escalation from being a myth-omane to being a demonopath. This type of person suffers from a form of insanity in which he or she shows morbid fear of evil spirits and believes him- or herself possessed of devils or demons. A social-psychological explanation of demonopathy (or the synonymous *demon-omania*) looks behind the facade of the presumably deranged person: it is role-playing over which the person has lost control; it is a self-inflicted pathology from which the person seems unable to escape. This category of insanity is not physiologically caused, as might be the case in brain injury or in neurochemical malfunctioning, but a condition that is socially caused and unfolds in situations where role-playing is expected. Despite the sociocultural causation and the situationally limited occurrence of the condition, the demonopath must be defined as a psychotic, if we judge reality by standards of empirical science.

The demonopath is far from being a passive victim of his or her affliction. This "victim of spells" was often an active initiator of witch panics and played an aggressive role in the persecution and prosecution of witches.

The Collective Imperative

There are at least two conditions that intensify the aggressiveness of demonopaths: *group reinforcement* (they often enact their roles collectively), and an *accepting audience*. In fact, there are no such things as private demonopaths; they are absolutely public figures who will only perform their roles when they are in front of an audience.

Almost all cases reported in the preceding chapters reflect these two elements. The most obvious case deals with Anneliese Michel, the star of the twentieth-century exorcism in the bishopric of Würzburg. The timing of attacks by the five demons tormenting her was predictable; they always occurred when family members, relatives, or neighbors were gathering in her home. Later, after the exorcists had initiated their work, the fits would occur whenever the priests were ready to minister to her torments. The full complement of a performance of "possession" required actress, manager, and audience.

The Warboys sisters had a credulous audience in their good-natured parents, in Lady Cromwell upon her visit to their home, and, most rewardingly, whenever the accused widow Mother Samuel was in sight. The girls' performance also showed the collective element. Initially it was only Jane, the oldest girl, who displayed the fits of the tormented, but soon her sisters joined her, and collectively they performed the role of the "afflicted by curse."

Probably the most intense show of collective suffering was performed by the Salem girls as they attended the hearing of Goody Cory, whom they had accused of bewitching them. When Martha Cory defended her innocence and tried to assure the court that she was a God-fearing "Gospel woman," one of the girls yelled "Gospel witch," a cry that was immediately taken up by the rest of the girls. At the same time they imitated every move the woman made. The significance of the two behavior forms, echolalia (compulsively repeating sounds in echolike fashion) and echomania (compulsively imitating bodily movements or gestures), was the collective method which served to reinforce each individual girl's behavior—in fact, one should not even refer to individual behavior; it was *group* behavior. Though modern sociology disavows the old notion of "group mind," it is tempting to use this example as an apt description. Gustav LeBon's idea that under such formidable conditions of mass reinforcement the individual's *superego* (the part of the mind containing culturally learned norms, the "conscience") and *ego* (the part of the mind conducting reality assessment) recede to give free rein to the *id* (the part of the mind containing basic emotional impulses). The impulses are thought to be more or less identical among the individuals of the species. Hence, the girls behaved not merely in accord, as a group of conspirators, but *identically*. They all had regressed to a common emotional-visceral denominator.

There probably is nothing more powerful to move the human psyche than the expression of a mass of people simultaneously proclaiming strong conviction. Woe to the dissenters, not only because they are risking punishment by the members of the frenetic crowd, but because they are at risk of abandoning their dissent and may be carried away by the mass excitement to become one with the mass. This may happen without the volition or the awareness of the individual. Classical examples of these dangers have been observed in a variety of collective hysteria: from witch panics to mass rallies of Nazis to the frenzies of lynch mobs.

More recent examples of mass ecstasy, especially as they involve young people and appear a lot less harmful than the examples mentioned above, come from sociological studies of teenagers' behavior in group or subcultural contexts.[4] The similarity of visceral expressions shown by teenagers carried away in a mass of peers adulating their heroes and by teenagers in the thrall of "possession" is unmistakable. In both situations, the inciting encouragement of a manager and of an audience is the sine qua non for ecstasy. Heroes often serve as catalytic managers for youthful behavior, triggering abandon and release. Typical settings were (and still are) the so-called youth concerts, where famous teen heroes make their appearance and provide opportunity for hero worship. The behavior at teen concerts is governed by completely different rules (and perhaps needs) than that at adult concerts, and consists of exuberant expressions of a visceral nature: screaming, shrieking, jumping, touching, moving rhythmically, and, in a number of cases, even fainting and collapsing. The Salem girls did not perform much differently. A good part of the behavior at teen rallies is not intended as listening but as testimony of *belonging* and has a mutually reinforcing effect on the participants. Most of the "performing" teenagers focus more on their peer audience than on their heroes, obviously wanting to make certain that they are seen screaming, jumping, fainting, and performing other prestige-inviting behavior. Research has discovered that back rows usually do not engage in such visceral performance, but merely applaud conventionally, since they are outside the field of observation and hence are lacking an audience.[5]

The classical examples of teenage crowd-reinforced behavior come from the early days of the rock 'n' roll era. Frankie Avalon's presence and singing would always induce some girls to faint—or to pretend to. It became the thing to do. During a Milwaukee performance by Avalon, twenty-one girls ostentatiously fainted. At another performance, when Avalon sang "Boy Without a Girl" the television camera focused on a number of sobbing teenagers. This set the norm, and from then on sobbing behavior became routine whenever the hero appeared and sang the song.

Avalon's record was broken in 1975 when 250 young girls fainted ritualistically at a concert given by a Scottish group, the Bay City Rollers. Michael Jackson's magnetism elevated the affliction to the international level when in 1988 he performed in Vienna: Approximately 130 girls (not one boy) fainted in homage to the U.S. superstar at a concert attended by fifty thousand devotees.[6]

These girls experienced the timeless phenomenon of euphoria generated by the individual's immersion into the group and the feeling of oneness with it. Today we recognize the social-psychological principle underlying this sort of behavior, but at the time of the Salem panic such behavior was thought to be an expression of supernatural forces.

Such experiences are virtually addictive. Once experienced, the lofty sensations will be craved again and again. University of Arizona medical professor Dr. Andrew Weil in his book *The Natural Mind* describes the human brain's need for occasional (perhaps regular?) ecstasy in order to purge and clear "congestion" in neurons and synapses.[7] Indulgence usually proceeds naively, meaning without the ecstasy seeker's awareness of its function, and can be achieved through a number of means—not necessarily recommended by Dr. Weil— such as psychedelic drugs, sex, alcohol, and indeed the type of group behavior exemplified by the Salem girls and their latter-day cousins in Milwaukee.

Returning to the focus on demonopathy, we note that this type of behavior can be contagious above and beyond the in-group. The Salem girls caused spontaneous, imitative behavior as they went from home to home visiting persons in their sickbeds, people also presumed to be bewitched. Sensing and "seeing" the demons surrounding the beds, the girls engaged in a display of commiseration and reacted with typical sobbing, shrieking, and writhing. At once, a number of onlookers started to imitate the girls' expressions and likewise "saw" the demons, "felt" them, and displayed demonic torment.

Playing, or, better said, living the role of the possessed can have a dramatic physiological impact. A powerful psychosomatic process begins. The basic assumption is that if a person programs his or her brain according to a certain role definition, the body will follow suit and express, often in a high-fidelity manner, the appropriate somatic symptoms. Dr. Nicholas Hall, professor of psychiatry and microbiology at the University of South Florida, has found evidence that some personalities are able to trigger specific biochemical changes, including allergies and other immune system reactions. While initially his research was limited to patients with multiple personality disorders, he has extended his experiments to actors and actresses. Currently he is doing blood assays on professionals as they enact the plays *It's Cold, Wanderer, It's Cold* and *I Love Lucy*. It is hoped that the experiments will yield data showing conclusively whether the actors experience different biochemical changes as they alternate between roles and emotional states that express fear, anguish, and disillusion in the first play and joyfulness in the second. A careful methodology has been employed to control for the effects of daily biological rhythms and other influences.[8] The study is probably the first scientifically controlled attempt to determine what occurs biologically when actors enact a role. Once the final data is collected and analyzed, the study may significantly demonstrate the holistic process of role-playing.

In the meantime, there are sufficient indications that the possessed children's organisms were in harmony with role expectations. Hence such somatic manifestations as vomiting, fainting, and suffocating may be true reactions of the body to the neural commands following the scripts of the drama.

Hunter and Hunted: A Common Psychiatric Mold

If we define the demonopath as one who is bodily tormented by a demon or a devil, then we should note that the difference between demonopathic children (such as in Bamberg, Salem, Warboys, and other places) and demonologists (such as inquisitors, judges, bishops, and other authorities) was only one of degree. Both adhered to identical belief systems, both considered physical torment and attack by evil supernatural figures real possibilities, and both have made such claims.

Demonopathic children have acted out the symptoms with artistic flair and some of the demonologists have similarly symptomized their belief in the reality of demonic torment by experiencing personal encounters with evil spirits. This is in harmony with Christian theology. According to the Bible, even Jesus had encounters with the Devil and "unclean spirits." The preacher at Mora in Sweden, a central figure in the witch panic of the 1660s, was convinced that demons disturbed his sleep and caused him aches and ailments. The renowned French jurist and witch-hunter Jean Bodin claimed the influence, sometimes benign, of a spirit who would whisper into his ear. Various other potentates, saints, and hermits of the church have given vivid descriptions of physical assaults by demons.

What underlies the torments of these afflicted persons is a mental disturbance that symptomizes itself in hallucinations, psychosomatic impairments, and obsessive-compulsive behavior. Some scholars have compared these demoniacally tormented to the chronic cases of hysteria shown in pioneer studies and experiments of the French neurologist Jean Martin Charcot during the late nineteenth century.[9] At La Salpêtrière clinic in Paris, patients exhibited classic hysteria. They lost feeling in parts of their bodies, writhed, shrieked, or fainted—the same reactions exhibited by the bewitched of medieval and early modern periods. Likewise, it was clinically found that such behavior can be "contagious" to suggestible individuals.

The Tripartite Format: Cultural, Social, and Personal

Instances of role-playing, whether occurring in the context of relatively passive mythomania or in the context of active demonomania, are neither private nor unique. The basic ingredients of such role enactments are taken from two sources: the cultural context (beliefs, traditions, norms), and the social context (the direct involvement in social interaction). What this means in regard to children is that they take the concerns of the day, interweave them with cultural images, and then mold stories from which they can derive personal benefit. They take advantage of the credibility accorded them and pursue personal goals, such as receiving prestige or praise, or enacting rebellion or revenge. These personal goals are rarely recognized as such by the children; they are largely on the unconscious level and rooted in a variety of emotions and needs.

The Salem girls Abigail and Betty, members of a Puritan preachers's family, for example, got away with insulting what probably constituted the most sacred thing in the home, the Holy Bible, by scornfully flinging it across the room. Here is a convergence of the *cultural, social,* and *personal* elements: the Bible as a sacred item in the culture of the Puritans, the family context with parental authority, and personal feelings of resentment against authority, sacred and parental. The result was the eruption of that resentment with impunity under the protection of enacting "the role of the afflicted." Betty Parris, brought up by the strictest of fathers, finally found a way to strike back.

Marion L. Starkey in her book *The Devil in Massachusetts* masterfully describes the background of Betty's resentment.[10] Here was a child brought up in a highly punitive religious environment, inculcated with the notion of human beings' sinful nature, manipulated by fear of the Devil and eternal hellfire, and suffering from inevitable guilt feelings. She ultimately used her mythomaniacal talent to forge the supernatural ingredients of Puritan culture into a plot that allowed her to rebel and to take revenge. When we consider the role of three powerful reinforcing factors, we may better understand the process whereby the initial prankishness escalated into a deadly game: (1) the complicity of other girls; (2) the psychological reward of being pampered as "afflicted" and honored as a martyr; and (3) the opportunity to make scapegoats out of persons who were representative of exactly the Puritan lifestyle that was the target of camouflaged rebellion.

When the Trier boy claimed to have beaten the drum at the witches' dance and to have seen certain townsfolk attending, he combined the cultural image of the witches' sabbath with the social element of peer-supported denunciation and the personal element of venting feelings of hostility. He and other children won a singular vendetta through their testimonies: they succeeded in implicating the top trial judge, Dietrich Flade, as a witch, with their denunciation resulting in his execution. In addition, two mayors, several councilors, and several of the associate judges were denounced and executed. For all this the boy and his peers reaped praise and congratulations.

When the young virgin Catalina approached the inquisitor Salazar y Frias to "confess" sexual intercourse with the Devil, the cultural element consisted of the religious belief that a personifiable Devil in fact existed and that witches fornicated with him. The social element was the circumstance that scores of other girls had stepped forth with similar claims and reinforced Catalina's decision to do likewise. The personal elements we can only guess. They may have consisted of a mixture of motives and drives, such as a perverted search for notoriety, a precocious sexual appetite, pubescent exhibitionism, or a form of rebellion against society's sexual strictures. Among the personal elements may also have figured a somatic condition that the young girl construed as a sign of having been violated by the Devil or his demons: menarche, the first menstruation. If this was what she experienced at the time, is it possible that she failed to understand its natural reason and gave it a supernatural meaning? In any case, whatever personal reason there may have been, the girl projected it into the cultural framework of demonology.

A final word about possession. What, from a strictly psychological point of view, seethed under its mask was a mélange of emotions normally unacceptable in social interaction: a reckless lust for attention, revenge against a community that—as really all communities must—imposed a myriad of dos and don'ts, and the targeting of specific individuals who represented the community. The latter point explains why the targeted persons often were community members of impeccable standing; only such individuals could logically serve as the scapegoats of the accusing children's pent-up opposition to the socializing process. The Trier case, with its punishment of judges and councilors, is classic in this context. The stricter the social environment, the more vehement the children's attack on it. Again, the Salem case comes to mind, where pent-up fears and guilt of Calvinist repression changed into anger and exploded into behavior that was vengeful and legitimate at the same time. The triumphant experience of releasing hostility and simultaneously reaping the community's compassion amounted to behavior reinforcement par excellence.

It truly is a social-psychological feat to receive the status of celebrity from the very people upon whom you heap punishment.

Notes

1. E. Dupré, *Pathologie de l'imagination et de l'emotion* (Paris: 1925). Cf. Julio C. Baroja, *The World of Witches* (Chicago: University of Chicago Press, 1965), pp. 250ff.

2. Cf. H. Weber, *Kinderhexenprozesse* (Frankfurt, Germany: Insel, 1991), pp. 101–102.

3. Quoted by Edward Dolnick in "The Great Pretender: What Makes a Pathological Liar Tick?" *Utne Reader,* November/December 1992, p. 67.

4. Hans Sebald, *Adolescence—A Social Psychological Analysis* (Englewood Cliffs, N.J.: Prentice-Hall, 1992), pp. 289–92.

5. Ibid., pp. 289–90.

6. Ibid., p. 290.

7. Andrew Weil, *The Natural Mind: A New Way at Looking at Drugs and Higher Consciousness* (New York: Houghton Mifflin, 1973).

8. James Hathaway, "Schizophrenic Show Calls on Actors to Play Unusual Roles," *Arizona State University Insight* 12 (March 2, 1992): 2.

9. Cf. Baroja, *The World of Witches,* pp. 248ff.

10. Marion L. Starkey, *The Devil in Massachusetts* (New York: Time, 1963), pp. xxiv, 4, 23–28, 31, 51.

12

Issues of Child Psychology

The Suggestibility of Children

The key element in both the processes of mythomania and demon-opathy is *suggestibility*. Pioneer researcher E. Dupré witnessed the creation of mythomaniacal profusion during numerous court hearings dealing with claims of child molestation. He noticed how a biased and one-sided climate was created through the unconscious collaboration of the questioner and the child, whereby the child emerged as if a proven victim of perverse crime.

In the majority of cases, concerned adults, particularly parents, showed anxiousness to know all about the assault—its nature, time, place, motive, and so on. The child may initially have been bewildered and embarrassed by all the questions, a reaction that was interpreted by the questioner, or the court in general, as a sign of shame or repentance. Right away the child was inundated with encouraging words and leading questions. The child followed the lead and would answer in such a way as to meet the more or less obvious expectations of the questioners. The hearing would turn into a veritable rehearsal of a story that the child began to learn by heart. In future rehearings, the child stuck to the version imprinted in his or her mind. The only changes the child would make consisted of adding new material conforming to this version.

Although we are speaking of the modern court of law, we are also speaking of the mind of children, which is timeless and has not changed since the days of the witch persecutions. What has changed, or at least is supposed to have changed, is the insight into the mental dynamics of children's testimony. In retrospect we are now better able to evaluate what happened in the trials of witch-children.

Modern psychological research has begun to pursue the subject of children's suggestibility. As we enter the twenty-first century, the topic has gained importance as increased claims of child molestations and child abuse in the United States have fueled parental and legal concerns. Many of the events presumably had taken place within the context of occult practices, the alleged scenarios teeming with demonic figures, including witches. One case, after lengthy investigations and hearings, was finally resolved because the "abused" children were shown to be referring to a teacher who appeared in a witch's costume at a Halloween party.

The majority of the cases include claims of sexual abuse. Research by psychologists David Raskin and Phillip Esplin found that children involved in parental abuse cases often take advantage of their power in court proceedings to fabricate, or at least vastly exaggerate, sexual abuse in order to punish or to side with one or the other parent. The researchers noted that such distortion was a strong tendency in cases that involved divorce, custody, or visitation disputes.[1]

While research into the actual forensic problems proved to be extremely difficult, a number of psychologists have chosen laboratory situations in an attempt to identify the principles underlying children's vulnerability to influence and manipulation. While the findings are far from complete, several insights have been gained.

Some studies have examined children's beliefs in extraordinary figures, some of them totally illusory, in order to see whether children behave in accordance with the meanings attached to these figures, whether they live up to the expectations culture has attributed to the figures, and under what circumstances their behavior can be influenced.

An example is children's belief in Santa Claus. Although clearly an illusory figure, it nonetheless is usually presented to young children as real. Studies by psychologist Norman M. Prentice have found that 85 percent of American four-year-olds believe that Santa Claus is real; at age eight, over one half of the children are still in a transitory stage in which they are torn between belief and disbelief.[2] But in situations where mothers discouraged the belief, young children adopted their mothers' disbelieving attitude.

Some researchers tried to determine whether a relationship existed between belief in imaginary figures and the ability to conduct make-believe.[3] No significant correlation was found between various fantasy scores that measured children's ability to engage in make-believe or imaginative play, on one side, and children's belief in fantasy figures, on the other. This means that a child's thinking is conditioned by what he or she learns to consider real and unreal, and not by any innate abilities. Belief in imaginary figures and imaginative play should not be confused. Imaginative play is simply a child's fanciful cerebration that can embellish life and make it more creative.

The implication for our understanding of seventeenth-century children is that they considered the witch a real person and the Devil a personifiable entity. Hence confessions and accusations were far from being playful or imaginative cerebrations, but were part of a belief system.

Two important modifications must be noted: (1) Mythomaniacal children combined belief *and* imaginative elaboration of the belief. (2) When modern parents present Santa Claus as a real person, they know they are being deceptive; they are lying to their children. When early-modern parents and authorities presented witches as real persons, they were convinced of their reality, and, rather than lying, they informed their children of an article of faith.

Suggestibility varies with age. Psychologist Maria Zaragosa found that young children (under eight years of age) have greater difficulty than older children and adults in distinguishing between imagined events and those they actually experienced. "Given the greater tendency to confuse imagination with perception, young children might also be more likely to confuse items that were merely suggested to them with those they had actually perceived."[4]

If, however, intrusion of extraneous information and the posing of leading questions are avoided—thus creating a sort of cognitively sterile environment for the child—children's recall of factual material has been found to be amazingly accurate, approaching in quality that of adults. Research data show that, "Children are capable of being good eyewitnesses, but that their recall appears to be more vulnerable to various distorting influences in the interview situation than does adult recall."[5]

Notwithstanding this finding, it must be kept in mind that the child brings to the interview or interrogation enough biased feelings and preconceived notions to be able to distort recall thoroughly and to engage in a form of auto-suggestion. As psychologist Jean Piaget once noted, "Any suggestion is a potent disrupter of truth."[6] Selective memory has been described as the process whereby "memory integrates the past with the present: desires, fantasies, fears, even mood can shade the recollection."[7] Gestalt psychologists emphasize the human predilection to integrate (mostly unconsciously) new experiences into an established structure of preceding experiences. The preexisting structure assigns to the new experience a meaningful place, that is, it interprets the meaning of the experience in the context of what already has been internalized and organized. We select what we observe, often by shutting out what does not appear to fit into the existing mental Gestalt. Remembering thus becomes an act of reconstruction, not reproduction, an act during which normal gaps and missing details often get filled in while other material gets ignored.[8]

The end result of the process is putting a boundary around one's views, establishing a *closure*: the mind's soothing reassurance that one's perceptions are joined together properly, without disharmony between details. Aspiring toward closure seems to be a natural process, indeed a need, of the human brain. And once closure has been completed, a definite reality view is established and becomes reluctant to undergo change.

Children's mentality is characterized by insufficient experiences and an unstable identity that is highly vulnerable to suggestion. We are often tempted to interpret certain symptoms of such inexperience and incompletion as children's impulsiveness or natural spontaneity. In reality it is an expression of the free-wheeling response of a tenuously integrated personality that develops by trial and error and all too readily responds to the suggestions of the social environment. According to Piaget, children approximately between the ages of two and seven are in a stage of cognitive development known as the "pre-operational stage." A child in this stage has difficulty being objective and sticking to the truth. "Without actually lying for the sake of lying, i.e., without attempting to deceive anyone . . . [they] distort reality in accordance with [their] desires and [their] romancing."[9]

Lying can take on two different modes. *Mnemonic distortion* presents false information with the person being unaware of doing so. *Nonmnemonic distortion,* on the other hand, is lying with the person being aware of giving false information.[10] Sometimes, as mentioned earlier, nonmnemonic lying can change into mnemonic lying, whereby the person gradually begins to believe in his or her lies. This is a form of self-brainwashing and has been observed in situations of social isolation and prolonged conditions of mental duress, as, for example, in situations of imprisonment and lengthy interrogation.

Self-brainwashing differs from brainwashing as experienced by prisoners of war. The former starts with a voluntary confabulation that gradually assumes truth value in the mind of the narrator. The latter starts with external pressure to persuade a person to change his or her mind and ends with a new conviction. Another difference is that, from the very beginning, the adults or the children in the hands of the Inquisition shared with the interrogators the same cosmology and its pantheon of supernatural figures. This meant that the convictions both parties embraced were closely related, a circumstance promoting the process of persuasion.

Psychologist Paul Ekman's studies focused on the truth-value of children's verbal behavior.[11] His survey findings from the 1980s in the United States show that most children are inclined to experiment with lies. Among the examples is an exchange that unwittingly mirrors a dialogue that could have been lifted straight from a witch trial. A little girl, Lori, decided one day to use her bedroom wall for trying out new crayons. Her upset mother shouted: "Lori, did you draw on your wall?" "No," Lori answered, completely straight-faced. "Well then, who did?" the mother pressed on. "It wasn't me," the girl insisted. "Was it a little ghost?" her mother asked sarcastically. "Yeah, yeah," Lori replied. "It was a ghost." Lori could not be swayed from that "confession," and her mother finally joined what she considered funny role-playing by saying: "Well, tell that little ghost not to do it again or she'll be sorry."[12] While the modern mother's words were cast in sarcastic levity, the same words could have been uttered by Renaissance inquisitors in absolute seriousness.

This vignette tells us that children will lie when feeling threatened—and they will lie within the framework at hand, particularly if it was initiated by powerful authority. Psycho-dynamics, largely of an unconscious nature, will sway the child's responses in a direction from which he or she expects the least unpleasant consequences.

Additional studies have focused on the truth-value of children's statements. Researchers at the Institute for the Study of Child Development at the University of Medicine of New Jersey have found that already at age three a majority of children will lie in certain situations. When the liars were challenged, only 38 percent of them admitted to having lied; it was interesting that facial expression, or body language in general, did *not* differentiate between the deceivers and the truth-tellers. The study also showed that boys were more likely than girls to admit their dishonesty.[13]

A study at Arizona State University corroborates some of the above findings. It was found that deception can normally be detected because lying produces unconscious body movements that differ from the person's normal movements. *But* differentiating body language is missing in "pathological liars or those who simply feel no remorse about lying."[14]

These findings bear on the credibility of children's testimony and accusations in more than one way. First, they remind us that a majority of children do lie; second, they proffer the disturbing fact that liars and truth-tellers cannot easily be told apart.

A revealing study showed some dangers that may arise from children's reports. Psychologist Karen Saywitz of Harbor-UCLA Medical Center and Gail Goodman of the State University of New York at Buffalo interviewed seventy-two girls, ages five and seven, about routine medical procedures they had received. Half were given full examination, including vaginal and anal checks; the rest were given just general physicals. When the first group was asked broad and nonspecific questions about the procedure, only eight mentioned the vaginal checks, and when the children were shown anatomically correct dolls, six pointed to the vaginal area. But of the girls who had undergone a merely general checkup, three claimed they also had had vaginal or anal examinations; one child even said that "the doctor did it with a stick."[15]

Bearings on Modern Life

It is obvious what sort of dangers such fantasies can cause in real life. They are reflected in court statistics and have assumed epidemic proportion. A number of cases from the 1980s and 1990s illustrate the star roles of children in human tragedies.

First it must be clearly said, however, that we are not assuming that all accusations made by children are false. Child molestation is unfortunately a fact of life. The real problem is to distinguish which claims are false and which are true. This distinction is often tragically delayed, if ever made at all. All too often, innocent persons, or at least unconvictable persons, have been punished so severely that the rest of their lives are in shambles. The irony usually is that in hindsight the children's claims should have been immediately recognized for what they were: malicious hoaxes or bizarre delusions. Their accusations were so fantastic, as we shall see, that it baffles one's mind that anyone would take such absurdities for the truth. It is this portion of trials that will be examined.

Most of the trials involve daycare centers, preschools, and divorce/custody disputes. Dr. Richard Gardner, professor of child psychology at Columbia University and author of *Sex Abuse Hysteria: Salem Witch Trials Revisited,* concluded that charges of sexual abuse have become a frequent part of custody quarrels. According to his estimates, spouses or ex-spouses raise this charge in about 5 percent of child-custody cases.[16] A 1988 study by the Association of Family and Conciliation Courts concluded that the charges are probably false 30 to 40 percent of the time.[17] Dr. Ralph Underwager of the Institute of Psychological Therapies in Northfield, Minnesota, researched the psychological profile of the accusers and discovered that 75 percent of them were afflicted with severe personality disorders.[18] Regardless of their problems, they usually are successful in using sex-molestation charges as a strategy to obtain custody and to achieve revenge against ex-spouses. The children become pawns in the process, and the opponents vie for their cooperation. The party winning is usually the one that is more successful in manipulating the children.

This brings to mind a disturbing parallelism between patterns of the past witch-hunt and patterns of the present court proceedings. In both scenarios children were often asked to report on their family life, especially whether it incorporated immoral (heretical) elements. And in both situations children catered to the inquisitiveness of the authority figures in order to be appreciated and made to feel important.[19]

New players have entered the battlefield and now profusely populate service-oriented postmodern society: counselors, lawyers, and therapists. They are the inquisitors of postmodern civilization and, for hefty fees, will belabor the suggestibility of the child. There are even heretofore unheard-of specialists among them, memory therapists, who will help patients, young or old, to recover long-lost memories of such traumas as incest, satanic ritual, and human sacrifice.

One such patient, a thirty-nine-year-old woman, sought respite from a prolonged depression and an explanation of its cause. During several weeks of treatment, a family counselor guided her awareness back to incest during her childhood, though the patient initially had no recall of such abuse. But the therapist kept prodding, and finally lurid details emerged, supposedly repressed memories about how her father had seduced her when she was a baby. Thereupon the woman confronted her father, broke off her relationship with him, moved away, and founded an incest-survivors group.[20] Later, after taking eye-opening psychology courses in college, she examined her "memories" more carefully and realized that they were entirely false. She asked her father's forgiveness and filed a lawsuit against the psychiatric hospital.

It goes without saying that if an adult's suggestibility can suffer such misguidance, what about children's? Even worse, misguidance at such a young age may result in an impression that no counselor or college course can ever delete.

Increasing numbers of schools for young children have become the target of child molestation charges. One dealt with San Diego Sunday school teacher Dale Akiki, whom nine children accused of rape, sodomy, and torture. The drawn-out court hearings heard the children's claims that the teacher had killed a baby, sacrificed rabbits, and slaughtered an elephant and a giraffe. The Superior Court finally concluded that the children weren't credible and released Akiki— after two and a half years behind bars.[21]

Another case in recent American history in which children's testimony wreaked havoc dealt with a teacher at a New Jersey day-care center. Margaret Michaels, twenty-five, was convicted on 115 counts of sexually assaulting twenty pupils at the Wee Care Day Nursery in Maplewood during the 1984-85 school year. The children ranged in age from three to five at the time of the alleged abuse and were six to eight when they testified. Michaels was convicted despite her lawyer's demonstration that the children's stories were fantasies, that they had been elicited by suggestive questions asked by overzealous investigators, and that there was no medical evidence of abuse. The jury, however, gave credence to the parents, who said "they observed marked changes in their children's behavior while they were in Michaels' care. They reported that some children experienced nightmares and fear of the dark, developed an aversion to peanut butter, and showed increased interest in sex play."[22] The convictions were ultimately overthrown; if they would not have been, the accused could have received a sentence amounting to hundreds of years in prison.

An example of media-suggested imitation was reported from Clearwater, Florida, where a nine-year-old girl gave testimony that convicted her mother's boyfriend of having raped her. The man spent more than a year in the county jail and could have faced life behind bars. At age eleven, the girl recanted her story and admitted that she had fabricated it after watching a television episode of the police drama "21 Jump Street" in which a rape case had been depicted. " 'I can't understand it,' the girl's mother said. 'She convinced me. She convinced a jury. She convinced my parents. She went through the whole bit.' "[23]

Perhaps the most destructive version of the genre commenced its fateful course in 1983 at a preschool in Manhattan Beach, California. Two teachers at the McMartin Preschool, Peggy Buckey, sixty-three, and her son Raymond, thirty-one, were accused by Judy Johnson, the mother of a two-and-a-half-year-old boy, who had attended a few of Buckey's classes, of having molested her son. An examination showed that indeed the boy may have been molested. Thereupon a public hysteria spread, nearly approaching the ones of old Mora or Salem, and soon forty-one children were involved and 208 counts filed against seven individuals. Johnson's complaints against the teachers grew increasingly bizarre. She accused Raymond Buckey of "sodomizing her son while he stuck the boy's head in a toilet, making him ride naked on a horse and tormenting him with an air tube."[24] Later, as the investigation was still under way, Johnson was found to be an acute paranoid schizophrenic. She died of alcohol-related liver disease. But by then the prosecution had stirred up enough other witnesses and felt no need to revise the initial witness's testimony, despite the fact that in retrospect it was considered unreliable. The police had written to two hundred parents stating that they were investigating claims of oral sex and sodomy that presumably had taken place at the preschool. This disclosure fanned the hysteria and set the stage for more children to come up with lurid tales of abuse. The children were interviewed by Kee MacFarlane, an administrator turned therapist at Children's Institute International, who soon established that 369 of the 400 children interviewed had been abused. Her technique was highly suggestive: she gave emotional rewards to the children who accused the teachers, and rebuffs to those who did not. " 'What good are you? You must be dumb,' she said to one child who knew nothing about the game 'Naked Movie Star.' "[25] The collection of stories she presented to the authorities as being credible accounts included: children digging up dead bodies at cemeteries, being taken for rides in airplanes, killing animals (including a horse) with bats, observing devil worship, being buried alive, seeing naked priests cavorting in a secret cellar below the school, seeing a teacher fly, and having been given red or pink liquids to make them sleepy.[26] Reminiscent of the denunciations made by children at witch trials during past centuries, the preschool children were driven around town and asked to point out molesters. The children pointed out "community leaders, store clerks, gas station attendants; one child picked out photos of actor Chuck Norris and Los Angeles City Attorney James Hahn."[27] Rather than discrediting the testimony of the children, the district attorney in Los Angeles pressed ahead with the prosecution and presented eighteen children to the grand jury, which in March 1985 returned indictments against Raymond Buckey, his mother, sister, grandmother, and three preschool teachers. They were arrested with television cameras whirring as they were hauled away from their homes, one of them from the desk in her high school class. In January 1986, charges against five of those jailed were unexpectedly dropped and they were set free as a new district attorney took over and declared a complete absence of evidence. However, Peggy Buckey and her son Raymond remained incarcerated and suffered the longest and costliest criminal trial in American history. It was not until 1990 that they were acquitted—after they had spent two years and five years, respectively, in jail.[28] It need not be elaborated what measure of emotional and material damage had been done to these victims of children's testimony and adults' credulity. Again, the dynamics are strikingly similar to the ones we described in the accounts of witch trials in previous chapters.

The California episode and its conclusion were ravaged by the mass media and produced a tremendous repercussion throughout the nation—but not the one of caution, as one might have expected. The reaction was one of children making similar claims. "Nationally, the attention generated by the case set off an explosion of reports claiming sexual abuse of children, increasing such reports from 6,000 in 1976 to an estimated 350,000 in 1988."[29] The main responsibility for this explosion must be placed on the mass media, which wallowed in lurid detail. The perils created by the media's suggestive power include the possibility that parents and authorities would use the malleable potential of children to bring about ulterior testimony to serve the biases and schemes of partisan adults. As one person warned: "Some parents, determined to damage each other in a divorce, are throwing abuse charges around. Those bent on destroying a reputation have a surefire weapon."[30]

This modern "surefire weapon" is the equivalent of the witch accusation of past times; again it is based on the testimony of children, a testimony whose truth value is hard to prove or disprove, and a testimony still too often credulously accepted in the modern world. These examples apply to the psychology of children just as well as to the psychology of witch trials. Unfortunately it seems that the occurrence of these examples will not cease nor their nature change in the near future.

The suggestive power of the mass media can have an international impact. Among the world's most avid observers of the American scene are the German media. No political, cultural, criminal, literary, or cinematographical happening of the slightest importance goes unnoticed. German television and the press (especially the tabloids) dwelled on the above-mentioned McMartin school tragedy with almost the same intensity as did the U.S. media and presented just as many details. The impact was predictable: an immediate, steep increase in the number of child abuse claims by children and their parents. One case stands out. In the city of Münster (ironically infamous for past witch-children trials [see map, pp. 52–53]) Montessori school teacher Rainer Möllers was arrested and tried on charges of child molestation. What ensued amounted to a rerun of the California McMartin school affair. The allegations by the German children described the occult corollary of the presumed molestation with such similarity that its origin could only have come from the media showing the American episode. The children accused persons totally removed from the setting, including taxi drivers, and talked about rituals that featured coffins, mortuaries, trap doors, chaining, and secret subterranean vaults.

As in the American setting, there was polarization of the experts into camps of believers and skeptics. The latter referred to the McMartin case and warned against hysteria (they might just as well have used the Salem witch-hunt as an example). Then the panic spread to other schools, with rumor and unsubstantiated allegations defaming innocent teachers. Finally, the investigation, which lasted from 1990 to 1993, resulted in the dismissal of the Möllers case for lack of evidence.

A key role in effecting the dismissal was played by a level-headed psychologist who submitted to the court an analysis of the children and their parents forming a "group mind" that had evolved through mutually reinforcing suggestion.[31]

At the core of all this lies a warning for the modern world: When analyzing children's allegations, we also must analyze the role of the modern mass media, not only within national boundaries, but on the international level as well. Only then can we understand the astounding cross-national similarities in many realms of public life, including Western societies' current epidemic of child molestation claims.

Research Findings

Enough examples. Let us continue with research findings. Generally, children under eight years of age tend to display an attitude of absolute righteousness, that is, "any type of lie is wrong." It is important, however, to realize that this is an *attitude* and not necessarily *behavior,* which means that children may say that lying is wrong in nearly all situations but still lie under many conditions. "By the age of four, or even earlier, children can and will lie—not simply make excuses or confuse fantasy with reality, but deliberately attempt to mislead, usually to avoid punishment."[32]

Children's absolutism and their almost simultaneous betrayal of it have been noted by Albert Bandura in his experiments in the Stanford University psychology labs. While all children in an experimental setting agreed that Rocky, a villain, was wrong or "mean" when he took toys away from Johnny, a good guy, the children of the group who were later found imitating Rocky's behavior excused their acts by saying they did so because Rocky's aggression "paid off" or "worked."[33] This incongruence of moral attitude and actual behavior favors anything but a Rousseauesque portrayal of children's innocence—the type of naiveté that suffused Jean Jacques Rousseau's philosophy about a presumed pristine nature of the child.

After approximately age eight, children no longer consider lying categorically wrong. Their attitude changes. Now it "depends on the situation." An example from Paul Ekman's surveys strikes a familiar cord and explains the tendency of children to denounce certain persons. In his interviews, Ekman asked the children under what circumstances lying would be okay. A typical response was that of Robert, an eleven-year-old, who said: "Say some kid is a real bad guy, a bully, who hurts other kids. Then if you lied and said he did it, even if he didn't, he would get in trouble, and since he hurts people it's okay if he gets punished."[34] To paraphrase the eleven-year-old's situational moral: lying is moral and right when it punishes bad people.

Most children do this only if they are cornered, when they try to avert punishment or unpleasant situations, and if they are quick enough to think of someone they consider to be deserving of punishment. Unfortunately, some children, without pressure to do so, choose to make up stories that are intended to harm others.

Several studies have shown that children's suggestibility is heightened and their tendency to confabulate intensified when they are fed misinformation requiring forced answers, particularly if that misinformation merely supplements, rather than contradicts, some aspect of the original event.[35] When, for example, the inquisitor asked Witchboy how he and his cronies got to the location of the wine cellar they had raided (had they walked? or flown by pitchfork?) the boy opted for air travel, because such locomotion was as plausible to him as it was to the inquisitor.

The implication for the inquisitorial situation is that the thought patterns of the accused were compatible with the cosmology of the inquisitor; hence the scenario suggested by the inquisitor's questions supplemented the thinking of the person interrogated. Such suggestiveness facilitates the incorporation of the interrogator's misinformation into the respondent's testimony.

Psychologist S. J. Ceci noted that the process of confabulation is significantly influenced by how the respondent perceives the interrogator's rank of authority.[36] The higher the status, the higher the vulnerability of children to go along with leading questions and sometimes even react with extraordinary stories. With what awe children must have viewed the inquisitors before whom they were brought. Children were examined by the same well and widely known officials as were adults. For example, in the case of Witchboy the prominent jurist Dr. M. Herrnberger, member of the prince-bishop's committee of lawyers, presided over the boy's "confession."

Another factor slanting children's testimony is the role of the interpretive questions, which are persuasive cues to the child about what people want to hear. A question such as, "In what way did he attack you?" already defines the child's status as victim of an attack without giving the child a chance to independently describe the event. Interpretive questions elicit compliant and cooperative answers. The stronger and more exclusive the interpretive questions, the more compliant the answers. Laboratory studies showed that after the interrogator's strong suggestions, "two thirds of the children switched from what they had seen to what the interrogator said."[37]

Questioning a child repetitively, as used to be done in the typical sequence of inquisitorial hearings, had an additional impact on the suggestibility of the interrogated. Psychologists Gail Goodman and Alison Clark-Stewart found that when a second interrogator was of the same type as the first, the suggestion planted in the first interrogation carried over to the second

> and by the end of the second interrogation only one child gave fewer than six out of six responses to the interpretive questions in line with the interrogation. Nor did the children change their stories when questioned by their parents at the end of the session: All the children answered in line with the interrogator's interpretation.[38]

What, in summary, can be derived from the variety of above studies that would help us better understand the dynamics of children involved in witch trials? The key concept is children's *suggestibility* and most points of the summary reflect this element:

1. The younger the child the more suggestible he or she is.

2. Recall can be thoroughly distorted by biases and notions internalized by the child prior to interrogation.

3. The incomplete mental Gestalt of children allows for un-encumbered responses, sometimes of an exceedingly inventive and imaginative nature.

4. The very incompleteness of children's mental Gestalt allows self-brainwashing, the belief in the reality of one's confabulations.

5. Closeness in worldview between the questioner and the questioned furthers the persuasion process.

6. Young children tend to experiment with lies, often testing the limits of adults' credulity.

7. Absolutism in attitudes contrasts with behavioral relativism; that is, children defend honest and fair play on the verbal level but violate them on the behavioral level.

8. Older children develop the type of situational ethics whereby they see nothing wrong with lying if it leads to the punishment of a "bad person."

9. Information or misinformation embedded in the questions deepens children's suggestibility if such material is supplementary rather than contradictory to the key issue.

10. Suggestibility is significantly enhanced by the interrogator's status: the higher the status, the higher the suggestibility.

11. Interpretive and leading questions are powerful magnets extracting the "right" responses.

12. Repetitive questioning deepens the child's tendency to cater to the leading questions.

13. Once suggestions are planted, children can carry them over to succeeding interrogators.

14. The stronger an interrogator conveys his or her view, the more suggestible the child becomes and the greater the compliance with the view.

15. The greater the ambiguity of the key event, that is, the more it resembles a social Rorschach situation with an amorphous structure, the more productive the impact of leading questions.

16. Children's testimony may contain personal motives, such as punishing certain individuals or sometimes simply reveling in the glory of feeling powerful.

17. Children believe in legendary figures, illusory as they may be, if told so by parents. Children whose parents tell them otherwise exhibit disbelief in the figures.

Considering these points in situations where children's testimony is supposed to establish the truth warns us that truth is a highly tenuous quality forged out of the interaction between questioner and respondent. In the inquisitorial situation the two parties harmoniously interwove their scripts—the inquisitor played his role, the child reacted with compliance and played his or her role accordingly.

At this time there is insufficient research on mythomaniacal children. Indirect evidence and plausible assumption indicate that when children endowed with a mythomaniacal talent become exposed to the key conditions discussed above, they begin to spin colorful tales.

Collective Suggestibility—A Field Study

It has been observed that in the course of human interaction certain social qualities emerge that assume an awesome dominance above and beyond the personality of the participating individual. Modern examples of children's hysteria, as exhibited at teen concerts, contain the same elements as the "hexed" behavior of children claiming to be afflicted by curses. In both situations the children are literally spellbound. They play roles that are reinforced by collective agreement, tacit and unconscious as such agreement may be. This means that being afflicted is not a personality trait but a social condition.

Unfortunately, manifestations of this type of collective and "contagious" behavior are difficult to arraign for scientific study. They are usually "natural," uncontrolled incidents that cannot be placed into a laboratory for analysis.

To the very rare exceptions belongs a field study completed at a primarily black Louisiana junior high school in the 1960s, where peculiar psychosomatic symptoms of young teenagers could be observed and measured by medical and psychological methodologies.[39] An outbreak of an epidemic of hysteria involved scores of pubescent and postpubescent girls aged thirteen to fourteen, and symptomized itself individually by hyperventilation, fluttering eyelids, tingling of fingers, dryness of the mouth, dizziness, tremors, and fainting. The attacks resembled epileptic seizures of the petit mal type and were locally called "blackout spells." Within a few weeks, the behavior spread through the school like a contagious disease, afflicting at least four hundred students. The state board of health investigating the epidemic initially confronted an enigma. It was unable to determine a physical cause of the "spells," and regional newspapers commented along the lines of "Mysterious Ailment Strikes Black Students."

The contagiousness of the condition was first noticed when one girl had an attack in church and a peer witnessing it imitated it the next day in school. Within three weeks over twenty girls and one boy simulated the affliction. On some occasions there were as many as seven girls having attacks simultaneously while the investigators were present. Students likely to have attacks were those who touched, supported, or carried to the lounge some girl who had had a "blackout spell." This indicates a principle of mass hysteria: the increased likelihood of becoming "infected" by physical contact or by proximity to the afflicted person—an intriguing similarity to the previously unaffected Salem youths catching the affliction when the conspiratorial girls visited them.

Another principle became explicit: the role of the audience as the triggering device. "[The] highest incidence of attacks was on the days when there were visitors in the school making inquiries regarding the hysteria outbreak. Some of the students also had attacks at home, in church, and in the movie theater."[40] Again there are clear parallels to previously discussed cases of hysterical affliction.

In the meantime the health officials had recognized that they were confronting a mass hysteria and now tried to dispel rumors of black magic that had started to course through the community. A more scientific etiology was suggested and concentrated on identifying certain socially "infectious agents" causing the trouble. In the final analysis the investigators realized that the outbreak had begun when school authorities discovered considerable sexual promiscuity among the students and when rumors started to circulate that all the girls would be given pregnancy tests and those found to be pregnant would be sent to the nearby state correctional school. The fear of punitive reaction by the authorities to the students' promiscuity caused the teenagers to plunge into acute anxiety.

Behavioral scientists took advantage of the panic and administered batteries of medical tests and psychological measurements to both the affected and the control (students not involved in the symptomatology) groups. To start with, IQ tests yielded a mean of 72.4, with a range of 55–92, for the hysterical group and a mean of 73.4, with a range of 40–105, for the control group. This represented a noteworthy absence of significant difference between the groups. The Minnesota Multiphasic Personality Inventory and the Rorschach test showed that the control group had slightly less emotional instability. Both groups were characterized by a low emotional maturity level and low levels of internal affective control ability. Electroencephalographic techniques revealed unusually high percentages of abnormalities in both groups: 53 percent for the hysterical students and 57 percent for the control students—a minor difference.

In short, none of the tests revealed any significant differences of innate ability or condition that would explain why some students should be hysterical. However, when a psychiatrist interviewed each student who was having "blackout spells" as well as each member of the control group individually, certain clinical differences began to emerge: (1) The affected students were far more interested in sexual matters; they talked more about sex and were much more seductive than the control students. (2) They were much more socially involved in "the scene," dating and interacting more with peers. (3) They showed greater appreciation of the attention given the matter and enjoyed talking about their affliction. In contrast, the control individuals showed little interest in talking about the subject or about their personal health in general. (4) The affected students had a much richer fantasy life and related more exciting plans for the future. They were more dramatic, expressive, and able to relate more easily. "The psychiatrist found rapport more easily established with the affected group."[41]

In sum, the etiology of the epidemic was rooted in a number of factors: guilt about misconduct, fear of society's reprisal, certain individuals' high suggestibility, and the efficacy of developing an illness as a way of handling conflict between authority and personal impulse.

The field study highlights the powerful role of guilt feelings and how individuals go about trying to manage them. There are various ways to come to grips with emotions that gnaw at our self-esteem. The teenagers chose one of them by invoking, as it were, a higher power to descend and intervene before actual authorities could reach them. "Blackout spells" served as self-imposed punishment and at the same time as protection against authority-imposed punishment.

Another guilt-reducing mechanism is to punish those who represent the source of guilt. This seems to have been the unconsciously guiding principle of the Salem girls. They rebelled against Puritan strictures, incurred guilt feelings as a consequence, and punished the entire community—the repressive Establishment—for it. This is not to say that this is the entire story of the Salem girls' motivation and behavior. Additional elements played important roles. But the management of guilt—or rather its mismanagement—is one of the noteworthy dimensions of the Salem case.

Notes

1. David C. Raskin and Phillip W. Esplin, "Assessment of Children's Statements of Sexual Abuse," in *The Suggestibility of Children's Recollections,* ed. John Doris (Washington, D.C.: American Psychological Association, 1991), pp. 153–64.

2. Norman M. Prentice et al., "Imaginary Figures of Early Childhood: Santa Claus, Easter Bunny and the Tooth Fairy," *American Journal of Orthopsychiatry* 48 (1978): 620–21.

3. J. Singer and D. Singer, "Imaginative Play and Pretending in Early Childhood: Some Experimental Approaches," in *Child Personality and Psychopathology; Current Topics,* vol. 3, ed. A. Davis (New York: Wiley, 1976).

4. Maria S. Zaragosa, "Preschool Children's Susceptibility to Memory Impairment," in *The Suggestibility of Children's Recollections,* ed. John Doris, pp. 27–39.

5. Helen R. Dent, "Experimental Studies of Interviewing Child Witnesses," in *The Suggestibility of Children's Recollections,* ed. John Doris, pp. 138–46.

6. Quoted by Anastasia Toufexis, "When Can Memory be Trusted?" *Time,* October 28, 1991, p. 88.

7. Ibid.

8. See a discussion on the dispute concerning the definition of memory traces and its application in Gestalt theory: Charles Brainerd and Peter A. Ornstein, "Children's Memory for Witnessed Events," in *The Suggestibility of Children's Recollections,* ed. John Doris, pp. 10–20.

9. Jean Piaget, *The Moral Judgment of the Child* (New York: Free Press, 1965), p. 164.

10. Stephen J. Ceci, "Some Overarching Issues in the Children's Suggestibility Debate," in *The Suggestibility of Children's Recollections,* ed. John Doris, pp. 1–9.

11. Paul Ekman, "Would a Child Lie?" *Psychology Today,* July–August 1989, p. 62–65.

12. Ibid., pp. 63–64.

13. Michael Lewis et al., "Deception in 3-Year-Olds," *Developmental Psychology* 25 (1989): 439–43.

14. Rebecca L. Jahn, "Detecting Deception," *Research at Arizona State University* 8 (Fall 1993): 6.

15. Quoted by Jerome Cramer, "Why Children Lie in Court," *Time,* March 4, 1991, p. 76.

16. Quoted by Robert Dvorchak in "Custody Fights Use Sex Charge as Weapon," *Arizona Republic,* August 22, 1992, pp. A1 and A8.

17. Ibid., p. A8.

18. Ibid.

19. Cf. Hartwig Weber, *Kinderhexenprozesse* (Frankfurt, Germany: Insel, 1991), p. 243n.

20. Leon Jaroff, "Lies of the Mind," *Time,* November 29, 1993, p. 52.

21. Associated Press, "Man Found Not Guilty of Molestation," *Mesa Tribune,* November 20, 1993, p. A7.

22. A United Press International report in *Arizona Republic,* April 16, 1988, p. A8.

23. Quoted in *Mesa Tribune,* January 28, 1990, p. 3.

24. Margaret Carlson, "Six Years of Trial by Torture," *Time,* January 29, 1990, p. 26.

25. Ibid., p. 26.

26. Ibid.; plus cf. Vern L. Bullough, "The Salem Witch Trials and the Modern Media," *Free Inquiry* 10 (Spring 1990): 6.

27. Carlson, "Six Years of Trial by Torture," p. 26.

28. Paul Eberle and Shirley Eberle, *The Abuse of Innocence: The McMartin Preschool Trial* (Amherst, N.Y.: Prometheus Books, 1993).

29. Carlson, "Six Years of Trial by Torture," p. 27.

30. Ibid.

31. Gisela Friedrichsen and Gerhard Mauz, "Jetzt ist niemand sicher," *Spiegel,* June 13, 1994, p. 105.

32. Carlson, "Six Years of Trial by Torture," p. 26.

33. Albert Bandura et al., "Imitation of Film-Mediated Aggressive Models," *Journal of Abnormal and Social Psychology* 66 (January 1966): 3–11.

34. Ekman, "Would a Child Lie?" p. 64.

35. Zaragosa, "Preschool Children's Susceptibility to Memory Impairment," p. 37.

36. S. J. Ceci, D. F. Ross, and M. P. Toglia, "Suggestibility of Children's Memory; Psycholegal Implication," *Journal of Experimental Psychology* 116 (1987): 38–39.

37. Gail S. Goodman and Alison Clark-Stewart, "Suggestibility in Children's Testimony," in *The Suggestibility of Children's Recollections,* ed. John Doris, p. 101.

38. Ibid.

39. James A. Knight et al., "Epidemic Hysteria: A Field Study," *American Journal for Public Health* 55 (June 1965): 858–65.

40. Ibid., p. 862.

41. Ibid., p. 863.

Epilogue

Of Cauldrons and Crucibles

When a community screams out in horror of witches, children are quick to seize the day by using accusation to transport all sorts of emotional want and distress. The plethora of emotions and motives include guilt, fear, rebellion, revenge, seeking status and praise, derring-do, the ecstasy of power, and sometimes pure malice.

It matters little whether the label of the accusation is witchcraft, satanism, or molestation. Any available label will do, as long as it packs enough social impressibility to move adults and the authorities into action. The suggestibility is two-sided: children manipulate adults as much as adults manipulate them, and neither side is usually aware of it.

The true art of counseling or judging is to expose who manipulates whom and what is the truth. The ingredients of the witch-maniacal scenario are difficult to sort out; they form a concoction of diverse emotions, resulting in an emotional broth not unlike the bubbling cauldron of legendary witches. If the ingredients are left to ferment long enough, the proper metaphor to describe the effect on the community becomes the crucible, wherein human ignorance and irrationality crush innocent people branded as conspirators and evildoers. The nexus between irrationality and a community acting as crucible is of hair-trigger sensitivity, and this work points to two historical settings: the early-modern period and present day of Western civilization. It shows how the triggering device creates a stage with angst and persecution mentality.

The parallels between the two settings are remarkable. When

237

children today talk about satanic ritual, they enjoy almost as much credibility as during the classic era of the witch-hunt. Today as then, there are books and manuals exposing a presumed conspiracy and giving advice about how to eliminate it. Lengthy criminal trials destroy the life and livelihood of persons ultimately freed because of lack of evidence.

The ideational underpinning in a majority of accusations is identical with traditional Christian theology: the assumption of the existence of a personifiable Devil. It matters little whether we call them witches, satanists, or molesters—any label will evoke the wrath of those in charge of the crucible.

Though Christian theology still plays a heavy role in society's crucible, the actual judicial power of the church has been curbed. Inquisitors and exorcists no longer can hand over heretics to jailer or henchman. Their power to excommunicate, banish, and condemn is limited to intramural churchly exercise.

These limitations are the consequences of the separation of state and church—no small achievement when we realize that Christian Europe still executed witches in the eighteenth century. Credit for the achievement goes to the rise of the spirit of humanism that checked Christianity's coercive monopoly and counteracted the denigration of humankind as characterized by innate sinfulness and threatened by an underworld teeming with demons and devils.

Glossary

BOUNDARY MAINTENANCE. The sociological principle assuming that social (including religious) integration is achieved by setting norms of acceptable behavior for members of society.

CANON LAW. The corpus of the laws of the church, based on theological assumptions; synonymous to *canon episcopi*. In the case of a prince-bishopric, the church laws merged with the secular laws and to a significant degree erased the distinction between church and state.

CLOSURE. Similar in meaning to BOUNDARY MAINTENANCE; but usually applied to the individual level (especially by GESTALT psychologists), whereby the brain integrates experiences into meaningful structures. A sort of unconscious "default" propensity of the brain.

CORPORUM MUTATIO IN BESTIAS. The belief that through black magic a person can change her- or himself into the form of an animal. Also called a *metamorphosis*. The classic version was the WEREWOLF.

CRIMEN EXCEPTUM. The legal status of the crimes ascribed to the witch was extraordinary, allowing procedures normally not used in other or "normal" crimes. Witch crimes were treated as secular as well as ecclesiastical crimes, since they were thought to be directed against humans as well as against God.

239

CUJUS REGIO, EJUS RELIGIO. The rule, developed after the Reformation, that citizens and subjects had to adopt the religious preference of their ruler.

DEMONOLOGY. The corpus of assumptions and descriptions dealing with evil spirits, demons, and the Devil. A *demonologist* was (and still is) a specialist expounding these assumptions, often preaching and writing about them in great detail. An *exorcist,* still recognized by the Catholic church, is a practicing demonologist, sometimes officially authorized by bishops to drive out the Devil. Many of the so-called learned doctors of the church (such as Thomas Aquinas, Jerome, Augustine, and many others) were pioneers in constructing complex demonological paradigms and advocating the persecution of witches.

DEMONOPATHY. Behavior interpreted as a manifestation of a person's suffering from diabolic possession or from being under attack by demons or the Devil. Synonymous with *demonomania.*

FAMILIAR. A demon in disguise of an animal, usually a pet, such as a dog or cat, or some farm animal. Witches were thought to keep company with them. Black cats had a particularly bad reputation, and in some instances were killed just as witches were.

GESTALT. Mental structure; the result of closure; with *prägnanz* dimensions as major support structures. Normal human beings aspire integration of experiences and impressions into a conflict-free, holistic mentality. A healthy brain naturally works that way. Closure means to draw lines around impressions that seem to belong together in sets of common meanings. *Prägnanz* dimensions are our major perceptions of and convictions about the world around us, facilitating the ordering of details and their integration into the Gestalt.

GNADENZETTEL. A special writ of mercy issued by the authorities, usually the prince-bishop, to grant the condemned death by strangulation or decapitation before burning.

HERESY. A religious orientation deviating from the "true belief," as held by church authorities. Witches' servitude to the Devil was considered the most evil heresy, for witches were thought to advance the Devil's work directly and knowingly.

HERETIC. A person preaching, practicing, or otherwise advancing a religious orientation that deviated from the "true belief." Such persons were severely persecuted, sometimes en masse, as in the case of the Waldensians or the Knights Templars. Witches were thought of as the worst of all heretics, because they served the Devil willingly.

HETERODOX. Deviation from *orthodox,* meaning the "true" religious belief; sometimes used synonymously with heretical, but often referring to other established denominations that could not be persecuted as heresies.

HEXENBISCHOF. The nickname of Prince-Bishop Johann Georg II, who ruled Bamberg from 1623 to 1633. A notorious witch-hunter, he built special witch prisons with torture chambers. He was responsible for the execution of over six hundred witches.

INDICIA. The presumed evidence for crimes of witchcraft (or any other crimes, for that matter), frequently including denunciations, conjectures, and theological interpretations.

INQUISITION. The organization established to combat heresy and witchcraft. Established by the pope around 1233, it had regional offices. In 1512 the name was changed to the Congregation of the Holy Office.

KIRCHWEIH. Originally referring to the annual commemoration of a church's inauguration, but over time turning into a secularized, strictly local festival with the character of a carnival.

LYCANTHROPY. The alleged metamorphosis of a person into a wolf; synonymous to the WEREWOLF phenomenon; an example of *corporum mutatio in bestias.*

MALEFICIA. Crimes ascribed to the witch. Characteristic of them was the black-magic method, the conspiracy with the Devil, and the nonutilitarian or purely malicious nature (serving no other purpose but wreaking harm) of the acts.

MALEFIZ-COMMISSION. A ruler's commission of lawyers advising him on legal matters. Members were personally involved in the prosecution and interrogation process. They carried out the Inquisition's judicial responsibilities and passed sentence.

MALEFIZ-PERSONEN. Persons accused of having committed destructive or murderous acts through black magic; synonymous with *witches*. (Note varying spellings in Middle High German.)

MALLEUS MALEFICARUM. Latin for "Hammer of the Witches," a book written by two German priests, Heinrich Kramer and Jakob Sprenger, published in 1484. It was one of many demonological works at the time, but became the best known and achieved the status of the Inquisition's manual describing the procedure for persecuting, prosecuting, and executing witches.

MARGINAL GROUPS/MARGINALITY. Categories or segments of the population outside the mainstream of society and stigmatized by undesirable character. Examples are juvenile gangs, beggars, vagabonds, religious fanatics, and the homeless. The emphasis is more on lack of social fit than criminality.

MYTHOMANIA. A compulsion to fabricate fantastic stories. Considered a psychopathology when enacted by adults, but usually not in children; not to be equated with hallucinations; to be understood as a specific child's skill used to gain personal benefits.

NIGHT FLIGHT. The assumption that witches could fly through the air on various crafts, mostly on broomsticks, pitchforks, rakes, or sometimes animals.

OSCULUM INFAME. A witch demonstrating her adoration of her master, the Devil, by kissing his posterior. Presumably one of the rituals performed at the witches' sabbath.

ORTHODOX. Referring to the "true" religious orientation; the opposite of heterodox or heretical.

PSEUDOLOGIA PHANTASTICA. A psychopathology, when observed in adults, symptomized by compulsive confabulation. Synonymous with MYTHOMANIA.

RATIFICATION. The final signing (or otherwise signifying) of a confession as being the truth. Presumably (according to the law) this was to be done voluntarily and without coercive torture. The act signaled the end of the inquest and sentence could be pronounced thereafter.

STRAPPADO. A method of torture whereby the victim is hung by the hands tied behind his or her back, dislocating the shoulders. In addition, heavy weights were often attached to the feet of the delinquent.

TERRITIO. This was the inquisitor's first reaction to an accused person proving to be recalcitrant at the beginning of an interrogation. It consisted of demonstrating the various instruments of torture and explaining how they might be used.

TRUDENZEITUNG. A flyer published in 1627 by Prince-Bishop Johann Georg II, the *Hexenbischof,* to warn against the evils of witchery. The publication was banned in neighboring Protestant Nürnberg to avoid spreading the witch panic.

VERMUTUNGSBEWEIS. A judicial practice allowing surmise and guessing as evidence in witch trials. The oxymoron ("evidence by surmise") was coined by Saxon jurist and witch-hunter Benedict Carpsov.

WEREWOLF. The mythology of a person changed into a wolf. Sometimes associated with the belief that witches could change into wolves or other animals. The Inquisition occasionally burned persons at the stake on the basis of this accusation. A form of CORPORUM MUTATIO IN BESTIAS. Synonymous with LYCANTHROPY.

WITCHES' SABBATH. The alleged assembly of the witches to feast, fornicate, and dance under the direction of the Devil. Authorities as well as the common people believed that it was celebrated at such hidden places as the infamous Blocksberg, or, closer to Bamberg, in the dank Hauptmoor Forest. Presumably the witches flew to these places on broomsticks or pitchforks. Synonymous with *witches' dance*.

WOTAN. The major god figure in the pantheon of the ancient Germanic people before Christianization took place.

Bibliography

Readers wanting to pursue the history of the witch persecution and its ramifications should note that they are embarking on an enterprise where the expression *caveat emptor* (let the buyer beware) is singularly appropriate. They should be careful in choosing the material. As a historian not long ago has said, a lot of utter nonsense and distorted information has been published on the topic. Sources by reliable authors and researchers are listed below.

Behringer, Wolfgang. "Kinderhexenprozesse." *Zeitschrift für historische Forschung* 16 (1989): 31–47.

Boyer, P., and S. Nissenbaum. *Salem Possessed: The Social Origins of Witchcraft.* Cambridge, Mass.: Harvard University Press, 1974.

Cohn, Norman. *Europe's Inner Demons.* New York: Basic Books, 1975.

Demos, John Putnam. *Entertaining Satan: Witchcraft and the Culture of Early New England.* New York: Oxford University Press, 1982.

Deschner, Karlheinz. *Kriminalgeschichte des Christentums.* Reinbeck bei Hamburg, Germany: Rowohlt, 1987.

Eberle, Paul, and Shirley Eberle. *The Abuse of Innocence: The McMartin Preschool Trial.* Amherst, N.Y.: Prometheus Books, 1993.

Gardner, Martin. "The False Memory Syndrome." *Skeptical Inquirer* 17 (Summer 1993): 370–75.

Hansen, Joseph. *Quellen und Untersuchungen zur Geschichte des Hexenwahns.* Hildesheim, Germany: Olms, 1901.

Harmening, Dieter. *Zauberei im Abendland*. Würzburg, Germany: Königshausen & Neumann, 1991.

Kuckertz, Beate, ed. *Kreuz-Feuere. Die Kritik an der Kirche*. Munich, Germany: Wilhelm Heyne, 1991.

Lea, Henry C. *A History of the Inquisition of the Middle Ages*. London: 1888.

———. *Materials toward a History of Witchcraft*. 1939. Reprint. New York: Yoseloff, 1957.

Levack, Brian P. *The Witch-Hunt in Early Modern Europe*. New York: Longman, 1987.

Looshorn, Johann. *Die Geschichte des Bisthums Bamberg*. Bamberg, Germany: Handels-Druckerei, 1906.

Macfarlane, Alan. *Witchcraft in Tudor and Stuart England*. London: Routledge & Kegan Paul, 1970.

Mackay, Charles. *Extraordinary Delusions and the Madness of Crowds*. 1841. Reprint. New York: Noonday Press, 1974.

Merzbacher, Friedrich. *Die Hexenprozesse in Franken*. Munich, Germany: Beck, 1970.

Midelfort, H. Erik. *Witch Hunting in Southwestern Germany 1562–1684*. Stanford, Calif.: Stanford University Press, 1972.

Monter, E. William. *European Witchcraft*. New York: Wiley, 1969.

———. *Witchcraft in France and Switzerland: The Borderlands during the Reformation*. Ithaca, N.Y.: Cornell University Press, 1976.

Ranke-Heinemann, Uta. *Eunuchs for the Kingdom of God: Women, Sexuality and the Catholic Church*. New York: Doubleday, 1990.

Richardson, James T., et al., eds. *The Satanism Scare*. Hawthorne, N.Y.: Aldine de Gruyter, 1991.

Robbins, Rossell H. *The Encyclopedia of Witchcraft and Demonology*. New York: Crown, 1959.

Sebald, Hans. *Witchcraft—The Heritage of a Heresy*. New York: Elsevier North Holland, 1978.

———. "Fire for the Female, Medicine for the Male: Medical Science and Demonology during the Era of the Witch-Hunt." In *Disease and Medicine in Modern Germany*, ed. Rudolf Käser and Vera Pohland. Ithaca, N.Y.: Cornell University Western Societies Program, 1990.

———. "Witches' Confessions: Stereotypical Structure and Local Color." *Southern Humanities Review* 24 (Fall 1990): 301–19.

Sebald, Hans. *Hexen damals—und heut?* Bindlach, Germany: Gondrom, 1993.

Soergel, Philip M. *Wondrous in His Saints: Propaganda for the Catholic Reformation in Bavaria.* Berkeley, Calif.: University of California Press, 1993.

Starkey, Marion L. *The Devil in Massachusetts.* New York: Time Inc., 1949.

Van Dülmen, Richard. *Theatre of Horror: Crime and Punishment in Early Modern Germany.* Cambridge, England: Polity Press, 1990.

Victor, Jeffrey S. "Satanic Cult 'Survivor' Stories." *Skeptical Inquirer* 15 (Spring 1991): 274–80.

———. *Satanic Panic: The Creation of a Contemporary Legend.* Peru, Ill.: Open Court, 1993.

Von Lamberg, Graf. *Criminalverfahren vorzüglich bei Hexenprozessen im ehemaligen Bisthum Bamberg.* Nürnberg, Germany: Rieger & Wiessner, 1835.

Von Riezler, Sigmund. *Geschichte der Hexenprozesse in Bayern.* 1896. Reprint. Aalen, Germany: Scienta Verlag, 1968.

Weber, Hartwig. *Kinderhexenprozesse.* Frankfurt, Germany: Insel, 1991.

About the Author

Hans Sebald is professor emeritus of sociology at Arizona State University in Tempe, Arizona. He grew up in Franconia, Germany, close to Bamberg, the locus of the trial of Witchboy (discussed in part two of this book), and is familiar with the language and the folkways of the region. Sebald's previous studies include an investigation of remnants of the old witch belief as they have survived not only in the folklore but in the actual practices of the peasants in the Franconian Jura Mountains, which have been under the ecclesiastical rule of the bishops of Bamberg for hundreds of years. Sebald's findings have been published in *Witchcraft—The Heritage of a Heresy* (New York: Elsevier, 1978) and *Hexen damals—und heute?* (Frankfurt, Germany: Gondrom, 1993, and Ullstein Berlin, 1990). Sebald has also published books on social-psychological issues, particularly on the dynamics of adolescence, and numerous articles in scientific journals. Besides being an academic, Professor Sebald is an avid outdoors person, backpacker, and conservationist. He built his home at the foot of the fabled Superstition Mountains in Arizona.

Index

251